PRESERVATION OF LIBRARY COLLECTIONS

PRESERVATION OF LIBRARY COLLECTIONS

By

Bhagwatiben Govindbhai Prajapati

M.A., B.Lib., M.Lib., B.Ed.

Librarian

Special Education College

Palanpur

(India)

DPH

DISCOVERY PUBLISHING HOUSE PVT. LTD.

NEW DELHI-110 002

Published by:
Tilak Wasan
DISCOVERY PUBLISHING HOUSE PVT. LTD.
4383/4B, Ansari Road, Darya Ganj
New Delhi-110 002 (India)
Phone : +91-11-23279245, 43596064-65
Fax : +91-11-23253475
E-mail : discoverypublishinghouse@gmail.com
sales@discoverypublishinggroup.com
parul.wasan@gmail.com
web : www.discoverypublishinggroup.com

***First Edition:* 2013**

ISBN: 978-93-5056-383-0

Preservation of Library Collections

Printed at:
Dynamic Printers
Delhi

Preface

The preservation services ensures the ongoing access to physical collections by undertaking assessments, treatments, housing, storage reviews, surveys and collection stabilization for exhibitions, loans and digitization projects. This work is achieved within the guidelines of the library's preservation policy. The library's collections are diverse and vast. Staff faces daily challenges to find ways of providing access to the collections whilst ensuring the condition of the collection is not compromised. A risk management approach to this work is essential, and the significance of collection items is used to help guide treatment approaches. The *Preservation of Library Collections* again became a subject of interest and activity after some decades of neglect. The subsequent growth in preservation literature has been notable. This book traces the revival of preservation awareness within the information profession.

This book is particularly relevant to libraries of all types facing the permanent issues of fast collection growth, limited space to house collections, and deterioration of collections. All libraries also face the issues of obsolete materials, limited budgets, changing user populations and needs, and new institutional programs, and will find the book helpful in dealing with those problems.

—***Author***

Contents

1

Introduction to Preservation

Cultural collections may include bound volumes, documents, scrapbooks, photographic prints and negatives, newspapers, maps, works on art on paper, motion picture film, sound and video recordings, and computer media. How should these materials be preserved? What preservation strategies are the most effective? What is the role of new technologies in preservation? *Preservation 101* will explore these issues and more, providing a basic overview of preservation issues for paper-based and related media collections, and giving you the tools to begin building an effective preservation programme for your institution.

WHAT IS PRESERVATION

What does the term "preservation" mean for libraries, archives, historical societies, and other institutions that hold paper-based collections? Can it be used interchangeably with "conservation," and if not, how are they different? What activities make up a preservation programme? How should preservation be implemented in different types of institutions with different types of collections? Does the advent of new technologies mean that traditional methods of preservation are no longer needed?

This part will provide you with some answers to these questions. You will learn how libraries and archives have traditionally defined preservation; how the meaning of preservation and other related terms has changed over the years; and what activities constitute a systematic preservation programme.

DEFINITIONS

The distinction between the terms "preservation" and "conservation" is somewhat unclear, as the use of these terms has varied over time, depending in part on the context of their use.

Since the 1980s, the library and archival communities have used "preservation" as an umbrella term for activities that reduce or prevent damage to extend the life expectancy of collections, while "conservation" refers more specifically to the physical treatment of individual damaged items. The term "restoration" is used mostly in the context of museum objects or motion picture films. It generally refers to the process of returning an object to its original state, or what is thought to have been its original state.

The American Institute for Conservation of Historic and Artistic Works (AIC) Definitions of Conservation defines these three terms as follows:

* *Preservation*: The protection of cultural property through activities that minimize chemical and physical deterioration and damage and that prevent loss of informational content. The primary goal of preservation is to prolong the existence of cultural property.
* *Conservation*: The profession devoted to the preservation of cultural property for the future. Conservation activities include examination, documentation, treatment, and preventive care, supported by research and education.
* *Restoration*: Treatment procedures intended to return cultural property to a known or assumed state, often through the addition of non-original material.

In the widest sense, preservation encompasses

* Activities that prevent damage to paper-based and media collections, such as proper housing, environmental control, and disaster planning; and

* Activities such as treatment, replacement, or reformatting that address existing damage.

Preservation involves keeping a balance between collection-level activities such as environmental control, which can be difficult and/or costly to manage but provide the greatest long-term benefit for the most materials, and item-level activities such as conservation treatment, which are often more easily understood and managed but can have limited effect, especially if the items are returned to a damaging environment.

HISTORICAL CONTEXT: LIBRARIES

While activities designed to keep collections in usable condition, including binding, repair, and reformatting, have always taken place in libraries, the evolution of systematic preservation practices for paper-based collections began during the 1950s and 1960s. By the early 1970s, the convergence of an obvious need for preservation and the development of infrastructure to carry out preservation activities resulted in the growing recognition of preservation as a separate library specialty.

Greater attention to the need for preservation in libraries and archives was driven by several catalytic events that occurred during the 1950s and 1960s. These fall into two general categories: the problem of brittle books and paper, and the recognition of the dangers disaster poses to collections. At the same time, preservation organizations began to spring up, and information and funding for preservation activities became more readily accessible.

The Brittle Book Problem

The 1950s and 1960s were a time of rapid growth of collections in research libraries, and librarians could not help but notice that materials in their collections were becoming yellowed and brittle. William J. Barrow, a pioneer in the research of the deterioration of paper collections, carried out the first major study of the condition of book paper in the late '50s. He found that only three per cent of the volumes studied would last more than 50 years.

In 1962, the Association of Research Libraries commissioned a survey of book deterioration in ARL libraries, conducted by Gordon Williams, which confirmed Barrow's findings. Late in the 1970s and into the '80s, additional studies were conducted at specific libraries, including Stanford University, the Library of Congress, and Yale University, which consistently showed that up to a third of collections were already dangerously embrittled.

The Dangers of Disaster

Several prominent disasters involving library and archival collections occurred during the 1960s and '70s, emphasizing the danger of disaster and culminating in the development of systematic techniques for disaster planning and response.

In 1966, the Arno River flooded Florence, Italy, damaging or destroying many valuable library and museum collections. Conservators from around the world joined in the salvage efforts and learned much about the effectiveness of various disaster response techniques. Flooding from Hurricane Agnes in Corning, New York, in 1972 and a water main break at Stanford University's Meyer Library in 1978, in which 50,000 volumes were damaged, drew additional attention to disaster planning and response in the United States. In both cases, wet library collections were frozen and drying techniques were tested, with vacuum-freeze drying emerging as the most effective strategy.

Development of Infrastructure for Preservation

For preservation action to occur, information, organizational support, and financial resources must exist, not merely the awareness of a problem. The *Council on Library Resources* (CLR), founded in 1956, and the Association of Research Libraries (ARL) both played a prominent part in early efforts to study and combat the brittle paper problem.

In 1961, CLR funded the creation of the Barrow Research Laboratory, headed by William J. Barrow, to study the permanence of the book. Other important research organizations include the Canadian Conservation Institute, founded in 1972, and the Image Permanence Institute, founded in 1985 to pursue scientific research on the preservation of visual materials and related collections. During the 1970s, two regional conservation centers were established—the Northeast Document Conservation Center (NEDCC) and the Conservation Center for Art and Historic Artifacts (CCAHA)—which provided conservation treatment and preservation education services.

Professional organizations also played a large part in the advancement of preservation programmes. The Research Libraries Group (RLG) was founded in 1974 by the New York Public Library and Columbia, Harvard, and Yale Universities. It has played an important role in conducting cooperative microfilming projects and devising guidelines for preservation microfilming. The American Library Association (ALA) established its first subcommittees on library preservation in 1970 and has continued to play an active role. The Book and Paper Group (BPG) of the American Institute for Conservation of Historic and Artistic Works (AIC) was established in 1980. The result of all these developments has been increased cooperation among libraries, archives, historical societies, museums and conservators.

Federal organizations-in particular the National Endowment for the Humanities (NEH) Office of Preservation, later reorganized into the Division of Preservation and Access—have played a leading role in providing funding for preservation activities in individual libraries and on the national level over the past 20 years. The independent Commission on Preservation and Access (CPA) was created in 1987 with a mandate to raise awareness of the brittle book problem and to encourage national efforts to address it. In 1995, CPA and CLR merged to become the Council on Library and Information Resources (CLIR). With the support of the NEH over the past two decades, a successful cooperative microfilming programme for brittle books and newspapers has grown. Local preservation programmes continued to develop as well, with the number of full-time preservation administrators in ARL libraries growing from three or four in 1971 to 52 in 1991.

HISTORICAL CONTEXT: ARCHIVES

All archival records might in some sense be considered permanent, or they would not be collected. But does that mean they all can or should be preserved? And if so, how should they be preserved? Early American archival repositories strongly emphasized the importance of ensuring the permanence of their collections. During the 19th century, there was a great impetus, partly as a result of the loss of some prominent collections to fire, to disseminate the information found in records by publishing them. As early microfilming technology was developed, archivists began to embrace this as well.

By the mid-20th century, however, archivists increasingly focused on the preservation of original documents that were clearly deteriorating. Archivists adopted many of the techniques for conservation of individual documents set forth by William J. Barrow, among them deacidification and lamination, a process later found to be damaging. In the middle of the 1960s, the acid-free box was developed, with partial support from CLR.

Faced with ever-larger collections of modern records, archivists began to see how severe the problem of physical deterioration was-and how little time and money was available to address it. As a result, they began to consider how to choose those records that deserved preservation in their original form, and those that should be dealt with in other ways, such as reformatting. Like librarians, archivists have increasingly focused on improving environmental control and storage facilities to ensure that their collections of enduring value have as long a life as possible.

Deciding What to Preserve

In libraries, it is relatively easy to identify important deteriorated collections in a particular subject category. Library collections are, by and large, well-cataloged, and there are tools available to assess the subject strengths and weaknesses of any particular library's collection. Assuming funding and other resources are available, librarians can determine what materials would make up a "comprehensive" collection in a subject, identify the libraries that hold those materials, and initiate a cooperative preservation programme for them.

Due to the nature of archival collections, archivists face more difficulty in ensuring that a particular subject or an area of society has been fully documented and the appropriate records preserved. The archival community has not yet developed a systematic programme for identifying collections in need of preservation that parallels the national brittle book initiative in libraries, although some steps have been taken. In the early 1990s the Commission on Preservation and Access supported the work of the Task Forces on Archival Selection, which began to address key issues in identifying and selecting collections for preservation.

PRESERVATION AND NEW TECHNOLOGIES

Preservation in cultural institutions over the past 30 to 40 years has been seen as fairly straightforward, involving specific activities such as environmental control, proper storage, disaster planning, reformatting, and conservation treatment. The increasing presence, however, of digital imaging and digital resources within cultural institutions in recent years has changed the way institutions perceive preservation. Digitization increases the complexity of the relationship between the medium and the message.

Digital preservation must be considered in two contexts:

* Can digital scanning be used to preserve the content of existing collections, and if so, does that mean traditional preservation activities are not needed?
* How should collections that are originally created digitally be preserved? What does it mean to preserve a digital object that can be easily changed without leaving any trace that the change was made?

Collection managers face difficult questions about technology's role in preserving collections. When is it sufficient to preserve just the information in an object, and when is it necessary to preserve the object itself? Is digital scanning of collections solely an access tool and a means of protecting collections from handling, or can it be considered a preservation strategy? Is digital scanning actually an effective means of protecting collections from handling, keeping in mind that the scanning process may involve much more handling of the collection than occasional use would? How does digital preservation fit into a traditional preservation programme?

Reformatting and Treatment, but it is crucial to understand that digital technology does not make traditional preservation unnecessary. Because of the difficulties inherent in preserving digital objects over the long term, digitization of collections is not a substitute for environmental control, proper storage, and other types of reformatting; it is simply another option in the preservation tool box. New technology does, however, make it even more difficult to allocate already-scarce resources among preservation activities.

ELEMENTS OF A PRESERVATION PROGRAMME

Although there is general consensus within the preservation community on the basic elements of a systematic preservation programme, where the emphasis falls will depend on the type of institution, since institutional and user needs will vary.

For example, the primary interest of a public library may be to keep materials in good repair so that they can be used until they become obsolete and are withdrawn, while a research library or an archives would emphasize preservation of intellectual content over the long term and/or preservation of original items with artifactual value.

The basic elements of a preservation programme are as follows:

* *Environmental Control*: Providing a moderate and stable temperature and humidity level as well as controlling exposure to light and pollutants. This should be a priority for all institutions, although control will usually be less tight for general circulating collections than for rare books, special

collections, or archival materials.

* *Disaster Planning*: Preventing and responding to damage from water, fire, or other emergency situations. Again, this should be a high priority in all institutions. The reasons are obvious for collections of enduring value, but even collections that are not meant to be retained over the long term represent a capital investment for an institution and as such must be protected from loss.
* *Security*: Protecting collections from theft and/or vandalism. This type of protection is needed for both special and general collections, since loss and vandalism of general collections results in unnecessary replacements and expense.
* *Storage and Handling*: Using nondamaging storage enclosures and proper storage furniture; cleaning storage areas; using care when handling, exhibiting, or reformatting collections; educating staff and users in proper handling techniques. Again, this should be a priority for all types of collections.
* *Reformatting*: Reproducing deteriorating collections onto stable media to preserve the informational content or in cases where the originals are fragile or valuable and handling is restricted. This category includes microfilming, production of preservation facsimiles, and duplication of audiovisual collections. These strategies are most appropriate for collections whose intellectual content needs to be preserved over the long term and/or where security copies are needed for unique items. Preservation microfilming is an excellent strategy for unique paper-based collections, but a low priority for institutions with general collections that are duplicated elsewhere.
* *Library Binding*: Rebinding of damaged volumes to provide sturdy use copies. This strategy is used by libraries with general collections in heavy use. It should not be used on any items that have artifactual

value.

* *Conservation Treatment*: Treating individual objects using the services of a trained conservator. This may be appropriate for a wide range of institutions, provided they hold unique materials that are of sufficient value to justify treatment.
* *In-House Repair*: Repairing objects that do not have artifactual value using a trained collections conservator or trained in-house staff. In-house book repair is used by public and academic libraries to keep non-unique books in good condition for use, and some institutions use basic paper repair techniques for historical materials. But for special collections libraries, archives, and historical societies, general preventive activities such as rehousing should be given a higher priority than in-house repair.
* *Digital Projects*: Using digital imaging to provide access copies of deteriorated original collections; creating digital objects that will act as preservation copies of original items; and/or preserving objects that are "born-digital". Digital projects may be appropriate across a wide range of institutions; the key in undertaking such a project is for the institution to have a good understanding of the requirements and limitations of digital imaging.

It is helpful to keep in mind that the primary goal of preservation is to ensure that collections survive in good condition for as long as they are needed. Preservation should never be limited to the treatment of a few select items. The most cost-effective way to establish longevity is to prevent or retard deterioration.

COLLECTION MANAGEMENT

There are several basic collection management activities that play a crucial role in the preservation of collections. These include development of an institutional mission statement and collecting policy, as well as organization and cataloging of collections.

Preservation planning requires a manager to set priorities and make choices by looking at the resources available for preservation and weighing the condition, needs, and value of materials against them. When time and resources are limited, it makes most sense to concentrate preservation efforts on materials that serve the mission of an organization. To do this, a repository must have a detailed understanding of its goals and objectives for its collections—exactly what it wishes to document, who it wishes to serve, and what types of material it will collect to accomplish those goals.

Making effective preservation choices also requires good intellectual control of collections, since relative values and preservation priorities cannot be assigned unless staff is familiar with the content of collections. In addition, intellectual control is crucial to providing access to your collections. Your collections may be housed in archival boxes, stored in a moderate environment, and protected from disaster, but if they are not accessible to users, you have neglected a basic responsibility.

MISSION AND COLLECTING POLICY

While it is easy to jokingly dismiss the institutional mission statement as a gathering of buzzwords with little real meaning, in fact, the importance to preservation activities of a carefully thought-out mission statement and collecting policy cannot be overstated.

In an ideal world, you would devise a basic statement of your repository's mission and collecting goals before actually identifying and acquiring collections. In reality, however, at least some collections may have been gathered haphazardly over time. Devising a mission statement and collecting policy will help you to look critically at all the materials you hold and decide whether they really belong in your collection.

Mission Statement

A mission statement should spell out your repository's overall goals. It may be short or extensive, depending on the size of your repository and the circumstances. In repositories such as public libraries, museums, or historical societies, where paper-based historical collections are part of a larger institution, it may be helpful to prepare a separate mission statement and collecting policy for the historical paper-based materials, because they need to be managed differently from general circulating books or museum objects. You must, however, ensure that these policies support the overall repository goals.

Your mission statement should articulate in general terms the purpose of the repository or collection's existence. What types of people, activities, and/or subjects do you wish to document? Will you focus on a specific time period or geographical area? Will you collect materials relating only to your institution, or will you collect materials from other sources as well? What users will you serve? If your repository is part of a larger institution, such as a university, how does your mission statement relate to that of the larger entity?

It is also very important to include a reference to the preservation of collections within your mission statement, along with references to collecting materials and making them available. For example, a historical society might be "dedicated to collecting, preserving, interpreting, and promoting interest in the history and culture of the local area." The presence of such a reference gives preservation equal status with other institutional activities, and demonstrates a commitment by the institution to long-term maintenance of collections.

Collecting Policy

A collecting policy expands upon the mission statement, providing specifics about the current scope of the collection, the areas in which additional materials may be collected in future, and the audience to be served. A good collecting policy will take into consideration the holdings and collecting activities of other local repositories. It is also crucial for a repository to have a clear sense of what it will not collect, since collections must be limited to those items that serve the real needs and mission of the repository.

Subjects to be discussed in a collecting policy include:

* The type of programmes and activities that will be supported by the collection (*e.g.*, research, exhibits, publications, outreach to the community);
* Potential user groups to be served (*e.g.*, scholars, genealogists, undergraduate students, local schoolchildren, the general public);
* Specific materials to be collected (*e.g.*, subjects, geographic areas, time periods, formats, languages) and levels of collecting (*e.g.*, existing strengths and weaknesses, desired levels of collecting in different areas, materials that will not be collected); and
* Information about acquisition policy, cooperative collecting efforts with other institutions, deaccessioning/weeding policy, and procedures for periodic review of the overall collecting policy.

INTELLECTUAL CONTROL: LIBRARIES

Effective selection of collections for preservation requires good intellectual control, since relative values and priorities cannot be assigned unless staff is familiar with the collections' contents.

An inventory of collections using standard library and archival descriptive practices can also assist systematic comparison of an institution's holdings with those of other repositories, especially when cataloging has been automated using the standard MARC (*M*achine-*R*eadable *C*ataloging) format. Whether or not materials are preserved elsewhere can be an important factor in determining your own priorities.

Organizing Library Collections

Most institutions with library collections will be familiar with standard procedures for cataloging and classification of library materials. Printed materials are cataloged and classified according to Library of Congress (LC) procedures that follow the *Anglo-American Cataloguing Rules*, Second Edition, or *AACR2*. This cataloging system was originally used to create catalog cards, but now computer files that are searched directly by the user are created using the MARC format. Call numbers are assigned for books using Library of Congress classification numbers or Dewey Decimal System numbers. The Library of Congress provides cataloging records for most U.S. and international publications.

The MARC format was established by the Library of Congress in the 1960s, when it began to computerize its catalog records. Using numbers, letters, and symbols to mark the information within a cataloging record, the MARC format has become the standard for library computer cataloging. Having undergone many incarnations since its inception, the version currently in use is called MARC 21; the Library of Congress maintains it and all its associated documentation. Computerized cataloging records are shared among libraries nationally and internationally through the Online Computer Library Center 's WorldCat database.

INTELLECTUAL CONTROL: ARCHIVES

This part will briefly review standard procedures for organizing and cataloging archival materials, which may be unfamiliar to some organizations, such as public libraries or historical museums, that hold archival materials in addition to other types of collections.

Archival materials are generally organized in groups, with related materials cataloged together as one unit instead of separately.

When arranging collections, archivists follow two primary principles:

* Provenance requires that records created or accumulated by the same source-whether an organization or an individual-be kept together, since as a whole they shed light on the activities of the records' creator. For institutional collections, maintaining provenance allows the researcher to discern where certain types of information might be found by determining what organization, department, or person would have produced that

information.

* Original order requires that the archivist maintain the original organization of documents within a collection. This can provide useful information about the routine activities of an organization and also help date documents or attribute documents to an author. If, however, there is no discernible order to the collection, the archivist will impose as straight forward an order as possible.

Archival description enables the researcher to find both the collection he or she needs and the information within the collection by using various types of written guides. The availability of written guides prevents users' rummaging through large numbers of boxes and documents, which can cause handling damage and general disorder. Furthermore, the researcher is not solely dependent on the personal knowledge of the archivist or other staff member(s) present to access the materials.

If you are starting with a significant backlog of material that has never been organized at all, you should begin with a basic collection-level inventory of all materials. This should provide information about the records' creator, the dates of the collection, the amount of material in it, and a general paragraph about its contents. Eventually you will arrange and describe all these materials in some detail, using standard archival practices.

Sharing Cataloging Data for Archival and Manuscript Materials

If possible, cataloging data for archival and manuscript materials should be automated at the local level using the MARC format. This might be done through an existing online library/museum catalog or through a stand-alone system that runs on a PC. In addition, there are a number of state-level databases of historical records that create automated cataloging records from information submitted by the repository.

For unique materials, cataloging records should be

entered into the OCLC bibliographic databases. For smaller institutions without the ability to input records into these databases, cataloging information can be submitted to the National Union Catalog of Manuscript Collections, a cooperative cataloging programme operated by the Library of Congress. Based on information submitted by the repository, NUCMC's catalogers create MARC records in the RLG database and establish pertinent name and subject authority headings. The submitting institution must then be prepared to make the cataloged materials available to researchers on a regular basis.

While the OCLC and RLG bibliographic databases are excellent resources, MARC records inherently provide limited detail. Access fees can also create a barrier to using these services. Archivists are now using the Web with greater frequency to provide comprehensive access to their collections by listing collections online.

Some have begun to put entire finding aids online, but this task requires an enormous amount of time and effort when done in a useful and standardized manner. Standards have been developed for encoding finding aids for the Web. The Encoded Archival Description (EAD) Standard is maintained by the Society of American Archivists in partnership with the Library of Congress Network Development/MARC Standards Office.

SELECTION FOR PRESERVATION

"Preservation" refers to all the activities undertaken by an institution to ensure that its collections survive in usable condition for as long as they are needed. While this sounds relatively simple, the process of deciding what to preserve and how to preserve it can be complicated and challenging. Which materials will be important in the future? What items or collections should be preserved, and how?

Even with a national cooperative microfilming effort, cultural institutions with paper-based collections have increasingly realised that it is not possible to preserve every brittle item. As a result, various strategies have been developed for selecting collections for preservation.

This part will explore the various criteria that you should consider when selecting collections for preservation action. Once you have decided what materials merit preservation, the choice of preservation method will depend on the intellectual content, the physical characteristics, and the condition of the materials. We will learn more about evaluating the condition of your collections and choosing the appropriate preservation method(s).

The key to making effective selection decisions is to realise that:

* You cannot save everything (even with cooperative projects);
* Priorities must be set among collections (*e.g.*, you must define your collection's strengths and concentrate on them); and
* Every item may not need to be preserved (*e.g.*, will a representative sample of certain materials be acceptable?).

SELECTION FOR LIBRARY COLLECTIONS

The selection process for preservation has been discussed and analysed extensively within the library community because of the growing need to develop strategies for selecting collections for repair, replacement, and reformatting.

Identification of damaged or deteriorated materials often occurs in the course of other library activities, although it may also happen as part of a special project. Consistent procedures for the identification of damaged items are necessary. When an item is identified for possible in-house or offsite preservation action, the librarian must indicate in the catalog record that the item has been temporarily removed from circulation and complete a form indicating what preservation action is needed. This form will accompany the item, which should be placed in a particular area and routed for further review or preservation action. Items must also be placed in a particular area and routed for further review or treatment.

In her article "Selection for Preservation," Carolyn Harris summarizes the most common methods librarians use to identify collections whose importance and condition justify preservation action.

Some of these methods are appropriate in the archival context as well:

* *Condition and Use*: Deteriorated items in need of attention are identified as they are returned after circulation or pointed out to staff by users or stack maintenance staff.
* *Condition and Library Processing*: Items in need of attention are identified during acquisition, cataloging, or other processing activities.
* *Condition at the Shelf*: Special projects that require inspection of materials at the shelf (*e.g.*, bar coding, shelf reading) can also identify deteriorated collections. For historical or special collections, a conservator may be needed for further review.
* *Collection and Condition*: An entire collection is identified as important for preservation and individual items within that collection are reviewed to identify materials in need of preservation attention.
* *Scholarly Review*: Faculty, researchers, or scholars identify deteriorated items with particular research value. This may be on an individual basis or part of a special project.
* *Vulnerability to Loss or Deterioration*: Materials that are particularly subject to deterioration, such as newspapers or items to be exhibited, are identified for attention.
* *Value or Uniqueness*: Items that are particularly unique or valuable (in monetary or other senses) are identified for attention.

Decision-making on the Collection Level

While it is easy to identify materials already in special collections as important, a research library may hold other collections of importance as well. In many cases, libraries have chosen to preserve only those collections that are circulated and used. But the library community has also realised that research libraries have a responsibility to preserve collections that may be important for research in the future, even if they are not currently used. Thus, strategies have been developed to select collections for preservation according to their quality and importance.

The criteria used to identify important collections include size of the collection; subject strength (*e.g.*, the depth and extent of the collection as compared to other collections on that subject); past, current, or projected future use; quality and extent of bibliographic control of the materials; available funding for preservation of the collection; media contained in the collection; cooperative responsibilities of the institution; and scholarly interest in the collection.

Decision-making on the Item Level

Before any item is preserved, it must be reviewed to make sure that preservation is the proper action to be taken. How is the item related to others in the collection? Are there additional copies or other items by the same author? Does the item fit the collecting policy? Are there other copies that are easily accessible in a close geographic area? Has the item been preserved (*e.g.*, filmed or treated) elsewhere? Is a replacement (*e.g.*, reprint, facsimile, microfilm) commercially available?

If these questions do not establish that the item should be discarded or replaced, additional analysis will be needed to determine the item's priority for preservation action and how it should be preserved.

SELECTION FOR ARCHIVAL COLLECTIONS

As in libraries, selection for preservation in archives often happens as part of other activities, such as acquisition, appraisal, arrangement, and description. The process of selection for preservation is closely related to archival appraisal, since it involves identifying the value and importance of collections.

While many of the criteria libraries use to select printed collections for preservation can be used in the context of archival collections, identifying important historical and archival collections also requires consideration of types of value specific to those collections. Since archivists have no more time or resources than librarians, they cannot save everything. Thus, they have developed methods for deciding which records have long-term research value and which do not.

Types of Value for Archival/Historical Collections

Most archivists follow, at least in a general sense, the guidelines for value T.R. Schellenberg established at the National Archives in the mid-1950s. On the most basic level, Schellenberg distinguished between primary value and secondary value.

The primary value of records is their ongoing business value for the organization that created them, to assist in carrying out its administrative, financial, legal, and operating activities; this is referred to as administrative, fiscal, or legal value. Secondary value refers to the value records may have to external organizations and/or private researchers.

Schellenberg defined two types of secondary value: evidential value and informational value. Note that these two types of value are not mutually exclusive: a record may be valuable for both evidential and informational purposes.

Evidential value refers to the value of records in documenting the organizational structure and functions of the institution or the activities of the individual that created them. Who created the records? Do they accurately reflect the activities of the organization or person? Do the records provide evidence of the structure and policies of the organization or institution or evidence of the changing interests of the person? In the case of an organization, are these records also maintained elsewhere within the organization? Do the records reflect policymaking or implementation of functions?

Informational value refers to the subject content of the collection.

Types of informational value include:

* *Uniqueness*: The information in the records must be more complete and useful than that found on this topic in other existing sources, whether public or

private. The records should also not be duplicated elsewhere, an occurrence that is fairly common in modern public records.

* *Form*: Records that provide concentrated information (*e.g.*, some information about many people, as in census records; or in-depth information about a few people, as in case files) are the best candidates for retention. The form of the record is also important: can it be accessed and understood easily by researchers?
* *Importance*: Value for long-term scholarly and public research is difficult to determine. Archivists generally try to document those subjects, people, and events that are considered important by the society within which the records were created.

Other types of value commonly encountered are:

* *Intrinsic Value*: This refers to records with characteristics that require them to be retained in their original form. They may be valuable because of their age (in general, older records have more significance, but this is not always the case), because the records have a unique physical form or aesthetic quality, because the records are directly associated with people or events of historical significance, because they might be useful for exhibition, etc.
* *Historical Value*: This term is used in many different ways; it might refer to materials that are valuable because of their age or association, or it might encompass both evidential and informational value.

Both value and condition must be considered in selecting archival and other historical collections for preservation. Additional considerations include whether the records are duplicated or maintained in another form elsewhere; whether they are complete (fragmentary materials can be frustrating for research); whether they need to be retained in their original form, or whether they can be reformatted (*e.g.*, onto microfilm); and whether there are donor or other restrictions on the use of the records.

2

Principles for the Care and Handling of Library Material

INTRODUCTION

What are the main threats to library material?

* The nature of the material itself
* Natural and man-made disasters
* The environment in which it is kept
* The way material is handled

Traditional library collections contain a wide range of organic materials, including paper, cloth, animal skins, and adhesives. Such organic substances undergo a continual and inevitable natural ageing process. While measures can be taken to slow this deterioration by careful handling and providing a sympathetic environment, it is impossible to halt it altogether. The chemical and physical stability of library material also depends on the quality and processing of the raw products used in their manufacture together with the design and construction of the final artefact. Over the centuries, the pressures of mass production have reduced the material quality of what is received in libraries. Much of the paper stock manufactured after 1850 is highly acidic, is becoming brittle, and will self-destruct in time. Binding techniques have been abbreviated for the sake of automation and many textblocks are now held together solely by adhesive. In fact, all books and, in particular, leather bindings, are far more susceptible to damage than most people appreciate. Modern media such as microforms, optical and magnetic disks, digital formats, photographs, and audio and visual media, all have inherent preservation problems and need to be stored and used carefully if they are not to perish prematurely. It is commonly difficult to accept is that a large amount of library material is reaching the end of its natural life, and the few years that it has left can only be prolonged by careful handling and storage.

WHY PRESERVE

* The type of library and how it is used reflect the preservation needs of its collections. The preservation requirements of a local public lending library are obviously different from those of a national library. However, both are obliged to maintain and keep accessible their collections, whether for a few years or indefinitely.
* Economically, libraries cannot afford to let their holdings wear out prematurely. Replacing library material, even when possible, is expensive. Preservation makes good economic sense.
* It cannot be easily predicted what will be of interest to researchers in the future. Preserving current collections is the best way to serve future users.
* Responsible and professional library staff should be committed to caring for and preserving the material with which they work.

WHO IS RESPONSIBLE

Everyone is responsible. While preservation and conservation specialists can advise and carry out specific activities, it is the duty of all library staff, from the head of the library downwards, to safeguard the welfare of their holdings. Preservation measures have to be endorsed, supported, and encouraged from the most senior level to the most junior in the library. Those who are responsible for managing the library and maintaining the external and internal fabric of the buildings must liaise closely with those who are responsible for the welfare of the collections. For example, if money has been set aside to rewire and replace the lighting of a building, then the opportunity should be used for ensuring not only that energy-saving lighting is used but also that it meets particular preservation lighting requirements. When plumbing is being installed or replaced, all concerned should be working towards ensuring that risks to the collections are reduced, and not increased by having pipes running through areas where library material is present. In such instances clear communication is the key. The preservation needs of a library have to be considered in line with the social and political climate in which the organisation operates. The organisation's purpose, collecting policies, and available resources also have to be taken into account.

Consequently, preservation policies must be made in consultation with various departments for the following reasons:

* The acquisitions and collecting parts of a library should be prepared to purchase additional copies of heavily used material, like reference works, when the cost of repairing such items is greater than replacing them. It is also necessary to calculate whether surrogate copies (*i.e.*, microform or electronic versions, and the machines to read them) are a more economical and effective way of providing access to heavily used material than 'hard' copy.
* A policy should be agreed with the cataloguing and record-creating activities of the library together with readers' services to direct users to surrogates rather than originals and to the most appropriate copy.
* Departments should plan for sufficient, good-quality accommodation for acquisitions.
* Reading room staff should be kept informed of any restrictions concerning the use of original material and briefed on limitations to photocopying.
* Resources should be provided for training staff on security for themselves and for library material, on how to handle library material correctly, and on how best to pass this knowledge on to users.

* An exhibition policy should be drawn up which ensures that items will not come to harm while on exhibition, whether within the library or on loan to other institutions. Librarians and conservation staff should agree on whether items are fit for display. Adequate support and security, and suitable environmental conditions for material to be exhibited, should be enforced.
* Preservation staff and those responsible for the collections, whatever their level of experience, should not only have some technical and scientific knowledge, but should also be familiar with the history of collections, the material they are made of, and the contents of the documents – so as to be able to understand better the preservation problems. Librarians, library staff at all levels, and students of librarianship should be acquainted with the importance of preservation within a library's overall function and policy.

WHERE TO BEGIN

Part of the process of formulating a preservation policy is to define whether, and to what extent, the library will acquire and retain material. There can be no general guidance for libraries on what material should be selected for acquisition and future preservation; this will depend on each individual library and its policy. However, national and regional libraries should cooperate in sharing the responsibilities of what to preserve and retain.

In order to be able to care for its holdings, a library must make a comprehensive and honest assessment of the physical state of the institution, the collections, and their preservation requirements. Moreover, to care for collections with a limited budget and limited resources, it is important that decisions are made on a clear and rational basis. Such an assessment can be done internally, by the library itself, or by independent consultants, whose expertise is established-both have advantages and disadvantages. Consultants are expensive and take up a lot of staff time. However, the final assessment should reveal the stark truth of the facts. An internal assessment will probably be cheaper but might be influenced by staff politics.

Unfortunately, it is also usually easier to accept recommendations from a body outside than from within. Such an undertaking must be a cooperative effort of all the departments and be endorsed at the most senior level. An assessment without authority is likely to be ineffectual. The final report is obviously critical to the success of any 'needs' survey. It should clearly identify the risks to the collections and be realistic in its proposals.

HOW TO BEGIN

It is important to have a clear idea of the objectives of the study before investigations into the state of the institution and its collections begin. Details on policies, operations and procedures may be found in written documents, the most likely sources will be through interviews with library staff at all levels, observations on how material is cared for and handled by staff and users, and risk assesments on the buildings and collections. Identifying major and immediate threats to the library's holdings or particular collections should be of primary concern.

Such threats will vary for different institutions, from renewing a fire and smoke detection system, through setting up an integrated pest management programme, to moving an important collection of photographs to an area with a more stable environment. Surveys are a fundamental tool for developing a library's preservation policy. However, while they should be comprehensive, they do not necessarily have to be too detailed.

Surveys can often result in enormous amounts of information being accumulated which later become very difficult to put into order and analyse. Short questions and answers are the key to successful surveys. The ensuing chapters will provide more ideas on what to look out for when planning the surveys.

Building

Building to identify any security or environmental threats that are posed by the location of the institution; to describe the history and use of the buildings; and to ascertain the condition of the external and internal fabric of the buildings.

Disaster Preparedness and Response

Disaster preparedness and response to describe potential risks-man-made or natural-to the buildings and collections; to review present precautions against these risks; and to examine disaster preparedness and response plans.

Environment

Environment to report on what environmental measures are in place to preserve the collections; what are the good and bad points of these measures; and who is reponsible for maintaining them.

Collection

Collection to ascertain the current condition of the collection and identify potential problems. Describing the type and quantity of items in collections will help to create a picture of the library's holdings and age range.

Further points that need to be covered include:

* What is the overall condition of the collections?
* Which collections are in particularly poor condition?
* Which collections are most valuable/important?
* Which collections are most at risk?
* How fast are the collections growing?
* What direction is collecting likely to take?
* Is space available or allocated for future or expanding collections?

Knowing which material is heavily used will help to determine the preservation needs of particular collections. For example, a run of local history journals which is frequently in demand and in poor condition may become a higher microfilming priority than another run of journals which is also in poor condition but not often used. Other areas, which are highlighted in subsequent chapters, also need to be documented, such as the security of the collections; how material is stored and handled; the condition of storage areas; reading room practice; and level of staff training and expertise.

WHAT TO PRESERVE

Once a preservation needs assessment has been carried out, the next step is to prioritise the recommendations which have been made.

Because of both limited resources and the potential scale of the problem it is necessary to be selective in deciding what is to be done in terms of.

* Securing the fabric of the buildings
* Improving environmental control
* Improving the storage and handling of the collections.

Such selectivity needs to be an explicit part of a library's policy if its responsibilities towards future users are to be properly undertaken. It is important to understand that selectivity does not preclude adopting an holistic approach to caring for library collections. All library material may not warrant special attention in the way of boxing or being stored in specific environmental conditions, but all should be safeguarded against man-made and natural disasters, theft and mutilation, pest and mould attack, and poor handling practices. Generally, selecting material for specific preservation processes such as reformatting or boxing is based on common sense. Boxing a collection which is in good condition and not used before attending to a collection which is in poor condition and heavily used is not common sense; neither is reformatting material which has been reformatted by an institution elsewhere.

WHAT ARE THE FINANCIAL IMPLICATIONS

Almost always, the amount of information held in libraries is greater than the resources available for carrying out their objectives with total success. It is not, and never has been, possible to save everything. A commitment to indefinite or permanent retention involves considerable financial expenditure on accommodation, special storage conditions, and possibly reformatting. Therefore, decisions have to be made as to what will be collected and preserved. Every library has a duty to ensure the welfare of its collections for present and future users.

There is no avoiding the fact that the maintenance and retention of collections costs money. For too long, libraries have spent a large proportion of their budget on acquisitions. Most libraries have no, or inadequate, funds set aside for preservation purposes. Spending time and resources on preventing damage to library material is almost always cheaper than repairing or replacing it. No library can afford not to take precautionary measures against fire, flood, theft, and mould and insect infestation, for salvaging material which has suffered from these disasters is extremely expensive in terms of human and financial resources.

The consequences of such disruptions are manifold. Serious disasters are often caused by circumstances which could have been avoided at little cost. Prevention is not only better but, more often than not, cheaper than cure. Caring for library material does not necessarily mean an excessive expenditure of library funds. There are many common-sense and economical solutions to preservation problems. However, all libraries must realise that preserving and maintaining their collections is as important as acquiring them, and that appropriate funds should be allocated accordingly.

WHY COOPERATE AND WITH WHOM

It is not simply sufficient for librarians to be aware of their responsibility for the preservation of their collections, although awareness is the first necessity. It is also important to raise awareness among the general public and those who are in a position to fund preservation programmes. Governments must play an active role in ensuring the welfare of a nation's heritage. National preservation offices, financially supported either by government or private funding, are essential if a country's written heritage, in whatever format, is to survive. These establishments should be in a position to encourage all libraries and institutions to adopt sound preservation policies. Very useful services, such as supplying literature on disaster planning, photocopying, or security matters on request are not enough. Active training and education should also be provided. Furthermore, national preservation offices can sometimes be appropriate bodies for coordinating retention policies on a national scale.

There is also the potential for them to be the political mouthpiece for libraries on issues like the mandatory use of permanent paper in publishing. Enlightening the general public through poster campaigns in schools and public libraries about the respect for and care of library material is another useful responsibility that can be assumed by national preservation offices. If a nation's heritage is to survive, then the coordination of national, regional, consortial, and institutional preservation programmes is essential. It is unrealistic to expect libraries and archives to address individually and resolve successfully the technical and financial problems associated with preservation on a national level. For instance, in 1996 IFLA and ICA established the Joint IFLA-ICA Committee for Preservation in Africa (JICPA) to raise awareness of preservation issues and coordinate activities in the region.

Libraries should cooperate not only with archives but also with museums and galleries. Considerable savings can be made and duplication of effort avoided by institutions consulting with each other over areas such as environmental control, building and collection evaluation, and disaster preparedness and recovery plans.

SECURITY AND DISASTER PLANNING

SECURITY

It is the responsibility of the library manager to intitiate, coordinate, and implement the development of a security policy within the library. When drafting such a policy other libraries, police, and staff should be consulted.

Securing Perimeters and Buildings

* Library perimeters and grounds should be kept tidy.
* Building exteriors should be assessed for ease of access by criminals. An alarm and closed-circuit television system should be seriously considered. All areas should be well-lit.
* Close attention should be paid to doors and windows in respect of locks, security glass, or film.
* The interior of the building should be kept tidy. It will present an image of care and supervision which will deter the potential criminal.
* All entry/exit points and routes should be kept separate if possible and staffed at all times.
* Any staff areas should be locked when not in use.
* Expensive equipment should be chained or bolted down and marked with security markings.
* All contractors should sign in and out of the library and wear passes at all times.
* The need for an alert attitude should be instilled in staff.
* All storage areas should be kept secure and clear policy guidelines provided on who has access to what areas.
* Specific measures, like the use of vaults, should be taken for the security of rare/valuable material.

Preventing Criminal and Anti-social Behaviour

Criminal and anti-social behaviour ranges from the rowdy visitor to the determined thief. Staff, books, equipment, and personal property are all at risk.

Starting-points in deterring criminal and anti-social behaviour include:

* Having a calm and ordered library
* Creating an environment which the genuine reader regards as helpful and efficient, but in which the villain feels anxious and wary
* Having prominent notices which clearly define what is unacceptable behaviour

* Training staff in how to deal with an awkward or aggressive user or a suspected book thief.

Security in Reading Areas

Points to consider:

* How are loose items issued and how are they checked on return?
* How well are reading areas invigilated?
* Are security devices in place?
* Are bags allowed in these areas and are they checked on exit?

Security of Library Material

All library material should be stamped in a way that clearly identifies it as belonging to a particular institution. Library stamps should be fast-drying, non-fading, stable, and indelible. Security tagging systems, if present, should be regularly inspected.

Emergency Information Booklet

It is useful for all staff to have easy access to an emergency information booklet which lists only the immediate steps to be taken, key personnel, and how they can be contacted in the event of:

* Accidents to staff and visitors
* Vandalism, theft, and assault
* Incidents like power failures, lift failures, loss of security keys
* Emergencies which threaten the welfare of people, the collections, and the fabric of the buildings – *e.g.* bomb threats
* Hurricane, earthquake, and flood warnings.

DISASTER PLANNING

It is vital for any library, no matter what its size, to take every precaution possible to prevent the occurrence of an avoidable disaster. Of equal importance is having measures in place to cope with the consequences of disasters, whether they be natural or man-made.

Natural:

* Hurricanes
* Floods
* Earthquakes
* Volcanic eruptions
* Sandstorms

Man-made:

* Acts of war and terrorism
* Fires
* Water (broken pipes, leaking roofs, etc.)
* Explosions

Numerous resources have been published to aid institutions in implementing disaster avoidance measures and formulating a disaster response and salvage plan. Only the key points are listed here.

It should be mandatory for every library to have a written plan in which all these elements are fully developed. A 'phased' approach can be used in disaster preparedness (as it can in preservation activities in general). That is, it is acceptable, as a first phase, to begin with a few parts (even in outline form), particularly if the institution focuses first on those issues that are of greatest concern.

In a subsequent phase, the planners can gradually add more detail and other parts as they become better educated, have time to pursue the plan, and are able to develop consensus on how the institution should organize its preparedness activities.

Disaster planning usually involves five phases:

* Risk assessment ascertaining the dangers to the building and its collections
* Prevention implementing measures which will remove or reduce any danger
* Preparedness developing a written preparedness, response, and recovery plan
* Response procedures to follow when disaster strikes
* Recovery restoring the disaster site and damaged material to a stable and usable condition.

RISK ASSESSMENT

Try to identify any external and internal threats that might cause problems for the collections and assess any shortcomings of disaster prevention measures which are already in place. Consulting with fire departments will help to find any potential hazards which are not immediately obvious.

Identifying External Environmental Threats

* Describe the district where the collections are housed (residential, industrial, shopping centre, rural, recreational).
* Are there any major industrial or natural hazards very close to where the collections are housed (airport, railroad/motorway, natural waterways such as the ocean, lakes, rivers, natural vegetation or bushland, other buildings)?
* What are the immediate surroundings or perimeters to the building (fences and gates, natural barriers such as rivers, lakes, ocean front, dark corners, overhangs, areas providing cover)?
* Are the surroundings secure (regular patrols, effective lighting, gates secured and access controlled, separate access for staff and visitors/users)?
* Is pollution (dust, gaseous pollutants) from factories, traffic, or the environment a problem?
* How safe is the building from fire and flood – are there hazards in the vicinity, either natural as in woodland and river or man-made, as in petrochemical plants?
* Have any major incidents or disasters occurred in the past five years (bomb threats and bombing, civil disturbances, riots, wars, natural disasters – flood, earthquake, fire, dust storm, vandalism)?

Identifying Internal Environmental Threats

* What materials are used in the structure of the building?

* Is the external and internal fabric of the building fire-resistant?
* Are there fire-resistant walls separating parts of the building and are there fireresistant doors?
* Are collections stored at a safe distance from plumbing, electrical and mechanical installations-water pipes, radiators, air conditioning, kitchens, laboratories?
* Is the area where collections are stored susceptible to leaks or flooding?
* Is smoking allowed in any areas?
* Are large amounts of flammable material (like chemicals in laboratories) other than books stored on site?

Assessing Current Preventive Measures

* Has the building a smoke, fire or water detection system?
* Is there an automatic fire extinguishing system in the area?
* What sort of manual fire fighting systems are in the area (extinguishers – water, foam, CO_2, fire hoses etc.)?
* Are the fire detection and/or extinguishing systems inspected regularly?
* Does the building have lightning conductors?
* Are special precautions taken when potentially dangerous activities are undertaken, such as rewiring and refurbishing of the internal and external fabric of the building?
* Is the building security system (if there is one) connected to fire/police departments?
* Does a written disaster preparedness and response plan exist for the library? Elements it should contain: description of emergency procedures; disaster response outline; emergency supplies list; recovery priorities; conservation experts; supplies stored off-site; list of staff volunteers; other.

* Are staff trained in emergency response procedures (delegated officer-in-charge, regular training, emergency evacuations)?
* Is computer data backed up daily?
* Are manually accessed catalogues, registration and accession records duplicated and stored off-site?
* Are electronic catalogues and records duplicated and stored off-site?

PREVENTION

Once the risks have been assessed, take all the necessary precautions to make the library buildings and their holdings secure. Consult with the emergency services (fire, police, and hospital).

Fire Alarm Systems

All parts of the building should be provided with a fire and smoke detection system, which simultaneously alerts occupants and the local fire brigade. Smoke detection equipment can provide early warning of a developing fire, thereby giving an opportunity of manual suppression prior to the activation of a sprinkler system. Manually operated fire-alarm call points, which can be used by occupants to indicate the presence of fire or smoke, should also be present throughout the building.

Manual Extinguishing Systems

If an automatic fire extinguishing system is not present, the following should be installed:

* Hose reels or racks so as to ensure that all parts of the building are within 6 m of the nozzle of a fully extended hose.
* Hydrant systems or rising mains on all buildings more than 30 m in height or where a single floor exceeds 1000 m^2.
* The hydrant or rising mains should be located so as to permit the fire brigade to pressurise the pipework from outside the building.

* Portable fire extinguishers should always be available, even if an automatic fire suppression system has been installed. There should be a suitable number of hand-held extinguishers (CO_2, water, or foam according to the likely cause of fire, *i.e.*, electrical or chemical) strategically placed.

Automatic Extinguishing Systems

Consideration should be given to the benefits offered by an automatic fire extinguishing system.

* A CO_2 gas system is only suitable for smaller compartments, *i.e.*, spaces which can be made airtight and which are not normally occupied by people.
* Halon gas systems are no longer produced as they are environmentally damaging, particularly towards the earth's protective ozone layer.
* Wet-pipe sprinkler systems are a reliable and safe extinguishing method and are relatively easy to maintain. Contrary to popular belief, the activation of one sprinkler does not cause all sprinklers to operate; and so danger of accidental discharge should not be over-estimated. The average sprinkler discharges 15-20 gallons per minute (90 litres per minute) while typical fire hoses release 120-250 gallons per minute (540-1125 litres per minute). It is important to remember that the environmental and human safety aspects of water are known, unlike the possible impact from various chemical agents. Furthermore, the recovery techniques for water-damaged material are also known.
* Dry-pipe sprinkler systems are essentially the same as wet-pipe systems except that the pipes in the protected area contain pressurized air. When the sprinkler is activated a valve opens allowing water to flow into the pipes. This lessens any threat of water leaking into collection areas.
* Micromist systems are being developed which discharge limited quantities of water at very high

pressures, resulting in exceptionally efficient cooling and rapid fire control with significantly little water. Tests have proved that water saturation, often associated with standard firefighting procedures, is avoided. Other anticipated benefits include: lower installation costs, minimal aesthetic impact, and known environmental safety.

Routine Maintenance

Fire alarms and suppression systems, the building fabric, plumbing, electric, and gas supplies and fittings, etc., should be maintained and routinely tested. All reports should be kept and any maintenance work documented.

PREPAREDNESS

The following should be prepared, reviewed, and updated regularly:

* Building floor plans which indicate storage areas, windows, entrances, and exits; fire extinguishers; fire alarms; sprinklers; smoke/fire detectors; water, gas, and heating pipes; elevator controls; electrical and water supply and cutoff points.
* Priority rescue lists made by departments, stating which items are to be salvaged from individual rooms. The fire services may allow entry into a building for salvage purposes for a limited time, and it is essential to know what items are to be saved and where they are located.
* Selecting and training an emergency response team comprising voluntary members of staff who live near the library. The team should be rehearsed in removing material and confident in making decisions about salvage techniques. It is essential for them to have participated in disaster workshops, where a disaster site is simulated and techniques can be practised.
* Detailed, step-by-step instructions on all phases of salvage operation, covering a range of incidents that

are possible (*e.g.*, roof/plumbing leaks, flooding, and fire) and the various media included in the collections, such as books and journals, manuscripts/ records, coated vs. uncoated stock, sound recordings, photographic media, computer/electronic media, etc.

* Instructions for long-term rehabilitation: procedures for activities including identification and labelling, smoke/soot removal, cleaning, sorting and rehousing, repair and rebinding, etc.
* A list of external contacts and names, addresses, and home and work telephone numbers of personnel with emergency responsibilities.
* Areas which could be used for recording and packing material.
* Locations for temporarily rehousing staff and material.
* Contracts with local freezer services.
* Contracts with vacuum-drying services.
* Arrangements with transportation services.
* Supplies for transporting, cleaning, and sorting material.
* *Record-keeping forms*: Multiple copies of all forms that may be needed in the salvage operation, including inventory forms, packing lists, requisitions, and purchase orders, etc.
* *Accounting information*: Description of institutional funds available in a recovery effort and procedures/ authorization for access to them.
* *Insurance information*: Explanations of coverage, claim procedures, recordkeeping requirements, restrictions on staff/volunteers entering a disaster area, and information on state/federal disaster relief procedures.

RESPONSE

* Follow established emergency procedures for raising the alarm, evacuating personnel, and making the disaster site safe.

* Contact the leader of the disaster response team to brief and direct the emergency response team.
* When permission is given to re-enter the site, make a preliminary assessment of the extent of the damage, the equipment, supplies, and services required.
* Correct the environment, if necessary, to prevent mould growth.
* Photograph damaged material for insurance claim purposes.
* Set up an area for recording and packing material which requires freezing, and an area for air-drying slightly wet material and other minor treatments.
* Transport water-damaged items to the nearest available freezing facility.

Drying Wet Material

As part of the preparation for a disaster plan it is essential to be familiar with the various procedures for drying different types of library material.

The following drying methods all have advantages and disadvantages:

* Air-drying
* Dehumidification
* Freeze-drying
* Vacuum thermal-drying
* Vacuum freeze-drying

If time must be taken to make critical decisions, books and records should be frozen to reduce physical distortion and biological contamination.

Air-drying

Air-drying is the simplest technique for drying damp-not totally wet-material. A damp book can be stood on its end and its pages fanned out or interleaved with blotting paper. Although this is an effective technique which does not require expensive equipment or materials (fans and interleaving paper), it is labour intensive, time-consuming, and generally results in some dimensional distortion.

RECOVERY

* Determine priorites for conservation work. Consult with conservators as to the most appropriate methods for cleaning and repairing material. Obtain cost estimates.
* Develop a phased conservation programme when large quantities of material are involved.
* Select items to be discarded, replaced, or rebound from those justifying special conservation treatment.
* Clean and rehabilitate the disaster site.
* Replace treated material in the refurbished site.
* Analyse the disaster and improve the plan in light of the experience.

It is worth liaising with local and district authorities/ councils about the availability of temporary storage facilities and other services they may be able to provide. Cooperating with other libraries, museums, and galleries in the area can save time, money, and resources.

ENVIRONMENT

The environmental factors of temperature, humidity, light, and atmospheric and particulate pollutants can all cause degradation reactions. The chemical, mechanical, and biological nature of these reactions may vary for different materials.

RELATIVE HUMIDITY (RH)

Relative humidity can be expressed as the ratio (in per cent) of vapour pressure in a sample of moist air to the saturation vapour pressure at the same temperature. Relative humidity is a difficult concept to comprehend and therefore warrants explanation. If the water vapour in one cubic metre of air, at normal atmospheric pressure, was extracted and weighed, the absolute humidity of the sample of air would be known and expressed as grams of water per cubic metre of air (g/m^3). The hygrometric chart shows the maximum amount of water vapour a cubic metre of air can hold at certain temperatures. As air temperature increases, the amount of water vapour air can hold increases as well. At 10 °C (50 °F) air can hold no more than 9 grams of water vapour. The air is at its maximum absolute humidity and is said to be saturated. At 20 °C (68 °F) the saturation point is 17 g/m³. Therefore, if a cubic metre of air in a closed container at 20 °C (68 °F) contains 9 grams of water vapour, the absolute humidity is 9 g/m³. If 3 grams of water is added to the container, it will evaporate and increase the absolute humidity to 12 g/m³. If another 8 grams of water is added, 5 grams will evaporate and 3 grams will remain as a puddle on the bottom of the container because air at 20 °C (68 °F) can only hold 17 g/m³. The relative humidity of the air in the container when only 9 grams of water vapour was present would have been:

$$\frac{\text{Absolute Humidity of Sample Air}}{\text{Absolute Humidity of Saturated Air}} = \frac{9}{17}\ 0.53, \text{ or } 53\%$$

The RH is temperature-dependent. If no additional moisture is added to the air, as the temperature increases, the RH decreases. So, if the air in the container is warmed to 25 °C (77 °F) – the hygrometric chart shows that at this temperature one cubic metre of air can hold 23 grams of water vapour – the RH would decrease.

$$\frac{9}{23} = 0.39, \text{ or } 39\%$$

Conversely, if the air in the container is cooled to 15 °C, the RH will rise, even if no more water is added. At 15 °C the air can only hold 12.5 g/m³ of water vapour:

$$\frac{9}{12.5} = 0.72, \text{ or } 72\%$$

If the air were cooled to 9 °C (48 °F), it would become saturated with water vapour, and the RH would rise to 100%. If the air were cooled any further, droplets would form on the side of the container because the air must give up some of its moisture as condensation. The temperature at which condensation first occurs (the temperature at which the air reaches saturation) is called the dew point. Indoors, in winter, the room air circulates to window panes, which are often cold enough to cool the air below its dew point. Drops of water then appear on the windows.

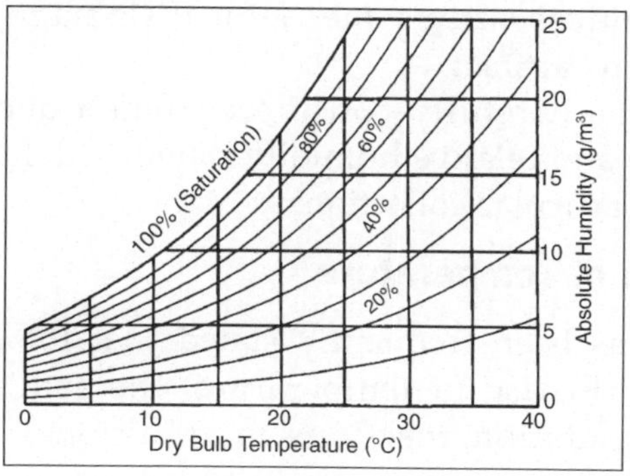

Fig. 1.1

TEMPERATURE AND RELATIVE HUMIDITY

The following statements need to be kept in mind whenever temperature and relative humidity are an issue.

* The first point that needs to be understood about temperature and relative humidity is that there is no one ideal level for all types of library material – only values and ranges that minimize specific types of change in materials and objects. A temperature or humidity that is acceptable for one object may be disastrous for another. For example, photographic film, magnetic recordings, and digital carriers require low storage temperatures and relative humidity levels if their longevity is to be ensured; whereas parchment and vellum items require an RH higher than 50% if they are to retain their flexibility.
* There is extensive scientific evidence to suggest that paper will retain its chemical stability and physical appearance for longer at a constant, low storage temperature (below 10 °C/50 °F)) and relative humidity (30–40%).
* However, while the paper text-block in a leather or vellum binding may benefit from being kept at a low

RH, the binding itself will inevitably suffer. Leather and vellum need an RH of at least 50% if they are to continue to operate mechanically. The argument of chemical versus mechanical damage or content versus artifact

has to be carefully considered when deciding what temperature and relative humidity ranges will have the most benefit for particular collections.

The Effects of Temperature

* It has been frequently stated that for every 10 °C (18 °F) rise in temperature, the rate of chemical degradation reactions in traditional library and archive material, such as paper and books, is doubled. Conversely for every 10 °C (18 °F) drop the rate is halved.
* Heat coupled with low relative humidity will eventually lead to desiccation and embrittlement of certain materials–leather, parchment/vellum, paper, adhesives, the adhesive binders on audio and video cassettes, etc.
* Heat together with high relative humidity encourages mould growth and creates an environment conducive to pests and insects.
* Cold (less than 10 °C/50 °F) together with high relative humidity and poor air circulation will lead to dampness and eventually mould growth.

The Effects of Relative Humidity

Organic matter is hygroscopic. It gains and loses water with increases and decreases in RH.

Consequently, materials expand and contract as moisture levels rise and fall.

* An RH of 55-65% minimizes mechanical damage as materials retain their flexibility.
* A sustained RH above 65% can eventually cause adhesives in both modern and traditional library material to soften and lose their adhesive strength.

* Above 70% RH, biological attack is a serious probability even if temperatures are low. In areas of poor air circulation RH should not exceed 60%; and even when air circulation is good RH should not exceed 65% in order to avoid mould growth.
* A low RH (less than 40%) minimizes chemical change but can cause materials to shrink, stiffen, crack, and become brittle.

The Effects of Fluctuating Temperature and Relative Humidity

* As has been stated, if the water content of a room is fixed, a sudden lowering of temperature will cause a rapid rise in the relative humidity, leading to condensation and possibly resulting in mould and other problems excess moisture causes.
* Moderate changes over a long period of time produce minimal stress in materials that are free to expand and contract.
* Fluctuations of temperature and relative humidity affect the dimensions and mechanical properties of organic materials and can lead to damage if they occur over a short period of time.
* Visible damage can take the form of flaking inks, warped covers on books, and cracked emulsion on photographs.

Measuring and Recording Temperature and Relative Humidity

Environmental conditions in all areas should be adequately monitored and recorded with reliable and regularly maintained thermohygrographic or electronic recording equipment.

Monitoring is very important because it documents existing environmental conditions; supports requests to install environmental controls; and indicates whether any climate-control equipment present is operating properly and producing the desired conditions. When monitoring equipment indicates notable changes in environmental conditions, reports should be given to authorities so that appropriate measures are taken immediately.

Recommended Levels of Temperature and Relative Humidity

* In general, library material should be stored and used in stable conditions which are not too hot, not too dry, and not too damp.
* Any attempts have been made to provide 'ideal' figures for temperature and relative humidity levels. However, it is now recognised that it is probably impractical and unrealistic to maintain a building or stack temperature at one setting throughout the year, especially in areas with extreme temperature variations, without incurring huge costs.
* If temperatures do rise above 20 °C (72 °F) it is vital that relative humidity levels do not rise or fall beyond acceptable levels.
* In institutions, temperatures are often dictated by what is deemed suitable for human comfort, around 20-22 °C (68-72 °F) for sedentary activities. Human beings are sensitive to changes in temperature but relatively insensitive to changes in humidity, while the opposite is true for most library material.

Setting relative humidity levels is always a compromise and is largely influenced by several factors:

* The nature of the collections
* Local climatic conditions
* Resources available to control the environment.

Taking into account these factors the following parameters should be observed:

* A level of moisture high enough to maintain flexibility
* A level low enough to slow deterioration of materials and control insects and mould
* A level that will do no structural harm to library buildings due to condensation in cold weather.

The Influence of Local Climatic Conditions on Relative Humidity

* In humid parts of the world, where relative humidity does not fall below 65% all year round and is much higher for long periods, it is unrealistic to expect a level much below 65%, unless the institution is air-conditioned day and night all the year round at great cost. In these regions good air circulation is imperative if mould is to be discouraged.
* In arid areas, where RH rarely rises above 45%, maintaining a level between 40-45% is all that can really be expected, unless great expense is incurred. Once again the key is to avoid fluctuations, to cool the air, and to keep certain materials like parchment and leather in an area where RH can ideally be maintained at no lower than 45%.
* Temperate regions with warm summers and cold winters often fare far worse than arid or humid areas. The RH in summer may be acceptable, but in winter, when central heating is used, it is often hot and dry during the day, and at night, if the heating goes off, it becomes cold and damp. Such fluctuations do far more damage than a constant high or low RH all the year round.
* In northern parts of America, Canada, and northeast Europe, maintaining 50% RH in winter without condensation is extremely difficult. Some institutions acclimatize their collections seasonally by gradually reducing levels of RH towards winter and increasing them towards summer.

ATMOSPHERIC AND PARTICULATE POLLUTION

Air pollution is to a large extent associated with towns and industry and is another cause of damage to paper and other organic materials. Air pollutants vary greatly in nature, from gases to particulates such as dirt and dust.

Gaseous Pollutants

Gaseous pollution is caused overwhelmingly by the burning of fuels. Pollutants such as sulphur dioxide, hydrogen sulphide, and nitrogen dioxide combine with moisture in the air to form acids that attack and damage library material. Ozone is a powerful oxidant which severely damages all organic materials.

It is a product of the combination of sunlight and nitrogen dioxide from automobile exhaust; it may also be produced by electrostatic filtering systems used in some air conditioners, as well as by electrostatic photocopy machines. Smoking, cooking, and off-gassing from unstable materials (cellulose nitrate film, paint finishes, fire-retardant coatings, and adhesives) may also produce harmful gaseous pollutants. Wood, particularly oak, birch and beech, emit acetic and other acids, and vulcanized rubber releases volatile sulphides that are especially damaging to photographs. The composition of all equipment, materials, and finishes used for the storage, transport, and display of objects should be tested by recognised methods to ascertain whether they are likely to produce harmful emissions.

Particulate Pollutants

Particulate pollutants, such as soot, dirt, and dust abrade, soil, and disfigure materials. Dust and dirt that have absorbed gaseous pollutants from the air become sites for harmful chemical reactions when they settle on library material. Particulate pollutants can also aid mould growth. Modern library material, such as magnetic and optical media, are very sensitive to dust and dirt.

Dust is commonly a mixture of fragments of human skin, minute particles of mineral or plant material, textile fibres, industrial smoke, grease from fingerprints, and other organic and inorganic materials. There are often salts such as sodium chloride (carried in from sea spray or on skin fragments) and sharp gritty silica crystals. In this chemical mixture are the spores of countless moulds, fungi, and micro-organisms which live on the organic material in the dust (fingerprints, for example, serve as good culture media). Much of the dirt is hygroscopic, and this tendency can encourage the growth of moulds, as well as increase the corrosiveness of salts, hydrolysis, and the release of acids.

LIGHT

Light is energy and energy is required for chemical reactions to take place. All wavelengths of light-visible, infrared, and ultraviolet (UV)-promote the chemical decomposition of organic materials through oxidation. Higher-energy ultraviolet is the most harmful. However, light in all its forms, especially in the presence of atmospheric pollutants, leads to a weakening and embrittlement of cellulose, adhesives, cloth, and skin materials. Light can cause some papers to bleach and others to yellow or darken; it can also cause media and dyes to fade or change colour, altering the legibility and appearance of documents, photographs, art works, and bindings.

The following factors concerning light should be known by all those responsible for preserving library material:

* Chemical reactions initiated by exposure to light continue even after the light source is removed and materials are put into dark storage.
* Light damage is irreversible.
* The effect of light is cumulative. The same amount of damage will result from exposure to a strong light for a short time as to a weak light for a long time. 100 lux (the unit of measure of illuminance) on a picture for 5 hours gives it an exposure of 500 lux-hours, equivalent to 50 lux for 10 hours.
* Visible and infrared light sources, such as the sun and incandescent light bulbs, generate heat. An increase in temperature accelerates chemical reactions and affects relative humidity.
* Daylight has the highest proportion of UV radiation and therefore must be filtered.

Types of Lighting

* Incandescent lamps are the most familiar type of electric light source. Light is produced by passing an electric current through a thin tungsten wire filament. Incandescent lamps usually have less harmful UV radiation output than fluorescent lighting, but they generate more heat through infrared radiation. Tungsten incandescent lights also burn less efficiently and must be replaced more often than fluorescent lights.
* Tungsten-halogen lamps (also known as quartz halogen or just halogen lamps) also produce light by passing an electric current through a thin tungsten wire filament but with the addition of a halogen gas in the bulb, which enables the filament to operate at higher temperatures yielding a 'whiter', more efficient light source. Halogen lamps have three to five times the life and UV output of tungsten incandescent lights.
* Fluorescent lamps are low-pressure mercury discharge lamps which produce UV radiation which in turn excites a phosphor coating that emits visible light. The use of different phosphors is responsible for the various colour characteristics these lamps exhibit. Although fluorescent lighting is high in ultraviolet content, it is usually installed in libraries because it generates less heat and is more economical to operate.

Measuring Light and UV Levels

It is necessary to measure and record light and UV levels at different times of the year, as readings will change with the seasons. A light meter or lux meter measures the intensity of visible light in lux (lumens per square metre). A camera with a built-in light meter can also be used to measure light levels indirectly. A UV meter measures the amount of UV radiation (wavelengths less than 400 nanometers) in units of microwatts of UV radiation per lumen.

Recommended Light Levels

Lighting in museums, galleries, and exhibition rooms is usually left to specialists. This should also be the case for library reading rooms and storage areas. While 200–300 lux are acceptable levels for reading rooms, attaining such levels with a combination of natural and artificial light, which satisfy staff and researchers, is difficult. In stack and storage areas 50–200 lux is sufficient. However, to achieve these levels it would be necessary to exclude all natural light and rely entirely on artificial lighting. Light sources with ultraviolet radiation emissions above 75 microwatts per lumen require filtering.

Light Levels for Material on Display

In exhibition situations, the light level falling on the surface of objects on display must be kept low. No more than 50–70 lux during an eight-hour day for a maximum of 60–90 days, is often recommended for light-sensitive materials like coloured paper, newsprint, and certain bindings (*e.g.* textile bindings), and media like manuscript ink and watercolours.

MOULD

The spores of fungi that become mould are always present in the air and on objects and will grow wherever conditions are favourable. In general, moisture (above 65% RH), darkness, and poor air circulation are ideal conditions. Warmth is a factor, but certain moulds and bacteria will thrive in cold temperatures too (think of what can happen in a refrigerator). Mould can weaken, stain, and disfigure paper and photographic material. It is generaly recognised that 'foxing' may be attributable to mould reacting with trace elements in paper. Cloth, leather, vellum, and certain adhesives are also affected by mould.

Attending to an Infestation

* Mould can be checked to see whether it is active or inactive. Generally, active mould is damp, slimy, and smears if touched. Inactive mould is dry and powdery and can be brushed off with a soft brush.

* If mould is discovered in large portions of a collection, isolate the area immediately and do not attempt to clean up without first consulting a mycologist to determine if toxic moulds are present. Certain moulds commonly found in libraries can pose serious health risks, causing headaches, nausea, eye and skin irritation, and respiratory problems.
* A conservator may have to be employed or at least consulted on the treatment of infested items and on the return of the affected area to a suitable condition for housing material.
* If only a few items are affected, place them in a dry paper-based box until treatment. If possible, include a desiccant, such as conditioned silica gel packets. This enclosure will prevent spores from circulating, but will not encourage the growth potentially created by the tightly sealed microclimate of a plastic bag.
* Alternatively, move the affected material to a clean area with relative humidity below 45%, separate from the rest of the collection, and allow them to dry.
* If immediate drying is not possible, or if many objects are wet, freeze them; later they can be thawed, dried, and cleaned in small batches. Material may also be freeze-dried and then cleaned.
* When dry, the items should be cleaned and stored under suitable environmental conditions. The storage environment is critical since even after cleaning, fungal residue will be present.

Cleaning Infested Material

* If the outbreak is small, and equipment limited, take the items outside – well away from the building – on a calm, mild day and brush them off with a soft white brush, away from you and downwind.
* Remove mould only with a vacuum cleaner that contains an HEPA (high efficiency particulate air) filter capable of retaining 99.97% of all particles down

to 0.3 microns. Conventional vacuum cleaners have drawbacks: often the suction is too strong; as the bag fills up the efficiency decreases; the exhaust can be contaminated with fine particles not trapped by the bag, therefore redistributing them around the room. An HEPA vacuum cleaner is an effective way to remove mould because it does not spread the spores around. Vacuum cleaners designed to filter air through water are unsuitable for capturing mould's small particles. Even if a fungicide is present in the water, this will not prevent particles of mould from being discharged back into the air.

While certain treatments can kill mould that is active, they are far less effective with dormant spores, which are protected by relatively impervious cell walls. Proper conditions will insure that dormant fungi remain inactive and will prevent germination of accidentally introduced active spores. If the environment is favorable to fungal activity, mould will grow. Even if complete eradication were possible, it would not be a permanent solution in storage spaces without climate controls.

More spores are always being introduced and would sooner or later become a problem.

* If it is not possible to remove mould outdoors, work in front of a fan, with the fan blowing contaminated air out a window, or work in a ventilation hood. Make sure the ventilation hood uses a filter that traps mould. Be sure to remove the mould in an area well away from collection storage and other people. Close off the room. If the building has central/mechanical air circulation, block the uptake vents so that spores are not spread through the building via the airhandling system. Take care when disposing of solid cleaning materials such as vacuum cleaner bags or filters. These should be sealed in plastic bags and removed from the building.
* To remove inactive mould from paper or books, use a multiple-filter vacuum cleaner. Small brushes and nozzles used for cleaning computers are useful for

this purpose. Papers can be vacuum cleaned through a plastic screen held down with weights. A brush attachment should be used for books. Covering the nozzle or brush with cheesecloth or screening will guard against loss of detached pieces. Remember active mould is soft and subject to smearing, and is easily rubbed into porous materials such as paper or cloth.

* Active mould is best removed from valuable artifacts with a small low-pressure vacuum cleaner. This delicate work is best done by a conservator.
* When fungal growth is visible on art objects or valuable items, it should be removed by a conservator. Staining caused by mould can often be removed or at least lightened. This is an expensive procedure and therefore most suitable for objects of significant value.

Treating an Infested Area

* It is important to find out what caused the mould outbreak in the first place.
* The room where a mould outbreak occurrs must be dried and thoroughly cleaned before the affected material can be returned to it. For moderate to large mould outbreaks contact a professional service that provides dehumidification or cleaning of the premises.
* If the RH is above 55%, it must be lowered before the collection is returned to the area. Adjusting the HVAC system or adding a portable dehumidifier may be all that is necessary. Also check for leaks or water condensation on outside walls. Inspect the heat-exchange coils in the heating/air-conditioning system, a notorious breeding ground for fungi, and clean them with a household disinfectant.
* Vacuum clean the shelves and floor with an HEPA vacuum cleaner, then clean them with a household disinfectant. Before returning the cleaned material to

the area, monitor the RH for several weeks to make certain it does not exceed 55%.

* After the items are returned, check daily for new mould outbreaks.

Preventing Mould Outbreaks

* Check new collections or shipments for the presence of mould.
* Maintain moderate temperature and relative humidity (below 20 °C/68 °F and 65% RH).
* Circulate air.
* Vacuum clean regularly.
* Do not shelve books directly against an outside wall. Owing to temperature and humidity differences between inside and outside environments, moisture may develop along walls. Allowing air to circulate against the walls will enable the moisture to evaporate.
* Do not allow plants into the building.
* Waterproof basements and walls below ground level.
* Place or adjust outside gutters and drains so that water does not collect near the outside walls. Check gutters and drains regularly to avoid obstructions.
* Place lawn sprinkler systems so that they do not soak outside walls.
* Regularly inspect collections for mould so that any infestation is detected before it becomes serious.

INSECTS AND PESTS

Insects

Insects which most commonly cause damage in libraries and archives throughout the world are cockroaches, silverfish, book-lice, beetles and termites.

* They feed on organic substances such as paper, pastes, glues, gelatine sizing, leather, and bookcloth; birds nests are also a major source of food for insects, and bird droppings are corrosive.

* They prefer warm, dark, damp, dirty, and poorly ventilated conditions.
* Their damage is usually irreversible – text and images lost by insects eating and boring through paper and photographs cannot be replaced.
* Termites can devastate buildings and collections.

Pests

Rodents such as rats and mice can devastate collections:

* They will destroy books in order to obtain paper for their nests.
* They can cause fires by gnawing through electrical insulation.
* They will pare their teeth on library furniture and fittings.
* Their droppings are corrosive and can leave permanent stains.

Treating Infested Material

* Always look for the least toxic alternative. For example, when faced with a box of books with silverfish, avoid chemical treatments and simply hand-clean the volumes using a vacuum cleaner and a soft brush. When uncertain if pests are active, clean the item, bag it, and examine it later for signs of fresh activity. Be sure to segregate collections from new accessions or items with possible pest problems.
* The least toxic approach is not only the environmentally friendly approach, but for many collections it is the only responsible approach:
  - Most fumigants will likely affect the long-term preservation of at least some materials.
  - There is no one fumigant which is known to be safe for all collections.
  - Collections may be damaged through contact with the water- or oil-based spray.
  - Fumigation offers collections no resistance to future pest attack.

* It is essential that after treatment, steps are taken to prevent any new infestation from being introduced. This will probably mean segregating new (and possibly infested) collections, strictly isolating collections with any signs of pest activity, cleaning, and improving storage conditions.

Some institutions have selected freezing as an alternative to chemical fumigation. By rapidly lowering the temperature to at least –35 °C and holding it at this level for up to several days, most life stages of most insects can be killed. While some commercial freezers are adequate for pest control, others are not able to lower the temperature quickly enough. A slow reduction in the temperature allows some insects to go into a state resembling 'suspended animation' and survive the treatment. Naturally, it is also important to ensure that the objects are not damaged by the low temperatures and that condensation is controlled.

Preventing Insect and Pest Infestations

It is now accepted that an integrated pest management (IPM) approach should form part of every preservation programme. IPM involves:

* Monitoring the building regularly for the presence of insects and pests
* Ensuring all staff, from cleaners to librarians, are vigilant and report any signs of fresh damage and activity
* Checking all material which is to be accessioned before it enters the library
* Using sticky traps. Traps have the advantage of catching insects before they can be found visually; they catch a wide range of species; they can be placed in areas which are difficult to inspect; trapped insects can be identified and counted; traps are good indicators of an increase in insect numbers in one area; they also highlight any failure of control treatment
* Understanding the biology and life cycles of insects

and pests, which helps to know when and where they are likely to breed, what they are likely to eat, where they are likely to live

* Eliminating or containing all sources of likely infestation-ideally food and drink should not be consumed on the premises; flowers and plants should not be allowed in the building
* Maintaining an environment not conducive to pests and insects, which is clean, cool, dry, and well-ventilated
* Preventing pests and insects from entering the building-making sure doors close properly, installing mesh screens for windows and doors, etc.
* Using appropriate exterior lighting, such as sodium vapour, which is less attractive to insects
* implementing a cleaning and hygiene programme – rubbish should be safely and properly disposed of; attics and basements regularly checked and cleaned.

IMPROVING THE ENVIRONMENT

If the objective is to retain a collection or specific individual items indefinitely, then very close attention needs to be paid to the environment in which the items are stored. The ideal environment includes controlled temperature and relative humidity, clean air with good circulation, controlled light sources, and freedom from biological infestation. Good housekeeping practices, security controls, and measures to protect collections against fire, water, and other hazards complete the range of environmental concerns. Library buildings should be designed as far as possible to meet preservation requirements.

These requirements affect many aspects of planning: design and orientation of buildings; building materials (which can, under some circumstances, be used to produce satisfactory internal climatic conditions in preference to mechanical air control systems); internal building and furbishing materials; and materials used for furniture, including shelving as well as lighting, both natural and artificial. Indigenous and traditional building methods and materials in subtropical and tropical areas often provide better storage conditions for library material than those that are imported. It is always worth considering constructing a sealed area within a building for material which needs tight temperature and relative humidity control.

Practical Measures to Improve the Environment

In many places heating, ventilating, and air conditioning systems (HVAC) may be too costly to install and maintain or may have to be restricted to specific collections. Nevertheless, there are many rudimentary measures and precautions that can improve a library's environment and protect collections. A first step in all efforts to improve the environment should be sealing the structure. This step alone will improve the physical condition of the building by reducing air infiltration, pest access, heating loss or heat gain, and air and particulate pollution.

Making the building watertight will also reduce the sources of moisture within the structure and may significantly reduce relative humidity levels.

* Use draft excluders and weatherstripping to make the building weathertight.
* Ensure windows and doors fit securely.
* Ensure good air circulation by appropriate use of fans and windows.
* Use dehumidifiers and humidifiers to reduce or increase relative humidity.
* Use insulation methods to reduce heat gain or loss.
* Use UV-filters on windows and fluorescent lighting.
* Use screens, blinds, shutters (preferably outside the windows, as this reduces solar heat gain), and heavy curtains to keep out direct sunlight.
* Ensure storage facilities are dark.
* Ensure buildings are properly maintained to keep out dampness during rainy periods.
* Use close-fitting enclosures (boxes and envelopes) wherever possible to protect important and valuable library material. These can create a micro-climate around the object, which delays the effects of changes

in temperature and relative humidity. They also shield the item from light, and can act as a buffer against atmospheric pollutants and prevent particulate deposits.

* Paint the outside of the building with a pale-coloured light-reflecting paint in hot climates.
* Be aware that while trees and vegetation near buildings can reduce heat gain, they can also encourage insect and pest activity.
* Locate plumbing and heating pipes outside storage areas.
* Locate sanitary premises and sinks outside storage areas.

HVAC Sytems

If the institution has a heating, ventilation, and air conditioning (HVAC) plant, then the following questions should be answered as part of any environmental survey:

* Does the air conditioning provide constant climate control throughout the year?
* Is the air conditioning system kept at a constant level 24 hours a day?
* Is the air conditioning turned down or shut off at any time?
* At what temperature and humidity levels is the air conditioning set?
* Are monitoring devices for temperature and RH regularly used in the facility?
* If there is no air conditioning system or, areas not covered by the system, how are rooms heated and/ or cooled?
* If there is no air conditioning system or, areas not covered by the system, how is humidity controlled?
* What sort of air filtration system is used?
* To what standard does it operate?
* Who maintains the air conditioning systems and how often?

House-keeping

To ensure the protection of the collections against particulate pollutants, a regular and sustained programme of cleaning should be maintained, undertaken with care and under supervision. Clean surroundings also discourage fungi, insects, and pests. The cleaning programme should include the examination of collections not only to provide early warning of biological or chemical damage but also to observe conditions throughout the area.

Cleaning the floors of storage accommodation and book stacks may be left to non-specialized staff under instructions to respect the collections and not to touch library material or shelves. Directions should be given to retrieve pieces of bindings, record slips, etc., from the floor (noting where they were found).

Library material on the shelves should only be cleaned by properly trained members of staff. It is important to provide appropriate materials and equipment which remove rather than redistribute dirt and dust. Cleaning cloths to which particulates adhere rather than dusters which merely spread them around in different places should be used to clean library fittings.

Floors should be vacuum cleaned (not swept) and damp-mopped once a week. Cleaning agents must be nontoxic and pose no threat to the collections from solvent fumes or abrasives. Products containing oil, chlorine, alum, peroxides, and ammonia should be avoided.

TRADITIONAL LIBRARY MATERIAL

PROCESSING LIBRARY MATERIAL

Written Notations

Written notations such as cataloguing and foliation inscriptions should be made as neatly and unobtrusively as possible with a soft (B) pencil, applying light pressure to prevent indentations. It is worth considering enclosing notations within brackets to indicate that the information was added by the institution. Inked notations (and accidental markings) are often permanent and cannot be removed. Many inks are acidic; others are water-soluble and will bleed and run when exposed to moisture, such as that encountered in a water-related disaster.

Shelfmarks (Call Numbers)

Shelfmarks should not be painted on books, nor should they be typed onto labels which are attached to books with pressure-sensitive tape or adhesive. Paint is unattractive and disfiguring; tape and adhesive may discolour, stain or otherwise damage the binding. For antiquarian material, shelfmarks should be written on the first fly-leaf with soft pencil. When using self-adhesive labels, care should be taken to ensure that the adhesive will remain effective over time. It is especially important that the adhesive does not desiccate, causing labels to come loose or fall off, and does not ooze, which will attract dirt and may damage other materials that come into contact with it. Ideally, labels should be on permanent paper.

Bookplates

If bookplates must be used in books, they should be made of low-lignin, alkaline paper, and should be attached with a stable, reversible adhesive, preferably riceor wheat-starch paste, or methyl cellulose; or polyester film jackets should be made and the bookplates attached to them. Circulation card pockets should be treated the same way, although books of special value usually should not circulate.

Inserts

All acidic inserts, such as loose bookmarks, scraps of paper, and pressed flowers, should be removed from books, assessed, documented, photocopied, and, if to be saved, then encapsulated in polyester. This is to prevent staining and acidity in the inserts from migrating into book pages and damaging them.

Fasteners

No attempt should be made to separate documents that are attached with lines or dots of paste or glue. If such items must be separated to allow for the safe handling, use, or filming of the records, a conservator should be contacted. Great care must be exercised when removing old fasteners such as staples, paperclips, etc.

Fasteners that have rusted or become strongly adhered to paper surfaces must be gently lifted; before removal, the line of contact between the paper and any encrusted rust must be broken. When removing fasteners, the document should be fully supported on a table, and one hand should be placed on the document to hold it in position and support the paper while the fastener is being removed. If the procedure is conducted in mid-air, documents are likely to be torn and damaged. Staple removers should not be used on fragile or brittle documents, as they can easily remove an entire weak or brittle corner along with the intended staple.

READING ROOM PRACTICE

Reading rooms should have sufficient numbers of staff to ensure security against theft, mutilation, and vandalism.

Supporting Books When in Use

Books are complex composite objects which open in a variety of ways and require different methods of support when opened. Very few books can be opened at 180° without being damaged. It is strongly recommended that no book is opened more than 120°, and tightly bound volumes no more than 90°. Bindings are far more vulnerable and fragile than is presumed and need to be handled with great care.

Board attachments are often precarious, with extremely thin leather over the joints. Such books should always be supported when in use and boards should never be flipped back 180° from the text-block. The traditional wooden lectern or reading stand has caused many volumes to be damaged by presenting the book at a steep angle which strains the sewing and does not support the joints, which will soon weaken and eventually split. Moreover, such steep lecterns are not comfortable for readers to use. For fragile and rare material, the foam book supports designed by Christopher Clarkson provide the most suitable way of supporting both tight- and hollowback volumes. A book can be set up at a comfortable reading angle of 20°, with an opening not greater than 120°, the joints fully supported, and the leaves restrained with strips of weighted fabric. As the reader progresses through the volume, the blocks can be adjusted to retain optimum support for the book's vulnerable joints. With a thicker book, the reader should add or remove one or more of the flat pads to fit the volume's changing profile as it is opened in different places. A larger wedge may be placed beneath the two side-supports, to form the base of the book-rest and provide a more comfortable reading angle.

Notices to Readers

Reading rooms should have notices clearly directing readers NOT to:

* drink, eat, or smoke in the library except in designated areas
* handle library material with unwashed hands
* use ink of any kind
* use correction fluid or highlighters
* annotate texts, or write on paper placed on top of the pages of an open book
* lean on library material
* touch illuminations, painted images, manuscript or printed text areas
* insert slips or notes in the gutter of a book
* leave items in direct sunlight
* leave out items not in use
* have more than a limited number of items out at a time for consultation
* pile items on top of each other
* shuffle loose items to fit them in an enclosure, but to handle them individually (in order to prevent

hidden edge tears from interlocking and causing further damage).

Assistance for Readers

Reading rooms should provide readers with:

* Information to encourage a regard for the welfare of library material
* Guidelines on how to handle library material
* Book supports and guidelines on how to use them
* Guidelines on how to remove and replace books on shelves
* Adequate space for the viewing of large items
* Cotton gloves for handling valuable material and photographs
* Clean work surfaces
* Polyester sheets for tracing maps
* Assistance with handling large items
* Clean, smooth weights to restrain unrolled plans.

Photocopying

Photocopying raises serious preservation issues. Flat-bed photocopiers and poor handling can cause severe damage to the structure of books and documents. Photocopy machines specifically designed for bound material and not office photocopiers should be provided. Overhead photocopiers, which allow a book to be copied face-up, are ideal but expensive. Ideally, photocopying should be carried out by the library's own fully trained staff, with each item being examined for its suitability. The criteria for restricting certain material and copyright regulations must be thoroughly understood by all staff members. Training parts in good handling practice and good copying practice should be mandatory for all new staff, with refresher parts for existing staff at frequent periods.

If it is not possible to allocate staff to carry out copying, there are some factors which can help to reduce wear and tear:

* Position the machines where they are within clear sight of staff.

* Post clear and concise guidelines on careful handling prominently by the machines. It is worth considering posters illustrating that the spine of a book should never be pressed down with the hand or the cover of the copier to ensure a good quality image.
* Make criteria for restricting material clear to users and discourage practices such as photocopying an item for the sake of a few sentences.
* Keep a record of what has been photocopied so that items which are frequently requested can be microfilmed.

The following material should not be photocopied:

* Fragile or damaged items
* Tightly-bound volumes
* Rare books and photographs
* Books stapled or stitched through the sides
* Fine bindings
* Vellum and parchment
* Items with seals attached
* Perfect bindings (books which rely on adhesive to keep the pages together and are not sewn)
* Oversize items that would have to be excessively manipulated to obtain a complete image.

STORAGE METHODS AND HANDLING

Storage methods have a direct effect on the useful life of material. While proper storage can extend life, slovenly, haphazard, overcrowded conditions soon result in damage to collections. Moreover, poor-quality storage enclosures can accelerate the deterioration of the material they are intended to protect. Handling by staff and users also directly affects the useful life of library collections. Damage to books is cumulative. Repeated poor handling can quickly transform a new book into a worn one, and a worn book into an unusable book that requires costly repair, rebinding, or replacement. By following the guidelines presented here, the library can make significant strides towards improving the welfare of the collection.

Shelving and the Shelving of Books

* Shelving should be designed to provide smooth, secure, clean, and convenient support. Any protrusions and sharp edges should be attended to. Ideally, book cases should be constructed of steel with a baked enamel finish.
* Volumes should be shelved a minimum of 10 cm off the floor to reduce the risk of damage from flooding or passers-by. When possible, use shelving units that have a 'canopy' on top, as this will deflect water, dust, and some damaging light.
* Good air circulation should be maintained in storage areas and around shelving.
* Book cases should be at least 5 cm away from walls and the books another 5 cm away from the back of the book case. This is especially important when book cases are positioned against the outside walls of a building.
* When books are stored in steel cabinets, ensure the cabinets are adequately ventilated. Holes should be in the sides and not on the top of the cabinets to avoid dust and debris falling on the books.
* Books kept on mobile shelving must be shelved carefully to avoid any possibility of them falling off or being crushed when the shelves are moved.

For the maximum protection of books, the following rules should be enforced:

* Shelve books so that they are not difficult to remove or replace. Books which are tightly shelved will soon be damaged when they are removed or replaced.
* Use bookends to support books when shelves are not full. Allowing books to lean will distort and strain the structures and eventually cause their breakdown. Bookends should have smooth surfaces and broad edges to prevent covers from being abraded and leaves torn or creased.

* Do not let books extend beyond the edges of shelves into aisles because they can be damaged by passers-by and trollies.
* Shelve books by size whenever possible. Avoid keeping large books next to small ones because the large book will be inadequately supported.
* Box, or at least separate with a piece of card or board, bindings with metal furniture (clasps, bosses, studs, etc.), which are shelved next to unprotected books.
* Separate paper and cloth bindings from leather bindings. Acidity and oils in the leather migrate into paper and cloth and hasten their deterioration. Furthermore, degraded powdery leather will soil paper and cloth.
* Shelve small, structurally sound books upright.
* Move the books or rearrange the shelves if books are too tall to stand upright. Do not store books on their fore-edges as this will damage the structure of a book and loosen the binding.
* Store oversize, heavy, structurally weak, or damaged books horizontally to give them the overall support they require. Additional shelves may need to be inserted at narrow intervals to avoid having to stack these books.
* When oversize books that are stored flat are removed, the upper volumes should be transferred to an empty shelf or book trolley. The desired volume should be removed by lifting it with both hands, and the removed volumes should then be transferred back to the shelf. Replacing the book on the shelf is done in the same way.
* Avoid stacking books in piles on shelves or tables as the books can easily topple over. Ensure the stacks contain no more than two to three books.
* Take special care to ensure that shelfmark flags or titles of books that are stored flat are visible so the books can be identified without moving them.
* Do not place a large book on a small book.

* When the binding must remain on view, such as in a period room in a historic house, the use of book-shoes (supports that cover the sides but leave the spines of books visible) or placement of a piece of polyester film between the books.

Poor handling procedures can cause irreparable damage to books.

* They should not be pulled off the shelves by the headcap, a practice that causes the headcap to fail, tearing the spine of the binding.
* If there is room above the book, reach over the top of the book to the foreedge and then pull it out.
* If there is no room, push back the books on either side of the one to be retrieved, to expose enough of the spine to allow for a firm grip on either side of the spine with the thumb and fingers.
* The book should be removed, and the remaining books on the shelf and the bookends readjusted.

Carrying and Transporting Books

* Do not carry more books than can be comfortably held firmly in both hands.
* Pack books flat in tough boxes when moving them out of a room.
* If necessary, pad the box with polystyrene or foam so that the books do not slide around.
* Transport individual books in card boxes. Carry the box in a polythene bag when going outside.
* Use water-resistant polypropylene containers with securely fitting lids when moving books out of a building.
* Whenever possible use two people to move containers.
* Avoid leaving library material in vehicles.

Book Trollies and Books on Trollies

Use book trollies that:

* Have large rubber wheels, for this helps stability, and manoeuvrability, and reduces vibration

* Have wide shelves or protective rails to secure the items in transit
* Have bumpers on corners to minimize damage from inadvertent bumps.

When putting books on trollies ensure that:

* They are shelved upright on the trolley and are properly supported as in the stacks
* Volumes do not protrude beyond the edges of the trolley
* The trolley is loaded so that it has a low centre of gravity.

ENCLOSURES FOR BOOKS AND PAPER MATERIAL

Enclosures should be lignin-free, sulphur-free, alkaline buffered, and have a high cellulosic content (above 87%). Enclosures include boxes, envelopes, and folders and are available commercially in a range of shapes and sizes.

Enclosures are crucial to library preservation, for they:

* provide protection from over-handling
* provide protection in transit
* provide protection on the shelves
* provide protection against fire, smoke, and flood damage
* keep out light
* keep out dust
* act as a buffer against fluctuations in the ambient environment
* act as a buffer against atmospheric pollution.

Types of Enclosures for Books

* Tailor-made boxes of bookboard and cloth are ideal but are expensive and require time and skill to make. They can be justified only for extremely rare, unique, and valuable material. They have the advantage of being able to provide all round support and are more robust than other types of enclosures.
* Phase-boxes are a cheaper alternative, which provide adequate short-term (15-20 years) protection, and are

much quicker and simpler to construct. They can be made in-house or commercially.

* Commercially made, archival-quality boxes and four-flap folders come in a wide range of sizes and can be purchased in small and large quantities.
* Book-shoes are appropriate for books that require structural support while being displayed on shelves.
* Slipcases should be avoided because they often abrade the surface of the binding and damage the text-block when the book is slid in and out.
* Envelopes are sometimes used for the storage of books. These generally do not provide the support books need and should be replaced with boxes.
* Wrappers of a permanent durable paper or card can be used to protect books that are infrequently used, if enclosures are too expensive or take up too much space on shelves.

Selecting Material to be Boxed

When prioritising books for boxing the following should be considered:

* Books with fragile and important bindings.
* Vulnerable and damaged books – books with loose or torn leaves, and books with loose covers.
* Books bound in vellum or with vellum text-blocks. Vellum responds readily to changes in relative humidity by expanding and contracting. This can result in warped covers and cracked joints. Boxing helps restrain vellum bindings and thereby minimizes warping.

Shrink-wrapping and Vacuum-packing

Shrink-wrapping and vacuum-packing, adapted from the food and packaging industry, are economical ways of protecting material. Both processes involve placing an item between sheets, or into pouches, of polyester/polyethylene film. The film is either shrunk using heat, as in shrink-wrapping, or a vacuum is created around the item and all air expelled, as in vacuum-packing. While they seem to be stable in the short term, further tests have yet to be carried out on the effects of long-term storage. Material which is to be moved and fragile items, in particular those with brittle paper, can be placed between boards and protected in one of the ways; the result is a rigid and strong enclosure. Shrink-wrapping and vacuum-packing are also being used as means of combatting insect and fungal attack and creating a stable micro-environment. Space can be saved as the process expels most of the air, thereby reducing the thickness of the item.

Newsprint

Commercially made, archival-quality boxes and vacuum-packing are both ways of preserving newspapers. However, because much of the newsprint produced after 1840 is made of short-fibred paper that contains lignin and other impurities, its long-term preservation is difficult at best and, consequently, microfilming has become the most common method of dealing with newspapers. Collections of newsclippings are usually important because of the information they contain and not because of the value of the clippings themselves. For this reason, again, photocopying and microfilming are the most practical preservation options. All photocopying should be done on low-lignin, buffered paper using an electrostatic copier with heat-fused images. Newsclippings that must be retained should be treated and then physically separated from better-quality papers in a folder or in an enclosure made of polyester film.

Periodicals and Pamphlets

Periodicals and pamphlets can be stored in boxes, folders, or card envelopes. Several items of the same cover size can be stored together in commercially made boxes. Items that differ in size can be placed in card envelopes and then boxed. If a single periodical or pamphlet must be shelved between books, it should be placed in a card envelope.

Scrapbooks and Ephemera

Many historical collections include scrapbooks and ephemera (*e.g.*, trade cards, valentines, patterns, paper dolls, etc.). These items pose challenging preservation problems because they often contain a variety of components and media. They may have raised surfaces, three-dimensional decoration, or moving parts. They are frequently unique, fragile, damaged, and of significant associational value. They should never be interfiled with other categories of library and archival material because damage may result from the different sizes, shapes, weights, and materials represented. Scrapbooks that are of special historic value in their original form should be individually boxed. Unbound ephemera should be grouped by size and type (*e.g.*, photographs, printed material, manuscripts, etc.), individually enclosed to protect items from acid migration and mechanical damage, if needed, and stored in a way that will support them structurally.

Single-sheet Material

* For paper collections, only objects of the same size and category should be stored together.
* Differences in bulk and weight are potentially damaging, so it is not advisable to store single sheets in the same box with books or pamphlets.
* Generally speaking, heavy objects should be stored separately from lighter ones, as should bulky objects (which cause uneven pressure inside boxes).
* As acid migrates from paper of inferior quality to any other paper with which it comes into direct contact, it is important to separate poor-quality papers from those that are better. Newsclippings and other obviously inferior-quality papers must be removed from direct contact with historical documents and manuscripts on better-quality paper.
* Documents and manuscripts should be unfolded for storage, if this can be done without splitting, breaking, or otherwise damaging them. If unfolding may result in damage, a conservator should be consulted before proceeding.
* Documents should be stored in file folders. Ideally,

no more than ten to fifteen sheets should be placed in each folder.

* Folders should be placed in document-storage boxes.
* All folders inside a box should be the same size and should conform to the size of the box.
* Boxes should not be overfilled because this can cause damage when items are removed, replaced, or reviewed.
* Boxes can be stored flat or upright. Flat storage will give the documents overall support and will prevent crumbling edges, slumping, and other mechanical damage to which upright storage might subject them. Flat storage, however, causes documents on the bottom of the box to suffer from the weight of those above. If boxes are stored flat, they should be stacked only two high in order to facilitate their removal from, and replacement onto the shelves.
* Upright storage is acceptable when documents and folders are well-supported to prevent slumping and edge damage. 'Spacer' boards made out of stable materials can be used to fill out boxes that are not quite full.
* Vellum documents and maps, etc., are highly susceptible to fluctuations in temperature and relative humidity and should be placed in an enclosure. Suitable enclosures include encapsulation, folders, mats, and boxes, or a combination of these.

Fascicules

Rare and unique single-sheet items, such as letters, have been traditionally bound into guard books. These are satisfactory if they are kept fairly thin and allow a support sheet for each manuscript page to ensure that the support and not the manuscript is handled. A simpler method is to make up fascicules. A fascicule is a single-section, pamphlet-sewn binding comprising support sheets of bifolia and hooked leaves (acting as compensation guards) with an acid-free stiff paper cover. Sizes are made to fit commercial boxes. All items are foliated and placed loosely in the fascicules by librarians. The leaves on which the items are to be attached are also foliated. A Japanese paper hinge is pasted onto the edge of the item. The hinges are then pasted and the items attached to the recto of the support sheets.

The fascicules are then boxed. Fascicules have several advantages:

* Each item is kept flat and supported.
* Items can be easily removed and replaced if necessary (*e.g.*, for exhibition).
* Flexing of the object is reduced.
* Abrasion between items is reduced.
* Handling is reduced.
* A variety of materials within a standard format can be accommodated.
* The contents are protected from light and airborne pollutants.

Oversize Single-sheet Material

Oversize material includes architectural drawings, blueprints, maps, large prints, posters, and wallpaper samples. These items are best stored flat in plan chests. They should be placed individually in folders cut to fit the size of the drawer. If several items are placed in one folder, interleaving with acid-free tissue paper is desirable, especially if the items have colours or are of special value. There should be sufficient space between chests to facilitate the safe removal and replacement of oversize material. There should also be an adequate surface on which to place items once they are removed or prior to replacement.

If they are not brittle or fragile, oversize material can be rolled when flat storage is not possible. Some items need to be rolled individually; others can be rolled in groups of four to six similar-sized items, the exact number depending on the size and weight of the paper.

A tube several inches longer than the largest item being rolled and at least four inches in diameter (larger diameters are preferable) should be used. If the tube is not made of low-lignin, pH-neutral materials, it should be wrapped in neutral or buffered paper or polyester film. Alternatively, place the items between two sheets of polyester film or acid-free tissue cut several inches larger in both dimensions than the largest item being rolled.

Roll the item or items onto the tube. Wrap the assembly with neutral or buffered paper or polyester film to protect it from abrasions. Using flat linen, cotton, or polyester tape, loosely tie up the wrapped roll. This assembly can be stored inside a larger rectangular box for added protection if desired. Tubes should be stored horizontally.

Handling and Transporting Oversize Single-sheet Material

* Use both hands when handling large items.
* Take care that large pendant seals are supported and turned with the document.
* Consider the route and destination before setting out, even if simply moving items from one room to another.
* Place maps, plans, and large single-sheet material in a portfolio or purposemade folder.
* Use two people for carrying large portfolios.
* Carry portfolios vertically.
* Use waterproof portfolios when moving items outside.

EXHIBITIONS

When exhibiting library material, special attention should be paid to the following:

* Selecting items which are fit for display.
* The security of the exhibit-cases should have locks, shatter-proof glass, be alarmed, and the room should be invigilated at all times.
* Materials used for case construction should be chemically stable and checked for offgassing.
* The climatic factors of temperature, relative humidity, light, UV radiation, and atmospheric

pollutants should be tightly controlled and monitored by appropriate equipment.

* Materials used for mounting exhibits should be chemically stable and pose no detrimental threat to the artefact.
* Books should be strapped with polythene to tailor-made card or acrylic cradles which acurately follow the profile of the opened or closed book. Books generally should not be displayed at an angle greater than 20° from horizontal, nor opened wider than 120°, and should be provided with a text-block support when appropriate.
* Acid-free card with an alkaline reserve should be used for window mats and mounts.
* Exhibits like paintings, not in cases, should be secured to walls or floors and cordoned off for security reasons so that visitors cannot touch them.
* A record of all items exhibited should be kept.

Loans to other institutions for consultation or for exhibition may involve risk or damage. The librarian has a duty to see that such requests, if granted, involve the borrower's making adequate provisions for safekeeping. All items should be protected against wear and damage in transit, and for security reasons the lending library may require such items to be carried both ways by personal courier, preferably a conservator or librarian.

The mounting of the exhibit should also be carried out or supervised by the courier. Loan items must be adequately insured, on an all-risks basis, again at the borrower's cost. The librarian needs to be satisfied that the conditions for exhibiting the item are appropriate on conservation grounds, and also that the security arrangements for the exhibitions are dependable.

Travelling exhibitions pose particular problems for conservation, because the likelihood of damage is multiplied. Lending institutions should make condition reports, including photographic records, of items being sent away for exhibition;

they also should consider making a complete microfilm of each loan, for the sake of security.

PHOTOGRAPHIC AND FILM-BASED MEDIA

PHOTOGRAPHIC MEDIA

Since the birth of photography in 1839, photographs have been made employing many different methods. Some of the materials used were extremely self-destructive, others were very sensitive to physical contact, and almost all photographic material is sensitive to the environment – not only temperature, relative humidity, and air pollution but also oxidising substances found from emissions in building materials, wall paints, wooden furnishing, cardboard, wall paints, and even the enclosures used to protect them. While the conservation of photographic material should be left to specialists, library staff can take certain precautions to safeguard the welfare of photographs within their collections.

Composition of Photographs

A typical photograph consists of three different parts:

* Support – the support layer may be of glass, plastic film, paper, or resin-coated paper.
* Binder – The emulsion or binder layer, most commonly gelatine, but also albumen or collodion, holds the final image material or image-forming substance to the support.
* Final image material – The final image material, made of silver, colour dyes, or pigment particles, is usually suspended in the emulsion or binder layer.

Many different final image materials and binders have been used over the years. Today, however, almost all black-and-white photographs are composed of silver suspended in gelatine.

Handling

Photographic media are extremely susceptible to damage from careless handling;

Staff and users should therefore:

* Provide copies rather than originals whenever possible
* Wear clean, lint-free cotton gloves when handling photographic media and never touch the emulsion side of any photographic image (*e.g.*, print, negative, transparency, lantern slide, etc.)
* Prepare a clean work surface
* Use two hands to hold a photograph, or support it with a piece of stiff card
* Not use adhesive tapes, staples, pins, paper clips, or rubber bands on photographic material
* Consult a photographic conservator on issues of storage and handling.

Enclosures

All enclosures should pass the Photo Activity Test (PAT) as described in ANSI standard IT. 2 1988. This stringent test evaluates the effect of housing materials on photographic media. Many manufacturers and suppliers of housing materials now conduct this test on their products. If at all possible, purchase products that have passed the PAT, or specify that any housing purchased must pass the PAT. Enclosure materials for photographs fall essentially into two groups: paper/board and plastic.

Paper and board should conform to the following criteria:

* High cellulose content (above 87%)
* Neutral pH (around 6.5–7.5)
* Undetectable reducible sulphur content
* Free of lignin, pH buffers, metal particles, acid, peroxides, formaldehydes, and harmful sizing agents.

Plastic enclosure materials should conform to the following criteria:

* Free of plasticiser
* Surface not glazed, coated, or frosted
* Polyester is recommended for most enclosures so long as the environment is stable. The exceptions are prints and negatives with delicate surfaces (such as flaking emulsion and hand-colouring), glass-based

material, Tintypes, cased photographs, and early film-based material.

Environmental Recommendations for Storage

Photographic media are exceptionally sensitive to environmental factors.

* Generally, storage temperatures should be kept as low as possible and measures should be taken to reduce exposure to light, UV radiation, atmospheric, and particulate pollution.
* Black and white prints and negatives should be kept below 18 °C (65 °F) and 30–40% RH.
* Colour material should be placed in cold storage (below 2 °C or 35 °F) and 30–40% RH if its longevity is to be ensured. Place material in cold storage only after consulting a specialist.
* For mixed photographic collections, 35–40% RH is recommended.
* Fluctuations of temperature and RH should be avoided.

Storage

Photographs

Photographs-it is best for each item to have its own enclosure. This reduces damage to the photograph by giving it protection and physical support. Because paper enclosures are opaque, the photograph must be removed from the enclosure when it is viewed; clear plastic 'L' sleeves (two sheets of polyester placed on top of one another and joined along two adjacent edges), with a piece of board behind the print for added support, have the advantage of allowing researchers to view the image without handling it, thus reducing the possibility of scratching or abrasion.

Special care must be given to the storage of oversize photographic prints mounted on cardboard. This board is often acidic and extremely brittle. Embrittlement of the support can endanger the image itself because the cardboard may break in storage or during handling, damaging the photograph. Such prints must be carefully stored, sometimes in specially made enclosures. They should be handled with great care. Once photographs have been properly housed in folders, sleeves, or envelopes, they may be stored upright or flat in drop-front boxes of archival quality. Horizontal storage of photographs is usually preferable to vertical storage, since it provides overall support and avoids mechanical damage such as bending. Vertical storage, however, may make access to the collection easier and decrease handling. With vertical storage, photographs should be placed in acid-free file folders or envelopes that are themselves housed in hanging file folders or document storage boxes. Overcrowding should be avoided. The use of hanging file folders will prevent photographs from sliding down under each other and will facilitate their handling.

In either case, care should be taken not to pack the photographs too tightly.

* *Prints in Albums*: May be interleaved with a photographic conservation paper if they appear to be suffering damage from adjacent prints or album pages. This should not be done if the binding will be stressed by the extra volume of paper. Modern albums of the type that have adhesive coated pages and plastic cover sheets should not be used.
* *Photographic Albums*: Should be stored flat, preferably in boxes lined with acid-free tissue paper padding.
* *Glass-plate negatives*: Should be kept in individual paper enclosures and stored vertically in suitably padded cabinets or strong boxes with a board separator after every fifth plate.
* *Film Negatives:* Can be stored in paper or polyester sleeves. They can then be placed in boxes or in a hanging file system in a cabinet.
* *Cased photographs*: Such as Daguerreotypes and Ambrotypes should be kept horizontally in their cases and these stored in cabinet drawers and/or boxes.

Boxes containing photographic material should be housed on metal shelves. Where possible, items of similar size should be stored together; the mixing of different sizes can cause abrasion and breakage, and can increase the risk of misplacing smaller items. Regardless of the size of the photograph, all enclosures within a box should be the same size and should be the size of the box. Boxes should not be overfilled.

FILM-BASED MEDIA

There are three main types of film-based photographic materials: cellulose nitrate, cellulose acetate, and polyester. These materials have been used as a support for negatives, positive transparencies, motion pictures, microfilms, and other photographic products. Cellulose nitrate and cellulose acetate are unstable. The by-products of their degradation can severely harm and even destroy photographic collections. In particular, institutions should isolate and properly store cellulose nitrate material because of its extreme flammability, especially when in a deteriorated condition.

Cellulose Nitrate-based Film

* It was manufactured 1889-1951 and in use 1900-1939.
* It is unstable and highly flammable.
* At room temperature and lower, it slowly and continuously deteriorates, emitting gases in the process.
* If these gases cannot escape from the container in which the film is kept, then decomposition accelerates-the base turns yellow, then brown, becomes sticky and then brittle, until it disintegrates into ashy-brown powder, resulting in the complete destruction of the picture/sound records.
* The reaction can lead to spontaneous combustion of the film with disastrous consequences for other adjacent material, people, and buildings.

Cellulose Acetate-based Film

* It was introduced in 1935, and from 1939 onwards almost totally replaced cellulose nitrate.

* It slowly decomposes at room temperature, giving off gases that resemble the smell of vinegar-vwhence the process is known as 'vinegar syndrome'.
* It eventually breaks down altogether.
* Until recently, cellulose triacetate films had been considered suitable for archival records; however, stability problems have become evident with this film as well.

Polyester-based Film

Commonly known as 'safety film'. For the most permanent photographic records, films incorporating a polyester (polyethylene terephthalate) base are currently recommended.

Handling

Film-based media can be damaged easily, even when in good condition. All three film types, and the gelatine binder on them, can be scratched, abraded, and creased. Oils and dirt from hands can also damage the support and binder, as well as the final image material. Once deterioration has begun, film-based media are even more prone to handling damage. Deteriorated media can become quite brittle; in this state, repeated removal from a housing can cause considerable harm. Furthermore, deteriorated materials may become sticky and adhere to other items. Ideally, film should not be handled at all by non-specialists and should be projected or copied only by a film conservator. Handlers should wear lint-free cotton gloves, handle the edges only, and work in a clean, well-lit, and well-ventilated area with enough room for processing. Eating, drinking, or smoking should not be allowed in the processing/examination area. Prolonged exposure to deteriorated negatives can be a dangerous health hazard, especially when in large collections.

Environmental Recommendations for Storage

Recent work at Rochester's Image Permanence Institute makes explicit the relationship between storage temperature/

relative humidity and long-term stability. The results, published in the *IPI Storage Guide for Acetate Film*, predict the life span of fresh and already degraded films under different combinations of relative humidity and temperature. The following chart illustrates the predicted life expectancies for the previously cited storage conditions. The first number of years in each storage condition is for new film and the second is for film that has begun to deteriorate.

Table. 2.1 Estimated Life Expectancy (in Years) for New and for Deteriorating Acetate Film in Selected Storage Environments

Office, Air Conditioned	21 °C D 70 °F at 50% RH	40–5
Cool Storage	18 °C D 65 °F at 35% RH	90–15
Cool Storage	13 °C D 55 °F at 30% RH	200–40
Cool Storage	04 °C D 40 °F at 30% RH	800–130
Cold Storage	–04 °C D 25 °F at 30% RH	1500–400
Cold Storage	–18 °C D 0 °F at 30% RH	1500–400

The Guide is a very practical tool for a collections manager, since the cost of an improved storage environment can be directly compared to quantitative benefits measured in years of additional preservation. As indicated by the Guide, cold storage is the only viable option to increase stability of material that already shows signs of deterioration and for keeping new material in good condition. If cold storage is not an option over the short term, the storage facility should be well ventilated to prevent the build up of acidic gases that drive the autocatalytic degradation reactions of cellulosic films. As much as possible, the environment should be stable, cool, and dry. Significant fluctuations of temperature and relative humidity should be avoided.

Segregated Storage

Ideally, each type of film-based material should be stored separately, isolated from other types of film supports. Organising storage in this way protects other photographic media from the harmful degradation products of cellulose nitrate and the cellulose acetates. In particular, the nitric acid formed by the degradation of cellulose nitrate can fade silver images, cause gelatine binders to become soft or even tacky, and corrode metal containers and cabinets. This type of materialbased organisation also makes monitoring the condition of the collection more efficient and effective. While it is important to separate different types of material if possible, it is also important to segregate deteriorating media from those in good condition. Deteriorating materials produce degradation products that can induce deterioration in other photographic media.

General Storage

Sheet film, like negatives and transparencies should be placed in sleeves, the sleeves in a box or drawer, and these boxes or drawers on metal shelves or in a cabinet. Roll film, such as motion picture film and microfilm, should be kept wound on cores, emulsion-side-in and placed in canisters which are free from plasticizers, chlorine, and peroxides. Acceptable materials include polyethylene or polypropylene. Any paper or card inside the can should be removed, as should any outside paper wrappings, and stored separately with appropriate documentation. Both flat and roll material should be stored horizontally on metal racking in cool, dry, dark conditions, with good air circulation.

AUDIOVISUAL CARRIERS

AUDIO DISK RECORDINGS

The most likely form of sound recordings to be found in libraries will be longplaying microgroove disks usually pressed on polyvinyl chloride, or the 78 rpm shellac disks.

Shellac Disks

The first shellac disks date from the 1890s, and this format was used until the 1950s, when it was gradually replaced by vinyl disks. Determining the causes of shellac degradation is difficult because a very wide range of qualities of shellac and 'fillers' have been used by manufacturers. In a proper storage environment, these disks suffer a slow, progressive embrittlement of the shellac. High humidity levels accelerate the embrittlement of shellac disks. This embrittlement causes a fine powder to be shed from the disk after each playback, effectively scraping away groove information. Organic materials in the aggregates are susceptible to fungus attack, while shellac itself is said to be fungus-resistant.

Vinyl Disks

Although vinyl is stable, its life is not indefinite. Vinyl discs are made of polyvinyl chloride (PVC), which degrades chemically when exposed to ultraviolet or to heat. Stabilization is therefore achieved by adding a chemical to the resin during manufacture. This does not prevent the degradation but controls it. Vinyl disks are resistant to fungal growth and are unaffected by high humidity levels.

Handling

* Remove grooved disks from the jacket (with the inner sleeve) by holding it against the body and applying a slight pressure with a hand and bowing the jacket open. Pull the disk out by holding a corner of the inner sleeve. Avoid pressing down onto the disk with the fingers, as any dust caught between the sleeve and the disk will be pressed into the grooves.
* Remove grooved disks from the inner sleeve by bowing the inner sleeve and letting it slip gradually into an open hand so that the edge falls on the inside of the thumb knuckle. The middle finger should reach for the centre label. Never reach into the sleeve.
* To hold a disk, place the thumb on the edge of the disk, and the rest of the fingers of the same hand on the centre label for balance. Use both hands on the edge to place disk on turntable.

Storage

* Store records in soft polyethylene inner sleeves. Avoid using inner sleeves made of paper, cardboard, or PVC.
* Do not leave recordings near sources of heat or light

(especially ultraviolet), as plastics are adversely affected by both.

* Do not place heavy objects on top of recordings. Recordings should never be placed on top of each other.
* Shelve recordings vertically, on edge.
* Do not use shelving units where supports put more pressure on one area of the recording or where supports are more than 10-15 cm (4-6 inches) apart.
* Do not interfile recordings of different sizes, as smaller items may get lost or damaged, while larger items may be subjected to uneven pressure.
* Remove shrink-wrap on long-playing gramophone records (LPs) completely. Shrink-wrap can continue to shrink, thus warping the disk.

Environmental Recommendations for Storage

A proper environment for the storage of sound recordings is essential to retard degradation. Elevated and rapid fluctuations of temperature and humidity can affect certain chemical properties of the plastics that make up recording media, causing distortion of sound quality and warping of the disk itself. 18 °C (64 °F) and 40% RH is recommended. Fungi on disk surfaces can cause pitting, which affects playback quality. Dust, combined with the pressure exerted on the grooves by the stylus, can permanently abrade the walls of the grooves, which affects playback quality; dust can also be embedded permanently into thermoplastic substances.

MAGNETIC MEDIA

Magnetic tapes (audio and video recordings on cassettes, audio and computer reel-to-reel tape, computer diskettes, etc.) are most commonly made of a magnetic layer of chromium or iron oxide bound with an adhesive onto a polyester film base. It is the adhesive binder which is susceptible to deterioration, through hydrolysis and oxidation. As the information is stored on magnetic tape in patterns formed by the magnetized particles, any loss or disarrangement of the magnetic oxide causes loss of information. Since the early 1950s, there have been more than forty video formats that have varied in size, speed, and the manner in which the tape is held. Cassette tapes are much thinner and weaker than reel-to-reel tapes, and their useable life expectancy is very short. Use reel-to-reel tape for long-term retention. Magnetic tape has a much shorter lifespan than is presumed. Magnetic tape that is over 15 years old almost certainly needs careful attention, and most tapes over 20 years old need professional help.

Handling

* Minimize handling.
* Avoid touching the surface of any tape or computer diskette. Oil from skin leaves a residue that can coat the equipment's playing head and attract dust.
* Do not touch the tape surface or the edge of the tape pack unless absolutely necessary, and then wear lint-free gloves.
* Do not use commercial products advertised to clean tapes and diskettes. Contact an experienced professional to clean or repair dirty or damaged tapes.
* Return tapes and diskettes to their individual boxes immediately after use to avoid possible damage and dust.
* Never use paper clips or adhesive tape to attach notes directly to cassettes, reels, or diskettes.
* Handle tape only in clean areas.
* Do not let tape or leader ends trail on the floor.
* Return tapes to their containers when they are not in use.
* Do not drop tapes or subject them to sudden shock.
* Cut off damaged tape or leader/trailer ends from open-reel tapes.
* Do not use general-purpose adhesive tapes to secure the tape end or for splicing. If necessary, use adhesive products designed for the purpose.

Use

* Label all tapes.
* Maintain machines according to manufacturer's specifications to ensure that equipment will not damage tapes.
* Clean the recorder tape path thoroughly at the recommended intervals.
* Discard tapes with scratches or any other surface damage, which causes significant debris to be left in the recorder tape path.
* Use a cleaning cassette after playing a damaged tape.
* Ensure tapes to be reused are thoroughly erased before they are put back into service.
* Fast forward and rewind tapes periodically.
* Do not leave a tape stopped in the middle – always rewind the tape fully.
* Protect the operating equipment and tapes from dust.

Backup and Refreshing

The loss of a single computer diskette can mean the loss of a large quantity of information. For this reason, backup copies are critical to ensuring the preservation of computer-based records. If maintaining an active computer database of records is part of an institutional operation, copy the information recorded on the system's hard drive onto backup diskettes or tapes on a daily basis. As a part of disaster prevention, store backup copies in another secure location. Audio, video, and computer tapes which are to be retained for long periods of time will require periodic copying/refreshing to ensure access to information.

Every three to five years, re-copy all master tapes onto high quality, polyesterbased tape in the currently established format for the media. Use this copy master only when making another 'use' copy. Make the copies of masters at different times so they do not age together. Use reel-to-reel audio tape for master audio copies. A written transcript of an audio or video tape can also be used as a 'use copy' or 'backup copy'.

A transcript may contain every word on the original tape, or only a general rendering of the discussion.

Migration

Information formats disappear as new technology emerges. Within the last twenty years, 8-track tapes, beta format video, ½-inch videotape, 3-inch, 5¼-inch and 8- inch computer diskettes and countless other formats have become obsolete. Access to information is limited when machines necessary to read these records fail and cannot be replaced. To ensure access to information, copy older formats onto a stable technology while playback machines remain available.

Storage

* Keep tapes and diskettes away from magnetic fields – do not stack tapes on top of electrical equipment.
* Keep storage areas clean and free from dust. Dust attracts and traps moisture and will precipitate hydrolysis, a common and serious cause of long-term magnetic tape degradation. Also, dust may cause permanent damage to the tape: the abrasiveness of the dust, along with the pressure exerted between the tape surface and the tape recorder heads, will scratch the oxide layer and the tape recorder heads.
* Do not leave open reel or cassette tapes exposed to the sun.
* Store open-reel and cassette tapes with the reels or tape packs vertical. Reels should be supported by the hub.
* Use high quality reels or cassettes, boxes/containers, and accessories.
* Use protective collars for open-reel tapes.
* Do not store the tapes in poor quality cardboard sleeves/boxes, which may be acidic, or vinyl boxes containing chlorine.

Environmental Recommendations for Storage

* *Tape storage areas should be cool and dry*: 15 ± 3 °C (59 ±5 °F) and 30–40% RH are safe practical storage

conditions. Extreme heat and frost will damage magnetic media.

* RH above 40% accelerates the deterioration of the tape binder.
* Avoid subjecting tapes to rapid temperature changes. If storage and operating area temperatures differ by more than 8 °C (15 °F), allow an acclimatization time within the operating area of four hours for every 10 °C (18 °F) difference.

OPTICAL MEDIA

Laser Disks

Laser disks were launched in 1978 and are usually 12-inch (30 cm) disks of glass or plastic. Millions of pits are etched into the surface which are read by a laser beam directed at the surface. A light beam is reflected, which is then converted into a conventional analogue signal.

CD-ROM

CD-ROM (compact disk – read only memory) originated from the audio compact disk which was available in the mid-1980s, and thus its physical dimensions and characteristics are the same. The main difference between CD-ROM and CDAudio is that CD-Audio contains only audio data, while CD-ROM may contain audio, computer, and video/picture data. The moulded plastic compact disk incorporates a continuous spiral of pits, which contain the data. An aluminium reflective layer allows a laser in the compact disk drive to read the encoded information. Data integrity is protected by a lacquer coating on one side and a plastic substrate on the other side.

Handling

The worst handling stresses for an optical disk are caused by severe flexing or application of a sharp point to the top surface. These actions deform the substrate, wiping out pits and causing areas of the disk to become unreadable. A sharp stylus – a ballpoint pen, for example – can cause compression of the polycarbonate substrate and the metallic reflecting layer in the area under the pen point. Do not leave disks in disk drives. Wear lint-free gloves when handling optical media.

Labelling

Applying labels of any kind may unbalance an optical disk and make it difficult for the player to read. Also, labels may peel in humid conditions. Once a label is on the disk, however, it is especially important not to try and remove it. The act of peeling off a label creates a lever action that concentrates stress in a small area. Such stress can cause delamination, especially in a writable CD. If it is necessary to write on the top side of a disk, a soft felt-tip marker is preferable to other writing instruments, but with some solvent-based markers there may be a danger of the solvents migrating into the protective lacquer.

Cleaning

Avoid using cleaning solvents. Light dust or dirt may be safely brushed off with a non-abrasive lens tissue, but the use of an air gun is preferable. Always be gentle and wipe from the centre hub towards the outside edge of the disk. The motion should be in a radial direction (like the spokes of a wheel), not circumferential.

Storage

The acrylic 'jewel cases' provided by many manufacturers and distributors are good protection against scratches, dust, light, and rapid humidity changes. Protect the individually cased CDs further by placing them in a closed box, drawer, or cabinet. This gives additional protection from light, dust, and climate fluctuations. If the manufacturer provides a spacer card or other material as part of the jewel case package, it should be retained.

Environmental Recommendations for Storage

Optical disks should be stored in a dust-free, cool (below 20 °C or 68 °F), and moderately dry environment (40% RH).

Warmer and humid conditions will lead to the oxidation of metallic reflecting layers, dark fading of dyes, and deterioration in polymer substrates and coatings. Do not leave disks in sunlight.

REFORMATTING

WHY REFORMAT

Although libraries can take steps to prevent damage to their collections and the rate at which they deteriorate, few institutions can afford the labour-intensive and costly process of conserving their collections. Preserving the intellectual content, by putting it into another, more durable format (reformatting), is all that is feasible and may be all that is required. Many publications are available which cover in detail the issues that reformatting raises and the methods and techniques involved. This part summarises some of the most common points and is concerned mainly with looking after the reformatting media. It is also a reminder that material which is to be reformatted needs to be handled with all due care.

Library and archive material is reformatted for numerous reasons:

* To preserve its intellectual content.
* To reduce wear and tear to originals.
* To save space-brittle and badly damaged material may be disposed of if it has no artefactual worth and if intellectual content is the only concern.
* To improve access-copies of microfilm and digitised media can be distributed to off-site locations, providing access to more than one user at a time.
* To duplicate certain records for security reasons, in case the originals are damaged, stolen, or destroyed.

Reformatting, if it is to be a truly successful preservation process, depends upon the cooperation of institutions on a national and international scale. Projects like that of the European Register of Microfilm Masters (EROMM), a database of existing microforms in the most important libraries of

Europe, must be set up. EROMM records what reformatted texts exist and where, so that institutions avoid duplicating their efforts (two institutions microfilming the same newspaper is a waste of valuable resources, as is one institution's reformatting a run of journals when a 'healthy' set exists in another town nearby).

Furthermore, cooperation is necessary between libraries in planning what is to be reformatted and by which institution. Many guides have been published to aid librarians in selecting material for reformatting and in setting up reformatting programmes. Generally, the following questions have to be asked:

* Is the item or collection unique or rare?
* Are there other copies of the item in the library or elsewhere?
* Does the item need to be treated (is the paper already, or is it likely to become, highly acidic and brittle)?
* Is it possible to replace the item?
* Is it, or is it likely to be, heavily used?
* Does it need to be retained in its original form?
* Has it been reformatted somewhere else already?

Reducing Wear and Tear to Originals

When the objective is to reduce wear and tear to originals, great caution has to be exercised in preventing damage occurring during the reprographic process. Reformatting increases the risk to an item because of the number of times it has to be handled in the process.

Selecting a Format

There are three main reformatting processes:

* Photocopying
* Microfilming
* Digitizing

Each has advantages and disadvantages over the others, but they can all serve different purposes, and all are worth having present in a library to some degree.

PHOTOCOPYING

Photocopying as a reformatting process is not a complete preservation tool since usually no master is made from which other copies can be taken.

However, it is particularly useful for replacing missing pages or text:

* Damaged or missing items in hard-copy periodical runs can be copied and bound for storage on open shelves.
* Photocopies may also be used when an embrittled item can no longer be used without risking damage, and a paper copy replacement (rather than film) is desired but is not available from a commercial publisher.

In each case, it is essential that photocopies be of the highest quality and on permanent paper.

Advantages

* There is no reading machine interface required other than the photocopier itself.
* The medium and format of the original can be retained.
* It usually costs less than other processes, particularly if the original is a monochrome document.
* Library patrons prefer paper facsimiles to the use of, say, microfilms, except where bulky documents, such as newspapers, are involved.

Disadvantages

* Photocopies made directly from a master photocopy are usually of poorer quality than paper prints of microfilms.
* The costs of making subsequent photocopies is higher than the cost of printing microfilms.
* There is some loss of information, especially for graphic objects other than line art.
* If the original is kept, more space has to be created.

Photocopy Paper, Toner, and Machines

* *Paper*: Photocopies should be made on paper that meets the American National Standards Institute (ANSI) standard for permanent paper, Z39.48- 1992 or ISO 9706, using a black-and-white copy machine, since colour photocopies are not stable over the long-term.
* *Toner*: Other considerations are toner quality (carbon black is recommended), and the fusion of the toner to the paper. Photocopy machines should be well maintained to ensure that the temperature is right for fusing the toner to the paper. If a freshly-made copy smudges when an attempt is made to erase the image, the machine is not fusing the image to the paper properly and must be adjusted.
* *Machines*: Photocopying bound items on common library photocopiers exerts enormous strain on bindings and inevitably damages them. Photocopiers which allow an item to be photocopied face-up are preferable. Overhead photocopiers which also digitise text and images are now available. They have great potential for being able to capture good-quality images of volumes which do not open well.

MICROFILMING

Microfilming Process

A wide range of standards covering all aspects of microfilm production and storage have been published.

Preservation microfilming comprises a number of steps:

* *Selection* – making informed decisions on what is to be filmed.
* *Preparation* – checking the item is complete; cleaning and repairing pages; preparing 'targets' that denote details such as title and magnification.
* *Filming* – similar to basic photographic procedures.
* *Processing the film* – after exposure, the film is processed to archival standards and tested to ensure residual processing chemicals are removed.

* *Inspection* – after processing, the film is inspected for blemishes, legibility, and completeness.
* *Record creation* – the creation and mounting of machine readable records (MARC) to promote use of film and prevent duplication of effort.

Commercial Microform Bureaux

Using a commercial microform bureau can be more economical than setting up an in-house operation. It is vitally important to evaluate the qualifications of any microfilm service company.

* Talk to other institutions, particularly archives, and enquire about their experiences with microfilming companies.
* Ask potential firms about their experience in filming records that are bound, fragile, or oversized.
* Ask for at least three references from other institutions.
* Contact the referees to see how the microfilm vendor handled records, met deadlines, and responded to refilming corrections.
* Inspect the microfilmer's operation. Ask questions about standards, procedures, and security.
* Draw up a contract between the institution and the bureau.
* Commission sample film.

Advantages

* A well-proven history – library material has been reproduced in microformats since the 1930s.
* Problems with the technology have largely been ironed out.
* Numerous standards exist for filming, processing, and storage.
* Microfilms can be economically created, duplicated, and distributed.
* Microfilms can be digitized if good-quality film has been used.
* Film is very compact.

Disadvantages

* User resistance – usually microfilm reading machines in libraries are of poor quality, and not designed for human comfort.
* Users must access the film manually by
  - Locating the film
  - Loading it onto a machine
  - Spooling through dozens of images to find the required one.
* If the film is not in the library, it may take weeks to be delivered.
* Film can become scratched when handled.
* Each generation or succeeding copy loses resolution (about ten per cent).
* Printouts may be of poor quality.
* Film creation variables are difficult to control.
* Image quality can be determined only after filming is complete.
* Bad pages must be re-filmed and spliced in.

Types of Microfilm

* *Silver-gelatine* – the only type for archival master negatives, which are to be retained indefinitely off-site in tightly controlled conditions. Master negatives are used solely for generating further copies and never for viewing.
* *Diazo* – an interim printing copy can be made from the master on diazo film, from which other copies are taken.
* *Vesicular* – positive copies can be made on vesicular film for use and circulation.

Storage and Environmental Recommendations

Most of the recommendations for film-based media apply to microfilm material. Many films in existing collections are on acetate-based stock. Such film chemically decomposes, giving off a vinegar smell and ultimately leading to shrinkage and emulsion damage. Indeed, all cellulosic films are susceptible to deterioration. The rate of deterioration of the film base proceeds gradually until it reaches the autocatalytic point, at which time the rate rapidly increases. Temperature and humidity have a significant impact on how long it takes the film base to reach the autocatalytic point. It is frequently claimed that properly processed and stored, black-and-white, silver gelatine film has a usable life of about 500 years, far longer than the useful life of many poor-quality originals. However, improper processing and storage conditions will reduce film longevity.

* Master negatives should be stored in fire-proof vaults (not safes, as these can not be kept at the required RH), free of dust and atmospheric pollutants and maintained at a temperature of 18 °C ± 2 °C (64 °F ± 5 °F), with a constant level of RH between 20% and 40% for silver gelatine on a cellulose ester base, and 30% to 40% for silver gelatine on a polyester base.
* Intermediate printing copies on diazo film and viewing copies on vesicular film can be stored in less stringent conditions. However, cool and dry conditions will help to prolong the life of these types of film.
* In all cases, rapid fluctuations of RH and temperature should be avoided.
* Diazo film images will fade, and exposure to light accelerates fading, so diazo film should be stored in darkness and always in its container when not in use.
* Vesicular film is particularly vulnerable to dust and the high temperatures produced by microfilm reading machines, so it is important to keep the machine clean and cool.
* Containers should be free from acidic, oxidising and reducing agents and meet the Photographic Activity Test (PAT), specified by ANSI Standard IT9.2- 1991.

DIGITIZING

What is Digitizing

Digitizing is a way of capturing and storing images using computer technology. A digital camera or a scanning device takes an electronic photograph, which is converted into binary digital code (essentially a string of zeros and ones), and can be viewed on a computer screen or printed out on paper. The data are stored within magnetic and optical media. The information content of digital images is not converted to alphanumeric form at the time of scanning and thus is not textsearchable.

Optical Character Recognition (OCR)

OCR software enables a scanned printed document to be converted into text which can be edited using word processing programmes. Unfortunately, the process is not completely accurate and time has to be spent rectifying misread letters. Moreover, OCR programmes are not capable of saving the original document's typography or page layout.

Advantages

* Digitizing offers quick access to multiple users world-wide.
* Images can be electronically restored and enhanced.
* High-quality user copies can be provided.
* Automated retrieval aids facilitate the finding of information.
* Digitizing provides an image which can be reproduced many times with no loss of quality.
* Digital images do not decay with use.

Disadvantages

* It requires an expensive commitment to supporting technologies used to convert and retrieve records.
* A digital image, displayed or printed, may not yet be acceptable as a legal substitute for the original.
* Standards are lacking in many areas.

* Digital storage is not yet accepted as truly archival – it requires continuous monitoring and eventual or periodic refreshing and transfer.
* The drive systems will become obsolete.
* There are relatively high but rapidly declining storage and production costs.
* The time needed to capture and store high-resolution archival images, and the costs of doing so increase as the quality increases.
* It is expensive to reproduce colour images.

Obsolescence Issues

The technological life span of any optical or electronic medium and its associated hardware and software is a major issue that does not exist when considering microfilming as a reformatting process. Computer hardware and software both change rapidly, with new versions of each coming out on a regular basis.

In addition, technologies come and go. Libraries will probably not be able to use many of the technologies of today in the future. Certainly, parts for the hardware will no longer be manufactured, and old software will eventually not work on new machines.

What this means is that libraries may not be able to retrieve information stored on optical media in 25 years, and this will almost certainly be a problem in 100 years. To deal with hardware obsolescence, archival copies of magnetic and optical computer media will have to be 'migrated' when newer technologies become the standard.

Digitizing and Microfilming Combined

The production of both microfilm masters for preservation, and digital masters for access, seems likely to become the preferred preservation strategy for the next decade. On the whole, a film-first policy is currently favoured. However, the rapid advancement of computer technology, the emergence of sophisticated equipment, which can produce microfilms and high-resolution digital images simultaneously and at low-cost, and the ever-increasing pressures of providing greater access will eventually see digital technology in the ascendancy. Nevertheless, until standards are in place, the use of digitizing for preservation will remain questionable.

3

Deterioration of Paper Collections

Conservation professionals spend many years studying the properties of collections materials and perfecting their examination and treatment skills. While you will not leave this part with a conservator's expertise, a general familiarity with the mechanisms of deterioration will be a valuable tool for evaluating the overall condition of your collections and focusing your preservation activities.

BASIC CONCEPTS

In order to understand the deterioration mechanisms of specific paper-based formats, you need to be familiar with several basic concepts and processes. This part will address the difference between organic and inorganic materials, the types of chemical reactions that affect paper-based collections, and the process of making paper by hand and by machine. A basic understanding of these subjects will inform the discussions of deterioration mechanisms throughout this part.

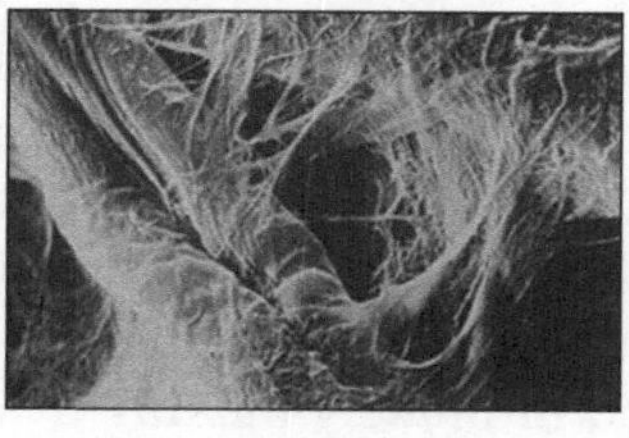

Fig. 3.1 On the Microscopic Level, Paper Consists of Fibres Bonded Together.

ORGANIC/INORGANIC MATERIALS

All materials are categorized as either organic or inorganic. Organic materials are made from plants or animals. Inorganic materials are made from rocks and minerals.

Organic materials include wood, paper, textiles, and animal parts. They also include some natural materials that are not obviously organic and some synthetic materials. All organic materials deteriorate over time.

Inorganic materials include stone, metal, ceramic, and glass, which are all made from rocks or minerals. Some inorganic materials are found in paper-based formats: photographs contain metallic particles; some pigments and inks contain minerals, metals, or metallic oxides; and metal particles are sometimes found in paper itself. Inorganic materials are generally stable individually, but they can react with other materials to cause deterioration. Some metals react with the cellulose in paper. Like organic materials, inorganic materials can be natural or synthetic.

CHEMICAL DETERIORATION

Chemical reactions are the driving force behind the deterioration of paper-based collections. The most common chemical reactions that you will encounter in this part are described in simplified fashion below. In practice, chemical reactions are very complex. Often one chemical reaction will initiate a series of others, and many reactions are closely related and occur simultaneously.

Hydrolysis

In the simplest terms, this is the chemical reaction of a compound with water to form one or more new compounds. In acid hydrolysis, which is the reaction that plays the largest role in the degradation of paper, acid within the paper reacts with water, causing breaks in the chains of molecules that make up paper and ultimately making it weak and brittle.

Hydrolysis is also a factor in the degradation of other materials, including leather. In leather, sulphur dioxide is absorbed from the atmosphere and converted into sulphuric acid in the presence of an oxidant. The sulphuric acid catalyzes hydrolysis of the collagen in leather, weakening the leather by breaking down the molecular chains within it.

Oxidation

Oxidation is a chemical reaction that involves the loss of electrons from an atom or a molecule. Oxidation requires an oxidizing agent, such as oxygen in the air, ozone, or pollutants such as nitrogen oxide. In some cases, light acts as a catalyst in activating these oxidants; this is referred to as photochemical deterioration. Oxidation causes paper to weaken, and oxidation of lignin plays a role in the darkening of poor quality paper. In addition, metal particles present in paper or inks can be oxidized, producing acids that degrade the paper through hydrolysis. Oxidants play a part in the acid hydrolysis of leather by converting sulphur dioxide into sulphuric acid.

Redox (Oxidation-Reduction)

The complementary reaction to oxidation is reduction, which involves the gain of electrons by an atom or a molecule. Redox reactions typically occur in photographs containing silver image material. In the oxidation-reduction process, the silver in the image is attacked by oxidants in the atmosphere. This forms new colorless silver compounds. During the reduction part of the process, the silver may be turned back into metallic silver but deposited in a different location in a different physical form. Resulting damage can include silver mirroring, loss of detail, and fading of the image.

PAPERMAKING

Paper and board are by far the most common material found in library, archives, and records collections. The invention of paper is credited to the Chinese in AD 105. The technique gradually spread to Japan, central Asia, and Persia over the next 600 years. The first hand papermaking mill was established in Spain in the 12th century, and papermaking spread throughout Europe over the next 300 years.

Hand Paper-making

Fig. 3.2 In Hand Papermaking, a Screen is Passed Through the Water to form a mat of Fibres, Which is Pressed Between Felts to be Dried.

In this process, a fibrous material is boiled and pounded to reduce it to its constituent fibres, and the fibres are suspended in water. A screen is passed through the water to form a mat of fibres, and the resulting sheet of intertwined fibres is pressed between felts to be dried. The sheet is then sized to make the surface suitable for writing, either by coating the paper by hand or dipping it into a tub of sizing solution.

Machine Papermaking

Fig. 3.3 In Machine Papermaking, Pulp is Poured onto a Continuous Roll of Woven wire Mesh, then run Through a Felt Roller to Dry.

The papermaking machine was invented in France in the late 18th century, and was further developed in England in the early 19th century by the Fourdrinier brothers, by whose name it is still known. The first Fourdrinier papermaking machine was put into operation in 1804. In machine papermaking, the reduced fibres are suspended in water, which is placed in a reservoir; the pulp is poured onto a continuous roll of woven wire mesh, which allows the water to drain through; the wire mesh is moved from side to side to form a mat of fibres; and the sheet then runs through a felt roller to dry it. This method has been refined to make it more efficient over the last 200 years, but the essential process remains the same. Explore The Wisconsin Paper Council's Papermaking Process Web site for a description of the modern commercial paper-making process. What do you think are some ways in which the materials used and the process itself might contribute to the instability of paper?

INHERENT VICE: MATERIALS

In this part, you will consider the basic materials that make up paper-based collections and the concept of "inherent vice". This refers to deterioration caused by agents present in the materials themselves, as opposed to deterioration caused by external forces. These agents may be inherent in the materials, or they may be added as part of the manufacturing process.

Over the course of time, a variety of materials and methods have been used to produce paper-based collections. Generally the primary goal of using new materials and different manufacturing methods was to make a particular process faster and easier. Unfortunately, many of these "new and improved" methods and materials were not a step forward in terms of the physical longevity of collections.

PAPER

Most papers produced from the mid-19th century to the present become brittle in about 25 to 50 years. Surveys done in the 1980s showed that yellowing and brittleness is present in about 25 to 40 per cent of research library collections.

Materials used to Make Paper

Fig. 3.4 Newsprint, Made from Groundwood Pulp Paper, Becomes Brittle and Yellowed over Time.

Early paper made from materials such as linen, cotton, and hemp rags was relatively stable and durable. However, there was a chronic shortage of these materials, which became steadily worse as the demand for paper grew. In the early 19th century, the invention of the cotton gin, provided additional relatively good raw material for papermaking. However, by the middle of the 19th century, papermakers began to look elsewhere for raw material.

In the 1840s, a process was developed to use groundwood pulp for paper. Groundwood papers contain more lignin than is found in fibres such as flax or hemp. Lignin is not only acidic, causing the paper to become weak and brittle, but upon exposure to light it oxidizes, causing the paper to darken.

Changes in Manufacturing

The desire to make paper more efficiently, quickly, and cheaply also contributed to the decline in paper quality over the course of several hundred years.

After about 1650, alum was added to the tub of gelatin size to harden it and keep it from spoiling. Alum is extremely acidic and leads to acid hydrolysis of the paper. In about 1680, the Hollander beater was invented, which was a mechanical device for chopping the rags to be made into paper. The Hollander, and later the Jordan resulted in shorter paper fibres and weaker paper, and left residual metal particles in the paper. Chlorine bleaching began in the late 18th century, resulting in the formation of hydrochloric acid within bleached papers.

In the early 19th century, alum rosin sizing was introduced to speed up the papermaking process. The paper was sized in the vat by adding rosin to the vat, followed by alum. Alum rosin sizing creates sulphuric acid as a byproduct of the reaction between the alum and the rosin, and in-the-vat sizing meant that acids were distributed throughout the paper, rather than just on the surface. Cumulatively, this resulted in more acidic, weaker, and more brittle paper. Alum rosin sizing was widely used by the 1840s, and in the 1870s a cheaper form of the sizing was developed

Permanent/Durable Paper

It is possible to make good quality machine-made papers from wood pulp by using a chemically purified wood pulp but this is a more recent development.

A standard for permanent paper was developed during the 1980s because of demands by interested parties concerned about the brittle book problem. Permanent paper is defined by the National Information Standards Organization in ANSI/NISO Z39.48-1992, Permanence of Paper for Publications and Documents in Libraries and Archives. The standard defines permanent paper as having a 2% minimum alkaline reserve less than 1% lignin, good tear resistance, and a pH of 7.5 to 10.0.

PARCHMENT AND VELLUM

Fig. 3.5 This Parchment Object Was Stored Poorly and has Become Dirty and Cockled.

The invention of parchment is often credited to King Eumenes of Pergamum, an ancient city in Asia Minor, in the second century BC, but writing on animal skins was common for centuries before that. The term parchment sometimes refers to any skin that has been prepared for writing, and sometimes refers specifically to sheepskin. The term vellum refers to calfskin only. Parchment and vellum were originally used for scrolls and other documents. They were also used as pages in books from the second century AD onward, and as bookbinding material. Until the fourth century AD, skins were treated with salt, flour, and other vegetable products to prepare them for writing; after this, skins were treated with lime water, an alkaline substance. Parchment is generally more alkaline and more stable than leather.

Characteristic Types of Deterioration

Beginning in the early 19th century, chemicals were added to the lime water baths to speed up the process of preparing the skin, but these made the skin weaker. Additional chemicals such as formaldehyde were then added to try to counteract this weakness, but only resulted in stiffer skins with less elasticity. In addition, sulphur compounds remained in the skin after rinsing and were converted into sulphuric acid, which in turn reacted with calcium carbonate to produce gypsum. The presence of gypsum causes parchment to turn a gray colour.

Parchment is also subject to photochemical reactions in which hydrogen peroxide forms, causing the parchment to break down and become brittle and fragile. If gelatinized parchment is brought into contact with water, it will disintegrate into loose flakes.

LEATHER

Fig. 3.6 Leather Fibres Break Down and Turn to red Powder, Known as Red Rot

Like parchment, leather is made from animal skins. Fundamentally, leather consists of a network of fibres made up of proteins, the most important of which is collagen. There are many different types of leather, and making leather is a complex process, for which different manufacturers have different methods.

Characteristic Types of Deterioration

Perhaps the most well-known leather damage is red rot, the process in which the leather fibres break down and turn into a red powder. In this process, sulphur dioxide is absorbed from the atmosphere and converted into sulphuric acid through oxidation. The sulphuric acid catalyzes acid hydrolysis, breaks down the molecular chains of the collagen, and weakens the leather.

Internal factors related to the leather manufacturing process also contribute to leather decay. Remnants of sulphur compounds used during the manufacturing process remain even after the leather is washed and convert over time into sulphuric acid.

Traces of metals from the rinsing water also remain behind, catalyzing the conversion of sulphur dioxide into sulphuric acid, which leads to acid hydrolysis. In addition, some vegetable tannins used during the tanning process seem to cause leather to decay more quickly. Finally, marbled decorations applied to book bindings in the 17th and 18th centuries can leave black corroded spots on the binding or damage the grain of the leather.

ADHESIVES

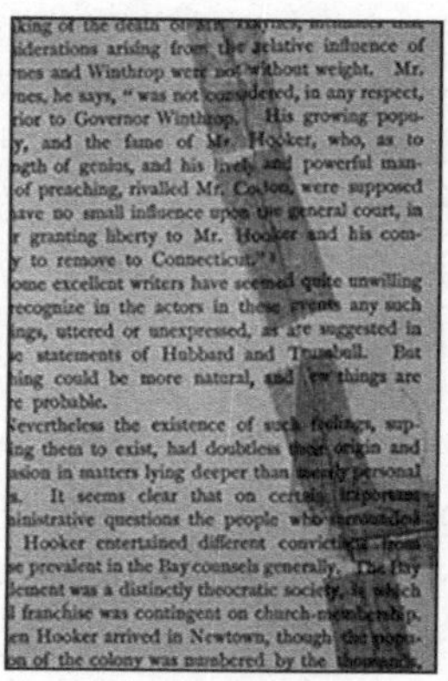

Fig. 3.7 The Use of Self-adhesive Tape to Repair Tears Causes Staining.

The term adhesive refers to a compound that bonds one material to another. Adhesives are encountered in various types of paper-based collections, most commonly in book bindings, scrapbooks, documents that have been repaired, and photo albums. Adhesives can be natural or synthetic; starch adhesives share common properties with cellulose, while synthetic adhesives are very similar to plastics.

Natural adhesives were first made from plant resins about 6,000 years ago. Later, animal, fish, and egg white-based adhesives were used. As modernization of adhesives continued during the 18th and 19th centuries, glues were made from various materials, including natural rubber and milk protein. Synthetic adhesives were developed in the early 20th century. Formulas for modern synthetic adhesives vary greatly, are often proprietary, and can change without notice.

Characteristic Types of Deterioration

Animal glues, traditionally used in bookbinding, break down over time, becoming discolored, dark, and brittle. They cause staining or simply crumble and fail. Synthetic adhesives react physically with water to produce swelling and chemically to produce structural weakening and acidic byproducts. In addition, evaporation of components within adhesives can cause them to become brittle.

Many adhesives used in collections in the past have not lasted well. Damage often includes discoloration, staining, and even failure of the adhesive, particularly in the cases of rubber cement and self-adhesive tape. While "archival" pressure-sensitive tapes that appear to be more stable than traditional pressure-sensitive tapes have been introduced, some problems have been observed with these tapes also. Natural adhesives such as wheat or rice starch paste are relatively stable and are often used in book and paper conservation.

COLOURANTS

Colourants of various types are encountered in watercolours, pastels, prints, architectural drawings and reproductions, writing and drawing inks, and colour photography.

General Characteristics

Colourants are divided into two categories—pigments and dyes. Both are colored substances that are dissolved in some type of liquid. A pigment is not soluble in the vehicle, but rather is dispersed or suspended in it. A dye, on the other hand, is soluble in the vehicle and colours an object by being absorbed into it, often with the assistance of another chemical called a mordant.

The science of colourants is quite complex. In some cases, a colorant can be either a pigment or a dye, depending on the vehicle used. Many modern pigments are made from soluble dyes by chemically bonding the dyes with a metallic salt.

Pigments and dyes are customarily classified according to their origins, such as organic or inorganic and natural or synthetic.

History

Natural inorganic pigments made from minerals were the first used by humans about 60,000 years ago. Natural organic pigments have been used since antiquity for many purposes, including cosmetics and textile dying. The first synthetic pigments were inorganic. After 1800, technology had developed sufficiently to produce these pigments on a large scale. In 1856, the first synthetic organic dye was developed from aniline, a chemical extracted from coal tar.

Characteristic Types of Deterioration

The primary form of colorant deterioration is fading, although some historical pigments also deteriorate upon contact with other substances, such as heat, acidic or alkaline materials, and chemicals. Some inorganic pigments of metallic origin may also cause oxidation and acidic deterioration similar to that caused by iron-gall inks.

Fading is a chemical change in which ultraviolet light reacts with the colorant, or triggers a reaction with oxygen or moisture, causing the colorant to change to a colorless compound.

Natural inorganic pigments were very stable and permanent, but due to the difficulty in manufacturing them, they have been replaced in modern times with synthetic inorganic colours. Natural organic pigments were very unstable and subject to light fading. The early synthetic organic colorants, while quite brilliant and intense, were also very unstable. Advances in organic chemistry during the 20th century have resulted in many modern synthetic organic pigments that are much less prone to fading.

Lists of historical pigments, as well as modern pigments that are ASTM-approved for artists' use, can be found in The Artist's Handbook of Materials and Techniques. These lists provide rankings for lightfastness in addition to other characteristics. The Watercolors Web site also provides information on the history and characteristics of pigments.

INK AND PENCIL

Ink is essentially a liquid in which one of many possible types of pigments or dyes is suspended. Pencils are made from graphite, a form of carbon. In paper-based collections, ink is encountered not just in documents but also in printed items and artworks. Pencil is generally encountered in handwritten documents and drawings.

History

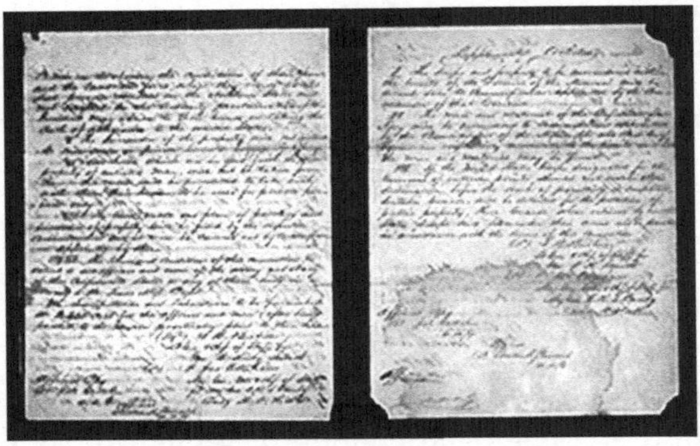

Fig. 3.8 Some Inks are Water Soluble, Leading to a Loss of Information if Documents Become Wet.

Inks for writing and drawing were probably first made around 2500 BC in Egypt and China. These were made from carbon suspended in water and vegetable gum. Through the centuries, many other inks were developed using berries, plants, and minerals to provide colorants. When synthetic aniline dyes were developed in the mid-19th century, they were soon used in inks. Since that time, a huge variety of ink formulas have been created, most of which are proprietary, and many of which are prone to fading, colour changes, and smearing.

Pencil is a stable medium. The process used to make modern pencils was developed and patented in France in 1795. Henry Petroski's *The Pencil* provides a history of the development of the pencil. Those caring for collections should also be aware of the existence of copying pencils. Markings made with copying pencils can be mistaken for those made with graphite pencils, but in fact the copying pencils contain not just graphite, but also aniline dyes that are water and alcohol soluble.

Deterioration of Ink

Carbon-based Inks

These are the earliest types of writing ink. Good quality early carbon inks do not discolor with age, but can smudge in high humidity. Poor quality carbon inks may turn a brown colour over time.

Iron Gall Ink

This was the predominant type of writing ink for many centuries. It was used as early as the fifth century and was common from the 12th century well into the 20th century. Iron gall ink is made by mixing tannic acid with an iron salt. Both high acidity within the ink and oxidation of excess iron compounds present in the ink make it very damaging to the support. In extreme cases the ink actually "eating through" the support.

Coloured Inks

Coloured inks are made using pigments or soluble dyes. In general, inks made using light-resistant pigments are of better quality. Inks made from soluble dyes are not lightproof and may be water soluble as well.

Traditional Printing Inks

Traditional inks used to make prints such as intaglio prints or lithographs, differ from writing inks in that they are oil-based, allowing them to adhere better to the printing surfaces and to perform well with printing equipment. While many of these inks were quite stable, others used fugitive pigments and were subject to bleeding. Also, if the ink was poorly manufactured, excess oil sometimes caused staining. Refer to How to Identify Prints for an explanation of printing methods. Refer to Bamber Gascoigne's *How to Identify Prints* for an explanation of printing methods.

Laser and Inkjet Printing

These were introduced on a large scale in the 1980s and have now become ubiquitous. Laser printing uses carbon inks and involves the same process as electrostatic copying. Black and white laser printing is quite stable. Most general-use inkjet printers use dye-based inks that are not very lightfast and are often water-soluble.

Fax Printing

Thermal transfer technology, used for fax printing and other purposes, became common during the 1980s. Printed documents using this technology tend to be very unstable.

INHERENT VICE: STRUCTURES

BOOKBINDINGS

The basic form of the book has not changed fundamentally over the centuries, but changes in the materials and methods used in bookbinding have sometimes compromised the quality of the resulting bound volumes.

Book Structure

The earliest books were in roll form, made from papyrus. As vellum began to be more commonly used, the practice of folding sheets and fastening them together began. Gradually the process of binding that is still used today was developed: individual folded signatures were sewn through the fold, then the signatures were attached to each other by sewing them to cords placed at right angles to the folded signatures. Boards were added to protect the pages, the cords were laced into the boards, and the boards were covered with protective material. Ideally, a binding should be strong and flexible, so that the book opens completely and the pages lay flat.

Decline in Binding Quality

During the latter half of the 19th century and much of the 20th century, poor quality paper was used for book pages. The quality of boards also declined, with wooden boards replaced by various types of boards made from compressed paper pulp that become acidic over time. Many modern bookcloths used as coverings fade easily and are vulnerable to attack by insects or mold. Adhesives used in binding are also often unstable. Sometimes different parts of a book respond differently to changes in the environment, causing distortion.

Changes in binding methods also contributed to a decline in binding quality. Gradually, hand-sewing of books decreased in favour of machine sewing. Books that are machine oversewn rather than sewn through the fold do not open well, and their pages tear easily if they become brittle. Inexpensive case bindings, in which the cover is prepared separately and then attached to the textblock by gluing the endsheet to the case, are less durable than traditional bindings in which the cords were laced in to the cover or slipped into a split in the cover board and adhered. Perfect bindings often fail. Pages or entire parts of the book may fall out.

REPRODUCTION METHODS

Beginning in the late 18th century, various reproduction methods began to replace hand copying of important documents. In the late 19th century, copying options were expanded and copying of original architectural drawings, plans, and maps also became common. Objects produced using some of these copying processes deteriorate more quickly than others, and some have detrimental effects on other collections if they are stored together. Therefore, identifying particular processes is crucial in making storage and other preservation decisions for these materials.

Letter Copying Process

Invented in 1780, this involved writing letters with a copying pencil and then pressing them against water-dampened thin tissue with a screw press. This process became popular in the 1850s and was used into the 1950s.

Hectograph Process

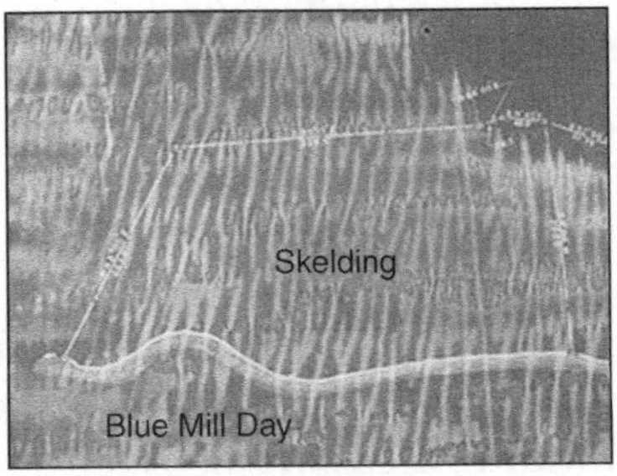

Fig. 3.9 Blueprints can Fade on Exposure to Light or Alkaline Materials.

This process, which became popular in the late 1800s, used aniline ink and was used both for copying documents and architectural drawings.

Writing was transferred to a gelatin pad from which copies were made. Various other processes for copying documents were invented in the late 19th and early 20th centuries, but many of these were not stable.

Blueprints

Invented in 1871, this process was used primarily to copy architectural drawings, plans, and maps. A translucent original was placed over sensitized paper containing iron salts, and then exposed to light. After exposure, the original was removed and the copy was washed to remove the unexposed compounds under the lines of the original drawing. The result was an image of white lines on a blue background. Blueprints are sensitive to alkaline environments, and light exposure. Similar processes include Vandyke prints, and Ferrogallic prints.

Diazotypes

This process became popular in the 1920s, and by the 1950s it was used to copy office records as well as maps, drawings, and plans. A translucent original was placed on paper coated with diazonium salts; this was exposed to ultraviolet light, which attacked the salts and turned the exposed area off-white. Depending on the specifc type of compound used on the paper, the lines on diazo prints can be various colours. Diazo prints are often processed using ammonia, which causes them to give off alkaline vapors that may harm other materials. The residual chemicals remaining in the print also cause oxidation and discoloration of the print itself, particularly on the edges. Sepia prints, a type of diazo print, can create greasy stains or pink stains on adjacent materials. Diazo prints are light sensitive.

Electrostatic Copying

Also known as xerography, this technology was introduced in the late 1940s and became popular in the 1960s. It makes a copy of the original by forming an image with toner powder using electrostatic charge and fusing the image to paper using a solvent, heat, or light. This is the most common copying process used today. If electrostatic copies are made on good quality paper and well-bonded to the paper, they are very stable. However, electrostatic copies of maps or plans made on matte or transparent Mylar are not permanent because the toner does not bond well to the Mylar.

PHOTOGRAPHIC PRINTS: BLACK AND WHITE

Among the materials collected and organized by cultural institutions, photographs are the most treasured and heavily used. Extensive technical and aesthetic changes have affected photography since 1839, when Louis Daguerre developed a practical method for creating permanent images.

Each photographic process has unique characteristics that affect its deterioration, storage, and handling. In order to care properly for photographic collections, you must understand how photographs are made and learn how to identify their various types. You must also become familiar with problems related to their physical and chemical composition.

The Basic Photographic Process

Photographs are composite objects, consisting of a base, a binder, and an image-forming substance. To produce a photographic image, light-sensitive materials such as silver salts are applied to a support made of paper, cloth, plastic, or metal, and exposed to light.

This forms either a direct visible image or a latent image, which can be developed using a chemical developer. The image is "fixed" in order to remove excess light-sensitive material and stop the darkening process. It is then washed to remove residual fixer.

Image-Forming Materials

As photographic techniques developed, a number of different light-sensitive materials were used to form the image. The most important was metallic silver, which was used in most 19th century photographic prints and is still used in modern black and white prints. Differences in appearance in the different types of prints are due to differences in the physical form of the silver particles.

Other types of image-forming materials used during the 19th century included:

* Platinum,
* Iron salts,
* Pigments, and
* Dyes.

Silver images exhibit several characteristic types of deterioration:

* *Sulfiding:* This is the formation of silver sulfide when silver reacts with sources of sulphur. This can result from the presence of sulphur in the atmosphere, but it is most often due to inadequate washing that leaves behind residual processing chemicals in the print. The result is yellowing, staining, and fading of the

image, usually beginning with the highlights.

* *Redox*: The visual results of redox reactions vary depending on the type of image, but generally they include loss of highlight detail, fading, and change of image colour to reddish, yellow, or yellow-brown. Silver mirroring is also a result of oxidation-reduction, and is particularly characteristic of silver images suspended in a gelatin binder.

Binders

Various materials have been used as binders for photographic prints. Albumen tends towards chemical reactions that cause it to yellow over time, which is exacerbated by the presence of residual fixative and mounting on poor-quality board. Albumen also becomes brittle and subject to cracking. Collodion is not flexible and becomes brittle, leading to cracks in the emulsion, but otherwise is fairly chemically stable and does not yellow. Gum arabic was used as a binder for gum bichromate prints, which are stable but rare because they were difficult to produce. Gelatin, the most common binder material, is made from animal proteins. It is fairly stable chemically but is quite sensitive to moisture in the air.

Supports

Nineteenth century prints generally had a primary support of high quality stable paper, although the secondary support was often poor quality. In the later 19th century, the primary paper support was often coated with barium sulfate in gelatin; this was known as the baryta layer. This layer was very stable, protected the paper from light damage, and provided some protection against damaging substances from poor-quality secondary supports.

Resin-coated paper was introduced as a support for photographic prints during World War II and became commercially available during the 1970s. This type of paper shortened photographic processing time because it required less washing and it was sturdy, allowing processing to be completely mechanized. Most modern colour prints are printed on resin-coated paper, which consists of a paper base between two layers of polyethylene, with titanium dioxide added to the emulsion-side layer.

Many early prints on resin-coated paper that were framed and exhibited developed cracking of the emulsion layer over time. Some black and white resin-coated prints on exhibit also developed redox, yellowing, and silver mirroring. These problems were due to the titanium dioxide in the emulsion and they occurred most commonly in framed photographs where the oxidizing agent could not dissipate. Stabilizers and antioxidants were added to later resin-coated papers during manufacturing to combat this type of deterioration, but this does not completely eliminate the risk of damage.

Daguerreotypes, Ambrotypes, and Tintypes

Strictly speaking, these photographic images are not paper-based, but they are positive images and are frequently found within collections of photographic prints. Daguerreotypes, positive images on thin copper plate with a silver coating, were popular between 1840 and 1860. They are usually found in small hinged cases and are quite fragile and subject to tarnishing due to exposure to pollutants. Ambrotypes and tintypes are both silver images in a collodion binder, but ambrotypes have a glass support sometimes coated with paint or lacquer, while tintypes have a thin lacquered iron support. Ambrotypes sometimes suffer chips in their original coating material. Tintypes are easily bent, sometimes causing the emulsion to crack.

PHOTOGRAPHIC PRINTS: COLOUR/DIGITAL

The primary difference between black and white and colour prints is in the image-forming material. There are two types of colour photography: chromogenic and nonchromogenic. Modern chromogenic colour photographs are the most common and use organic cyan, magenta, and yellow dyes as the image-forming material. The chromogenic process forms a black and white silver image, which causes the developing chemical to react with dye couplers to form a dye image around the black and white image. The black and white image is then removed with bleaches and the colour image is fixed and washed.

A different type of dye is used in nonchromogenic photography, which was introduced in 1955. This process is known as silver dye bleach and produces photographs with excellent dark stability and better light stability than chromogenic photographs. However, chromogenic materials are cheaper and more versatile, and thus much more common.

Deterioration of Chromogenic Colour Prints

Dye Fading

Fig. 3.10 Dye Fading is Common in Early Colour Photographs.

Unfortunately, the dyes used in chromogenic processing are inherently unstable. The three dyes do not fade at different rates, so there is often an imbalance of colour in deteriorated colour photographs. It is also very important to note that some dyes that fade faster in the light may be more stable in the dark, and vice versa. In general, early colour photographs were very unstable; many lost 30% of their dyes within 10 to 15 years. Even colour photographs from the 1980s will reach the 30 per cent mark within 20 years. Advances in dye stability were made during the 1980s and 1990s, and contemporary colour materials can be expected to survive 30 to 50 years at room temperature.

Highlight Staining

This appears as a yellowish staining in the highlight areas of the photograph, and is due to residual dye couplers for the magenta dye, which form these stains as they decompose.

Digital Colour Prints

The increase in digital photography in the last decade means that many photographs are now printed on photo printers rather than processed in the traditional way. These prints are created using dyes and inks, some of which are not stable and long lasting. Waterproof pigment-based inks are more stable than dye-based water sensitive inks, but they usually have a smaller range of colour. Many types of paper supports are also used, including laser/copying paper, general purpose inkjet paper, fine art papers, and coated inkjet papers.

Ultimately, using the right combination of paper, printer, and ink is most crucial to digital print longevity. Wilhelm Imaging Research has tested many papers, inks, and printers on the market today. In addition to providing guidance on the life expectancies of various digital prints, these tests have shown that using third party inks and paper will not provide the same durability as using ink and paper recommended by the printer manufacturer.

EXTERNAL FACTORS

External factors such as high, low, or fluctuating temperature and humidity; light exposure; the presence of pollutants; and poor storage and handling exacerbate the deterioration of collections. While these external agents affect all paper-based collections to a certain extent, some of them are particularly damaging to specific types of materials, which will be your focus here.

CLIMATE

Temperature

Generally speaking, higher temperatures accelerate the chemical reactions that cause deterioration in paper-based collections. Thus, cooler temperatures are preferred for collections with long-term value.

Temperature plays a particularly crucial role in the fading

of chromogenic colour photographs. The higher the temperature, the more movement there is on the molecular level, and the more likely it is that the molecules will be rearranged, resulting in dye fading. For this reason, cold storage is recommended for long-term preservation of colour photographs.

Relative Humidity

Fig. 3.11 The Parchment Pages of This Volume have Rippled on Exposure to Water.

Humidity provides water to fuel the chemical reactions that cause deterioration. The more moisture there is in the air, the more quickly chemical deterioration proceeds.

High humidity is a primary factor in hydrolysis, which accelerates the deterioration of paper (causing ferrotyping, shiny blotches on the emulsion that result from pressure on the softened binder material; and accelerating), black and white photographs (softening gelatin binders, causing ferrotyping and accelerating the yellowing of albumen binders), and colour photographs (accelerating dye fading). Parchment will ripple in overly humid conditions. Mold and many insects also flourish under hot and humid conditions. Mold causes staining and, in extreme cases, disintegration of paper, while insects can eat holes in paper-based collections.

If humidity is too low, materials such as adhesives and book leathers may become brittle and more susceptible to cracking, particularly during handling. Extended storage at low humidity can cause photographic emulsions to shrink and crack, supports to curl, and mounts to warp. Parchment will split and warp in overly dry conditions. Fluctuating humidity levels also cause damage. Most materials expand and contract with small changes in relative humidity (RH). These changes weaken physical bonds and set up stresses that can shorten the life of most materials

LIGHT

Light energy, in the form of waves, is absorbed by molecules within an object. This absorption of energy activates a variety of chemical reactions that have the potential to damage paper-based collections. This is termed photochemical deterioration. Shorter wavelengths of light such as UV light have more energy than longer wavelengths. They bombard an object with more energy in a shorter time and so cause photochemical deterioration to accelerate. This is why UV light is more damaging than visible light, although all light is damaging.

Fig. 3.12 Lignin in this poor Quality Paper Caused it to Darken when Exposed to Light During Exhibition.

Practically speaking, light causes paper, bookbindings, and many media (such as inks and dyes) to fade, yellow, or discolor. Light exposure accelerates the oxidation of lignin, which causes paper to darken. Light also contributes to the weakening and embrittlement of paper fibres, textiles, and leather. Some types of light (incandescent lamps and direct natural light) also produce significant heat, accelerating the rate at which materials deteriorate. Materials that are particularly sensitive to light include colour photographic prints, early black and white images (especially salted paper and albumen prints), cyanotypes, blueprints, diazo prints, and hand-colored images.

POLLUTANTS

Fig. 3.13 The Outside Edges of the Pages in this Book have Darkened Because of Exposure to Pollutants When the Book was Stored Closed on the Shelf.

Airborne contaminants in the form of gases and particulates jeopardize the preservation of collections.

For repositories in urban areas, gaseous pollution from sources such as industrial discharge, motor vehicle exhaust, and other combustion products can be a serious concern. Gaseous pollutants can also originate indoors, given off by common substances such as paint, cleaning supplies, untreated wood, photocopiers, and certain kinds of adhesives and plastics. Various types of gaseous pollutants initiate chemical reactions that contribute to the deterioration of paper-based collections. These reactions are usually worsened when high relative humidity is also present.

Particulates come in the form of tiny solids-grit, grime, smoke, dust-which originate largely in industrial processes, vehicle engines, wood-and coal-fired heating systems, smoking, and cooking. They are generally abrasive and acidic and often highly reactive chemically. Photographs in particular are extremely sensitive to atmospheric pollutants. Particulate pollutants may cause abrasion of emulsions and attract mold or insects. Gaseous pollutants such as sulphur dioxide, nitrogen oxides, ozone, and formaldehyde contribute to sulfiding, redox reactions, and dye discoloration.

STORAGE AND HANDLING

Fig. 3.14 The Sewing in this Volume has Broken Due to Excessive Handling.

Poor storage and handling can also cause physical and chemical damage to collections.

Physical damage due to poor storage and/or handling might include tears, creases, dog-eared corners, scratches or abrasions, or damage to book bindings. In some cases disfiguring marks may be made on items (*e.g.*, vandalism or writing on the back of photographs that either bleeds through or creates indentations). Rusting staples and paper clips can stain and deform paper documents.

Chemical damage due to poor storage and/or handling might include staining due to acid migration from acidic storage enclosures or adjacent materials such as news clippings or bookmarks.

EVALUATING YOUR COLLECTIONS

You have explored how the components of paper-based collections deteriorate; you have considered the complexities of some of the composite objects found in paper-based collections; and you have briefly examined the role of external factors in collection deterioration. Now you will begin to relate this information to your own collections.

IMPORTANT

This examination of your collections is not meant to serve as a formal collection condition survey, but it will assist you in determining which materials need further attention. You may decide that one or more collection condition surveys are required for specific subsets of your collection (*e.g.*, rare books, photographs, scrapbooks). This type of inspection most often takes the form of an item-by-item survey by a conservator with detailed knowledge of that particular type of material

BOUND MATERIALS

Fig. 3.15 These Books are Held Together by Rubber Bands (which can Themselves Cause Damage) Because their Spines and Covers are Damaged or Detached.

Bound materials in your collection may include printed books (general or rare), handwritten record books, and bound pamphlets of various types (*e.g.*, catalogs, directories, guidelines). Common types of physical damage to printed books and handwritten record books include page damage (*e.g.*, tears, dog-eared corners, missing pages, markings from vandalism, damage from iron gall inks), binding damage (damaged sewing, detached signatures, deteriorating adhesives, broken or loose joints, wholly or partly detached covers, endcap damage), and distortion (caused by climate fluctuations or previous water damage). Older pamphlets are often very deteriorated due to handling and acidity, and may have been placed in acidic pamphlet binders to protect them.

Common types of chemical and biological damage include fading or darkening/discoloration of pages (due to light damage and acidity), acid migration from acidic inserts such as bookmarks, fading of binding materials, red rot of leather bindings, holes from insect damage, and staining caused by mold. Note that darkening of pages due to acidity often shows up first on the edges of the textblock, which are more exposed to pollutants and climate fluctuations.

DOCUMENTS/MANUSCRIPTS/EPHEMERA

Documents and manuscripts found in cultural institutions can range from medieval manuscripts to 18th century letters to modern office files. They may be copies or originals, and they may have been produced using a variety of inks, papers, and copying processes. Ephemeral materials may include cards, postcards, brochures, patterns, papers dolls, etc., some of which may have raised surfaces or three-dimensional decoration, and may include adhesives. Common physical damage to flat paper items includes tears, folds, and creases; dog-eared corners; abrasions; staining from rusted paper clips, deteriorated rubber bands, or pressure-sensitive tape; loss of parts of the paper (usually around the edges); and distortion and staining from previous water damage.

Fig. 3.16 Foxing (Small Brown Spots Probably caused by Mold or by the Presence of Tiny Metal Particles) Often Occurs When an Item is Stored in a Poor Climate.

Common chemical and biological damage to paper documents includes brittleness and fragility due to acidic deterioration and light exposure; discoloration or darkening due to acidity and light exposure; staining and weakening from mold growth; holes from insect infestation; foxing (small brown spots that appear on paper, probably caused by mold or by the presence of tiny metal particles in the paper, in combination with high humidity and temperature); and acid migration, where better quality papers are stained by poor quality papers stored with them.

NEWSPRINT

Newsprint is generally found in several formats within cultural collections:

* Newspaper clippings within general document files, bound newspapers,
* Loose newspapers,
* Newspaper clipping scrapbooks.

Newsprint is almost uniformly made from poor quality paper and is usually very brittle, fragile, and darkened. Recent news clippings may still be in good condition, but they will ultimately be subject to the same deterioration processes. Clippings in scrapbooks may be further deteriorated due to the use of poor quality adhesives.

OVERSIZED AND FRAMED MATERIALS

Most cultural collections include at least a few maps, plans, and architectural drawings. Perhaps they are maps of the surrounding area or plans of buildings within the institution. Many cultural institutions also hold collections of artwork on paper, which may include posters, watercolors, pastels, and drawings of various kinds.

In general, these materials are subject to the same types of deterioration as paper documents. Many of these materials are oversized and may have been stored rolled for many years, complicating the problems of acidic deterioration. If materials that have been rolled seem too brittle to unroll for examination without causing damage, do not unroll them;consult a conservator for assistance. You may also encounter maps or other items that have been coated with varnish or other coatings, which has darkened and deteriorated.

Various copying processes used for maps and architectural materials have different vulnerabilities, and different processes stored in proximity to each other may damage each other, resulting in discoloration or fading.

Artworks on paper also exhibit a range of deterioration problems, which include fading or alteration of watercolor pigments smearing of pastel, charcoal, or pencil drawings; yellowing, fading, or browning of the paper support due to acidic deterioration; foxing; surface mold growth; cockling due to climate fluctuations; and tide lines or stains due to water damage.

Framed materials (which might include artworks on paper, documents, or photographs) often show characteristic signs of deterioration: browning and yellowing due to acid migration from poor quality backing materials (these might be wood, corrugated board, newsprint, or cardboard); knot patterns or a dark central stripe down the paper due to wooden slats used in backing; mat burn (darkened lines around the margin where the beveled edge of acidic matboard meets the paper); tape stains due to poor quality tape used for repairs; and adhesive stains due to poor quality adhesives used to hinge or mount the item to the backboard.

SCRAPBOOKS

Various types of scrapbooks are found in cultural collections. News clipping scrapbooks are common, as are personal scrapbooks that contain a variety of materials, including documents, photographs, pamphlets, and pressed flowers. Scrapbooks, being composite objects, exhibit various problems common to documents, bound volumes, and photographic materials. Their pages may be brittle and weak, photographs may be faded and stained, news clippings may be yellowed, items may have become detached from the pages due to adhesive failure, the pages may have been stained by adhesives, and the bindings may be broken or otherwise damaged.

PHOTOGRAPHIC PRINTS

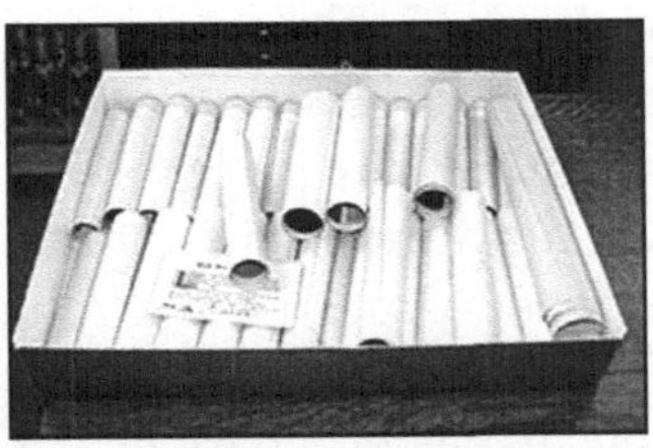

Fig. 3.17 Older Rolled Photographs Can be Difficult to Unroll Without Damaging them; Always Consult a Conservator if in Doubt.

The most common types of photographic prints found in cultural institutions are cased photographs, albumen prints, silver gelatin prints, and modern colour photographs. These may be stored with documents in files, in boxes or albums, or even loose in drawers. Different types of photographic processes have specific vulnerabilities. However, there are some major categories of damage to photographs that you may observe within your collection. As with paper documents, photographic prints are subject to physical damage such as tears, creases, dog-eared corners, and mold or insect attack. Special concerns for photographs are abrasion and scratching of emulsions (binders), cracking emulsions, emulsions that are peeling away from the support layer, and indentations or staining caused by writing on the back of photographs.

Fig. 3.18 Damage to this Photograph has Been Caused in Large Part By the Brittle and Acidic Board on Which it was Mounted.

Chemical damage to photographs may manifest itself in black and white images through fading of the image, loss of image detail, yellowing of the image, silver mirroring of shadow areas of the image, and/or staining. For colour prints, colour change and fading are the primary results of deterioration.

Rolled photographs are often found in collections. As with documents, these should not be unrolled if it seems this may cause damage; a conservator should be consulted. Photographs mounted on acidic boards are also common (these are frequently albumen prints, which tend to curl up if not mounted). There is often physical damage to the board and chemical damage to the photograph.

Photograph albums pose additional problems, since the albums themselves may damage the photographs. Many older albums have acidic pages that can accelerate photograph deterioration. Adhesives used to attach photographs often cause staining and sometimes fail, leaving the photograph unattached. Modern "magnetic" albums in fact use adhesive to hold the photograph to the page; this adhesive darkens and stains photographs over time. Modern albums with plastic pages made from polyvinyl chloride (PVC) also accelerate photograph deterioration. Polyester, polypropylene, and polyethylene are the only acceptable plastics for photo album pages.

4

Deterioration of Film and Electronic Media

This chapter will focus primarily on the reasons that film-based and electronic media deteriorate. Some related materials, such as glass plate negatives/transparencies and early sound recordings, will also be addressed briefly. You will explore how the interaction among the individual components of each format contributes to deterioration. You will also examine how exposure to external agents of deterioration, such as climate extremes, further accelerates deterioration. This part will continue the process of evaluating the overall condition of your collections and focusing your preservation activities.

GLASS SUPPORTS

In the mid-19th century, photographic negatives and transparencies began to use glass as a support. Glass provided a sharper negative and a more detailed positive print, and soon replaced paper negatives. Like photographic prints, glass negatives and transparencies are composite objects, consisting of a glass support, a binder, an image-forming or recording substance, and, in some cases, a cover glass.

COMMON FORMATS

The lantern slide was invented in 1849. Lantern slides were often hand-colored and had a glass covering, which was taped around the edges. Lantern slides were in use until the middle of the 20th century, when smaller transparencies on film were introduced. Eventually lantern slides were completely replaced by 35mm colour slides. The autochrome process, also produced a positive image on glass. Dyed starch grains were applied to a varnished glass plate, with a silver halide emulsion then applied on top. Once the plate was exposed and developed, it was varnished and given a cover glass.

In 1851 the collodion glass plate negative was introduced, which used glass as a support and collodion as a binder (these were also known as wet-plate negatives, because it was necessary to expose and process the glass plate while the binder and sensitizing solution were still wet). During the 1870s gelatin dry plate negatives, which used a glass support and a gelatin binder, became commercially available. These eventually replaced collodion glass plate negatives because they required less exposure time and the plates did not have to be developed in the field. Gelatin dry plate negatives allowed for the production of ready-to-use glass plates with a longer shelf life than collodion glass plate negatives. Gelatin dry plate negatives were gradually replaced by nitrate film negatives and were rare after the late 1920s.

CHARACTERISTIC TYPES OF DETERIORATION

The flaking of the emulsion layer from the glass plate is frequently seen. In glass collodion and gelatin dry plate negatives, the binder sometimes peels away from the plate if the plate was not properly cleaned. The most common type of damage to glass plates, however, is breakage due to poor handling.

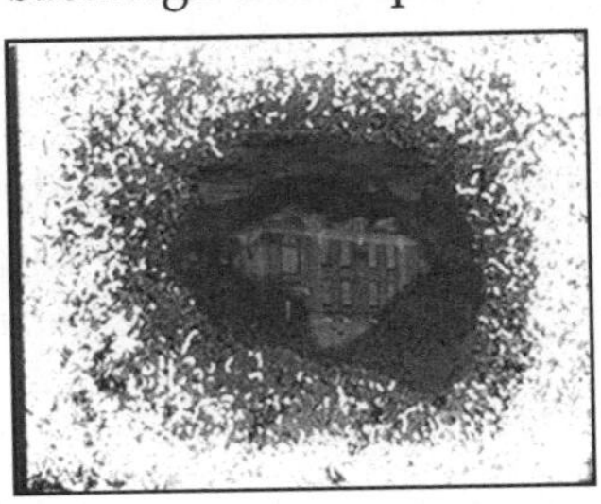

Fig. 4.1 Flaking Emulsion is Characteristic of Deteriorating Gelatin dry Plate Negatives, Most Often as a Result of Storage Under Poor Environmental Conditions. The Brown Portions are Residual Processing Chemicals.

Collodion glass plate negatives and early gelatin dry plate negatives were also sometimes vulnerable to chemical decay due to excess amounts of alkaline chemicals in the glass. This type of glass was termed soda or soda-lime glass. This chemical decay is known as alkali leaching or "weeping glass." At high relative humidity, the surface of the glass develops an alkaline hydrated layer (this manifests as moist droplets) that can damage the binder and the silver image. If the moisture remains on the glass for some time, a fine network of cracks (called crizzling) can develop on the surface. By the 1920s, the addition of aluminum oxide resulted in more chemically stable glass. Weeping glass is also frequently found in daguerreotypes.

FILM SUPPORTS

Like photographic prints and glass negatives/ transparencies, film-based media are composite objects, consisting of a film support and a binder/emulsion with an image-forming or recording substance suspended in it. Film has been used as a support for many different types of media since the late 19th century, including various types of still photography film (such as 35 mm roll film, portrait and commercial sheet film, x-ray film), slide film, microfilm, amateur movie film (8mm and 16mm), and motion picture film.

Three types of film have been used as supports: nitrate, acetate, and polyester films (with the latter being the most stable). Many modern film-based media use a polyester film base, but not all. The characteristic deterioration of these films will be discussed in this part, along with typical deterioration mechanisms of the binder and image-forming materials.

Film is also used as a base for magnetic tape (audio, video, and computer tape), but these media are discussed separately in this part because of their unique characteristics.

NITRATE FILM

Nitrate film was invented in the late 19th century in response to the need for a more lightweight and less fragile support for photographic negatives. The first nitrate sheet film negatives were made from celluloid (an primitive form of plastic made from cellulose nitrate combined with a plasticizer). Celluloid was first created in 1846 and was used for many purposes, including making billiard balls and combs. In 1887, the first sheet film negatives were made by coating a thick sheet of celluloid with a layer of gelatin emulsion. Within a few years, gelatin emulsion roll film made from a thinner and more flexible form of celluloid became available.

Cellulose nitrate film was used as the support for many different types of film, including portrait and commercial sheet film, x-ray film, 35mm roll film, and motion picture film. It was not used for colour film or for 16mm or 8mm film (both of which were made for the home and educational markets). Nitrate film was eventually supplanted by cellulose acetate film, and the Eastman Kodak Company stopped producing nitrate film completely in 1951.

Characteristic Types of Deterioration

Nitrate film is extremely flammable, which eventually led to its discontinuation and replacement by cellulose acetate film. Its chemical instability was less apparent at first, but six progressive stages of its deterioration have been extensively documented over the years:

Fig. 4.2 This Nitrate Negative is in Stage 5 of Deterioration.

* No deterioration.
* The film turns yellow and the image exhibits silver mirroring.
* The film becomes sticky and gives off a strong nitric acid odour.

* The film turns an amber colour and the silver image begins to fade.
* The film becomes soft and may adhere to adjacent materials, and the image becomes illegible.
* The film breaks down completely, turning into a brown powder.

The chemical decay of nitrate film is irreversible and is made worse by high temperature and high relative humidity. Duplication onto stable film and cold storage of originals is recommended.

Identifying Nitrate Film

If film exhibits, it can be easily identified as nitrate film. Nitrate film can sometimes be identified by date (*e.g.,* almost all film manufactured between 1889 and 1920 was nitrate), but detailed date information is not always available. Other means of identifying nitrate film include:

* *Edge Printing*: Located on the edge of the film is the name or type of film base, such as "NITRATE"; the name of the manufacturer; and/or notch codes, which were notches of various shapes meant to identify the type and the emulsion side of the film)
* *Curling*: Early nitrate roll films tend to curl very tightly; in 1903, manufacturers began to coat the reverse side of the film with gelatin to prevent this problem
* *Destructive Tests*: Procedures such as the diphenylamine test, floatation test, or burn test can be performed; these destroy the material being tested and should be performed only by a professional

ACETATE FILM

Cellulose acetate film was first invented in the late 19th century to replace cellulose nitrate film, which was already recognized for its dangerous flammability. However, the first acetate was not practical for use. Acetate is an umbrella term that encompasses several different types of film: cellulose diacetate, acetate propionate, acetate butyrate, and cellulose triacetate. Cellulose diacetate was developed first and was used for both sheet and roll film between 1923 and 1955, but it had a tendency to shrink a great deal.

Acetate butyrate and propionate films were developed during the 1940s as alternatives to cellulose diacetate; these were used for home movie roll film, x-ray film, sheet film, and aerial film. Nitrate was still superior to these films, however, for 35mm motion picture film. Cellulose triacetate was developed in the late 1940s. It was used for sheet film, various sizes of roll film (particularly 8mm and 16mm, which are commonly found in cultural collections), and motion picture film. It is still used today for most types of roll film, including transparency film (slide film). During the 1970s, however, polyester film began to replace it for sheet film.

Characteristic Types of Deterioration

While cellulose acetate films do not have a problem with flammability, they are just as chemically unstable as nitrate films. The hydrolysis of acetate is referred to as "vinegar syndrome" due to the distinctive vinegar odour it produces. Vinegar syndrome proceeds quickly at room temperature, and it is accelerated by higher temperature and relative humidity.

The stages of deterioration are:

* No deterioration.
* The film gives off a vinegar odour (due to acetic acid) and begins to become brittle and shrink.
* The film begins to curl and may have blue or pink staining.
* The film loses flexibility and warps.
* The film develops liquid-filled bubbles and crystalline deposits, sometimes obscuring the image.
* As the film base continues to shrink, the emulsion becomes separated from the base in some areas, known as channeling.

The deterioration of cellulose acetate is autocatalytic, meaning that as the film becomes more acidic, this acidity further accelerates the deterioration process. Cold or frozen storage is recommended to slow deterioration. The Image Permanence Institute (IPI) has developed a product called A-D Strips that can be used to determine the extent of chemical deterioration in acetate films.

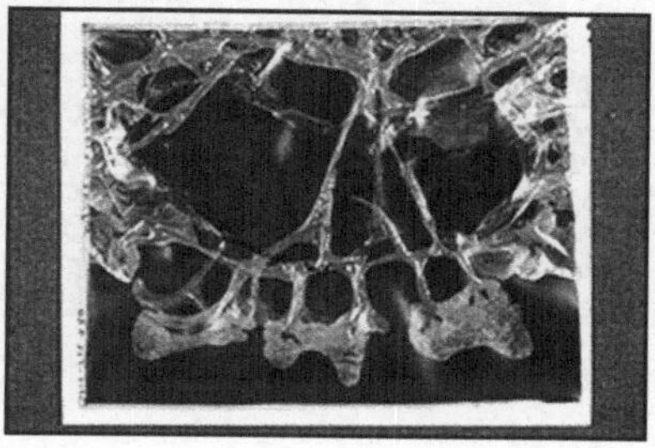

Fig. 4.3 This Acetate Negative, in the Last Stage of Deterioration, Shows Channeling where the Emulsion has Separated from its Base.

Identifying Acetate Film

It can be easily identified as acetate film. Other methods for identifying acetate film are similar to those for nitrate film: dating, edge printing (acetate film is usually marked as "SAFETY" to differentiate it from nitrate film), notch codes, and destructive tests (the flotation and burn tests). Polyester roll film may also be marked as "SAFETY." When held up to the light and viewed edge-on, however, acetate roll film transmits very little light compared to polyester roll film.

POLYESTER FILM

Polyester film, a generic term for polyethylene terephthalate (PET), was developed in the mid-1950s. During the 1960s and 1970s, it gradually replaced acetate for sheet films. Polyethylene naphthalene (PEN, a modification of PET) was introduced in 1996 for amateur roll film, under the brand name Advantix, but other roll films are still made from cellulose acetate. Polyester film is a synthetic polymer, unlike cellulose acetate and cellulose nitrate, and it does not contain solvents or plasticizers. Thus, it is inherently very chemically stable. Polyester film is also used for archival quality enclosures for collections.

Identifying Polyester Film

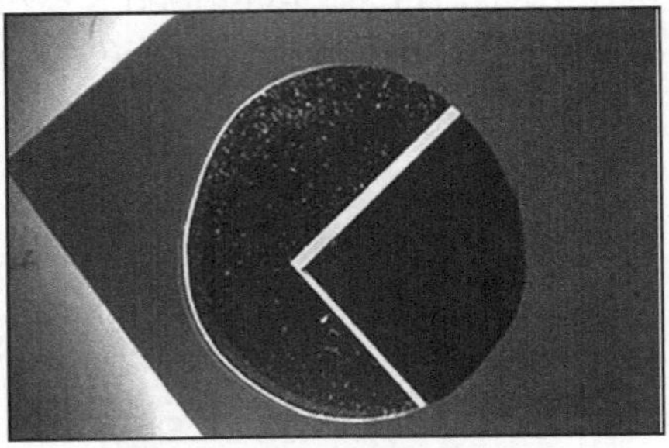

Fig. 4.4 Rainbow Colours Can be seen Along the Edge of Polyester Film when it is Viewed Between two Polarizing Filters in a Mount.

Polyester film, like acetate film, may be marked with "SAFETY" on the edge. Polyester can also be identified by viewing it between two polarizing filters, which produces rainbow colours. In addition, polyester roll film will transmit much more light than acetate roll film when held up to the light and viewed edge-on.

STRUCTURAL LAYERS

While degradation of the substrate is usually the primary cause of damage to film-based collections, the binders and image forming materials are also subject to deterioration.

Binders/Emulsion

Collodion was used as a binder for collodion glass plate negatives and lantern slides. Gelatin was introduced about 20 years later and used for gelatin dry plate negatives and transparencies such as lantern slides and autochromes (an early colour process).

Lantern slides first used an albumen binder and later wet collodion and dry gelatin binders. Since lantern slides and autochromes had a glass covering that was taped around the edges, their emulsions are somewhat more protected. However, broken tape seals and cracked or broken cover glass do occur and can allow moisture to enter and emulsions to crack and peel.

Fig. 4.5 The Gelatin Binder on this Glass Plate Negative has Dissolved as a Result of Exposure to Water.

Collodion glass plate negatives sometimes had a subbing (a thin coating, usually albumen), which was applied to the glass plate to help the collodion adhere to the glass. In addition, a varnish coating was placed over the emulsion for protection, since it was very fragile and subject to abrasion. Gelatin dry plate negatives were also coated with a subbing, or they were chemically etched to help the emulsion adhere to the glass. Gelatin dry plates were usually not varnished. In general, gelatin binders are subject to softening and mold growth in high relative humidity, as well as flaking due to shrinkage of the gelatin in low relative humidity.

Fig. 4.6 High Humidity has Caused the Emulsion on this Nitrate Negative to Become Soft and Sticky; Parts of the Enclosure Remain Adhered to the Negative.

Nitrate, acetate, and polyester films all use gelatin as their binder material. Nitrate and acetate films also had a subbing of diluted cellulose nitrate to help the binder adhere to the film. In addition, nitrate (after 1903) and acetate had an anti-curl layer of gelatin applied to the back of the film. The tendency of gelatin to soften in high humidity is made worse by the byproducts of nitrate deterioration, which cause the emulsion to become very soft and sticky. In acetate and polyester films, the gelatin is vulnerable to softening and mold growth in high humidity, but is otherwise not a major contributor to deterioration.

FINAL IMAGE MATERIALS

Silver Particles

In black and white negatives, transparencies, and films, the image is made up of silver particles suspended in the binder material. As in photographic prints, the silver particles are formed by the exposure and development (using chemicals) of light sensitive silver salts.

In gelatin dry plate negatives and collodion glass plate negatives that were not coated with a varnish to protect the image, oxidation of the image is common, resulting in silver mirroring. In nitrate film, the byproducts of deterioration cause the silver image to fade.

Fig. 4.7 This Deteriorated Nitrate Negative Exhibits Silver Mirroring.

Colour Dyes

The colour dyes used in autochromes are subject to fading. Colour negatives and films—which use chromogenic colour dyes and were produced on acetate and polyester bases—are subject to the same problems with dye fading and highlight staining as are colour photographic prints.

These materials are not permanent, and some older negatives are already faded to the extent that they cannot be printed. Cold or frozen storage of colour materials is recommended to slow deterioration.

EARLY SOUND RECORDINGS

Before the advent of magnetic tape (and later, compact disc), sound recordings were made by picking up sound vibrations and transmitting them to a stylus, which etched them into the surface of a rotating cylinder or disc. The earliest recordings were acoustic, which, in simple terms, means that changes in air pressure were channeled through a horn to a diaphragm attached to the stylus and thus transformed into mechanical motions. Later recordings (after about 1925) used microphones, which transformed the changes in air pressure into changes in electrical voltage, which in turn made the stylus move.

Fig. 4.8 This Early Tin Foil Phonograph Recorded onto a Cylinder Covered with tin Foil.

The first phonograph, which recorded onto cylinders and played back the recordings, was invented by Thomas Edison in 1877. Emilie Berliner patented the Gramophone (which used a disc instead of a cylinder) in 1887, and in 1892 he began producing discs commercially.

Both types of machines were sold commercially until the early 1920s, but discs soon surpassed cylinders in popularity. Commercially recorded cylinders were discontinued in 1929, but cylinder recorders were still used at least through the 1940s for live recording of ethnographic field notes and for office dictation. These types of recordings are not as common in cultural collections as magnetic tapes, but discs, in particular, are encountered fairly frequently.

CYLINDERS

The first cylinder recordings consisted of a brass cylinder covered with tin foil. These were soon replaced with wax and plastic cylinders of various types, which could be either prerecorded or recordable. "Soft wax" cylinders are usually original (not-prerecorded) recordings. They were actually made from a variety of materials, including wax, resins, soaps, and oils. Colorants, plasticizers, lubricants, and/or hardeners were sometimes added. Prerecorded cylinders ("molded cylinders") were first made from hardened wax or metallic soap and later from celluloid plastic.

Fig. 4.9 Wax Cylinders were Made from a Variety of Materials, Including Wax, Resins, Soaps, and oils. This Illustration Shows a Custom Storage box.

Characteristics of Deterioration

The grooved surfaces of cylinders (particularly wax cylinders) are very vulnerable to damage, so cylinders should be handled only using the holes at the end of the cylinder, and they should always be stored standing on end. Wax cylinders are also very susceptible to mold at high relative humidity. Finally, it is important to note that wax cylinders should not be touched when they are cold, since warmth can cause the cold wax to fracture.

Cylinders made from hardened wax, metallic soap, or celluloid can become very fragile and brittle over time. Exposure to light, particularly UV light, will accelerate this deterioration.

Discs

Disc recordings made from a variety of materials were produced and used throughout the late 19th and early 20th centuries. Acetate discs were primarily used for making recordings, while other types were used for pre-made commercial recordings.

Acetate Discs

Acetate discs are very unstable due to their coating of nitrocellulose lacquer plasticized with castor oil. The plasticizer gradually evaporates off, causing the lacquer coating to become brittle and shrink. This coating is bonded to a base (usually aluminum) that cannot shrink, so the coating cracks and peels off the base. Acetate discs are also subject to chemical reactions that result in the formation of acids, which further accelerate deterioration. As with other materials, these chemical reactions are made worse by high temperature and humidity.

Vulcanite Discs

These were made from vulcanized rubber (vulcanization made the rubber stronger and more elastic) and were first marketed by Berliner in the 1890s. Vulcanite discs are quite stable when stored in the dark, but very unstable when exposed to light and/or heat and humidity.

Light facilitates the oxidation of the rubber, forming sulphur oxides and sulphuric acid in the presence of humidity. This acidity eventually causes the plastic to decompose. Vulcanite discs also have characteristic problems such as warping, blisters, and particles that are a result of the production process.

Shellac Discs

Shellac discs were first introduced in the early 1900s. Early discs were made with an organic shellac binder (produced from insect secretions) that covered a core. Later shellac discs were made from a plastic resin that was slightly more stable. Cores were made from many types of fillers with a wide range of quality (*e.g.*, powdered limestone or slate, carbon black, lubricants, oils, resins). Therefore, making generalizations about the causes of deterioration is difficult.

Shellac discs are relatively stable, but are prone to slow embrittlement of the shellac coating. The curing process during the manufacture of shellac discs causes chemical reactions that eliminate water or ammonia molecules, causing embrittlement. This process continues, although more slowly, throughout the lifetime of the disc, and it is accelerated by high temperature and humidity.

Edison Diamond Discs

In 1911, the Edison Company began marketing a new disc made from a synthetic plastic called phenol. This plastic material formed the core of the disc, which was then coated with thin layers of varnish.

These discs were quite stable and not prone to warping like others. However, prolonged contact with moisture or high humidity may damage them. These discs were designed to be played on Edison phonographs only and they were incompatible with other players., While they enjoyed significant popularity for some time, they were eventually supplanted by other types of discs. By 1929, they were no longer being produced.

Vinyl Discs

Vinyl discs were first introduced in 1930, but did not become popular until the late 1940s, when both $33^{1/3}$ rpm long play vinyl records and the 45 rpm format were introduced. Vinyl discs are quite stable, even though they are made from polyvinyl chloride (PVC), which deteriorates upon exposure to light or heat.

The deterioration process produces hydrochloric acid, which further accelerates the corrosion. To control this, a stabilizing chemical that consumes the hydrochloric acid is added during the manufacturing process. This generally provides enough protection for several decades.

Fig. 4.10 Vinyl Disc Recordings are Fairly Stable Chemically, but Must be Handled Carefully.

MAGNETIC MEDIA

The term magnetic media encompasses a variety of materials, including early wire recorders, numerous formats of audiotape and videotape, computer tape, computer hard drives, and computer floppy discs.

The first machines to record sound magnetically were developed around 1900 by Danish inventor Valdemar Poulson. They included the wire recorder (used for office dictation and recording of telephone messages), as well as a machine that recorded onto steel tape. Both technologies were used well into the 20th century, but magnetic tape eventually became the dominant medium. By the early1950s, magnetic tape had been almost universally adopted in radio and commercial sound recording.

Videotape was developed during the 1950s and quickly became popular. A number of different formats were developed-many of which did not become commercially successful. Magnetic tape has also been used to back-up and store computer data since the 1950s. More recently, magnetic disks in the form of hard drives, 5¼ inch floppy disks, and 3½ inch floppy disks have been used to store data on personal computers.

STRUCTURE

All magnetic tape is made up of two layers: a substrate (backing) and a recording layer (a binder containing magnetic particles). When the tape is passed through a recorder, the magnetic particles are permanently aligned within the binder to produce a copy of the sound waves being recorded.

Magnetic hard disks consist of a metallic base (usually aluminum) coated on both sides with a recording layer similar to that of magnetic tape. Floppy disks and diskettes have a plastic base with a magnetic recording layer on one or both sides.

The newer 3½ inch diskettes are enclosed in a rigid plastic protective jacket, while the older 5¼ inch diskette enclosures are more flexible. For both types, a slot in the jacket allows the read/write head to access the disk.

TAPE SUBSTRATES

The first magnetic tapes used a backing (carrier) made of steel. During the 1930s, German companies developed an audiotape that used a plastic carrier coated with a powder made from material that could be magnetized.

At that point, the recording quality of magnetic tape had improved enough to compete with the best disc recorders, and after the end of World War II it gradually became more widely used.

Fig. 4.11 Acetate Tape is Easily Distinguishable from Polyester Tape: Light Shines Through an Acetate Tape Pack.

The backing for magnetic tape provides support for the magnetic recording layer as it travels through the tape recorder. Magnetic tape for sound recordings was produced on both acetate and polyester backings, while videotape was produced only on polyester. In magnetic audiotapes, the plastic backing is much thinner than in film, making it much more fragile.

Characteristic Types of Deterioration

Acetate magnetic tapes, like:

* Acetate films,
* Suffer from vinegar syndrome.

The tapes will emit a vinegar smell and eventually the backing will become brittle and shrink. Polyester tape is much more stable chemically (it is very resistant to oxidation and hydrolysis), but it is subject to physical distortion and mistracking of the tape due to poor winding of the tape pack and/or changes in temperature and relative humidity.

TAPE RECORDING LAYER

Magnetic tapes have a recording layer of magnetic particles (iron oxides in acetate magnetic tape; iron oxides, metallic iron, or chromium dioxide in polyester tape) suspended in a polyurethane binder. The binder may also include lubricants and other agents used to improve tape performance. Some tapes also have a binder coating on the back of the tape to reduce friction as the tape moves through the player and to make the tape wind more uniformly on the reel.

Binder Deterioration

The primary means of deterioration for all types of magnetic tape is binder degradation, also known as sticky shed syndrome. The polyurethane binder is subject to hydrolysis, in which moisture is absorbed by the binder material and longer molecules within the binder are broken up into shorter ones. The result is a softening of the binder and the presence of a gummy surface residue on the tape. The residue makes the tape stick in the recorder and causes uneven playback, sometimes making the tape jam completely. Occasionally, cleaning or baking the tape will make it usable for long enough to copy it, but this must be done by an experienced professional.

An additional problem with the binder is the loss of lubricants over time, which can be due to evaporation, to use of the lubricants during playback, or to hydrolysis or oxidation of the lubricant itself. Lubricant loss will also cause sticking, uneven playback, or jamming of the tape. Relubrication of tapes is possible, but must also be done by an experienced professional.

Magnetic Particle Deterioration

The magnetic particles that store the recorded information are subject to changes in their magnetic properties that can result in loss of the recorded signal. Although the extent of their vulnerability varies, all tapes are subject to demagnetization from exposure to a strong magnetic field, so care must be taken to avoid exposure.

Some magnetic particles are more stable than others (*e.g.*, they keep their magnetic properties longer and are more able to resist demagnetization).

Iron oxide particles are the most stable; these are generally used in lower grade audiotapes and low to high grade VHS/ Beta videotapes.

Metal particulate and chromium dioxide particles provide a higher quality output (hence they are used in high quality audiotape), but they are less stable. Metal particulates are also used in 8 mm videotape and digital audio and videotapes. The rate of metal particulate and chromium dioxide deterioration is dependent on temperature.

DISKS AND DISKETTES

Diskettes have a notoriously short lifespan; the plastic base can deform and cause problems with reading the disk, while the magnetic particles that record the data can become unstable.

Hard drives are more reliable, but still susceptible to failure (sometimes catastrophic). Disks and diskettes are also, of course, vulnerable to strong magnetic fields, which can demagnetize the magnetic particles that store the data. While there is no hard data about the longevity of magnetic disks and diskettes, their lifespan is estimated to be less than 10 years.

Fig. 4.12 Estimates of the Lifespan of Magnetic Disks and Diskettes Extend Less than 10 Years at Most.

In addition, magnetic disks face the problem of technological obsolescence. It is very likely that the hardware and software to read the data, particularly from diskettes, will be outdated and perhaps unavailable before the disks themselves become unreadable. Solutions for this problem, including copying and migration of data.

OPTICAL MEDIA

Optical disc technology was invented in the 1960s and is the basis for the CD and DVD formats that are familiar to us today. In the 1990s, prerecorded compact discs (CDs) became the most popular medium for recorded sound. Various CD formats have since become popular for other applications as well, with CD-ROM (read only memory) and CD-R (recordable) both introduced in the 1990s for computer applications.

DVD (originally digital video disc) technology was introduced in 1995 as a medium for playing full-length movies and gradually became dominant over the videotape. There are various formats of DVD, which are likely to replace CD formats in the near future. These include DVD-ROM for computer data, DVD-RAM (a writeable version of DVD-ROM), and DVD-Audio.

STRUCTURE OF OPTICAL DISCS

Optical discs are multilayered objects that store digital data; they are used for audio, video, and computer data. Some are prerecorded, and others allow the user to record data. To record data onto an optical disc, a laser passes through a polycarbonate support and etches marks (known as pits and lands) into a data layer to represent the bits and bytes of digital data. To read data, the laser passes through the support and the data layer and is reflected off a metal reflective layer (sometimes these are separate layers and sometimes not).

Different types of discs have different structures and composition. A DVD is essentially two CDs glued together; that is, it has two layers of polycarbonate that are joined with adhesive in the center. Thus, CDs can be read and written on one side only, while DVDs can be read and written on one or both sides, depending on the format.

GENERAL STABILITY

The optical disc technology would prove to be very stable, but this is not the case. Like other media found in cultural collections, optical media are vulnerable to physical deterioration. In addition, they face the problem of media obsolescence—in many cases the technology to read the media will become obsolete and unavailable before the medium itself deteriorates.

The specific materials that make up the various CD and DVD formats (and their vulnerability to deterioration) will be discussed in this part.

CD/DVD SUBSTRATE

Fig. 4.13 Damage Caused by the Adhesive on a Barcode has Rendered this Bootleg Video CD Useless.

Both CDs and DVDs have a polycarbonate (clear plastic) substrate (CDs have one layer, while DVDs have two layers joined with adhesive). This stabilizes the disc, keeping it flat, and provides the depth necessary for the laser to focus on the data layer and the metal reflective layer. Thus, in a CD, which is read by the laser from the bottom, the data layer is actually near the top of the disc. In a DVD, the data layers are better protected due to the presence of a polycarbonate layer on both sides of the disc.

Characteristic Types of Deterioration

Although the polycarbonate will deteriorate over time, the other elements within a disc (*e.g.*, the data layer or the metal reflective layer) will deteriorate more quickly. The polycarbonate layer is vulnerable to poor handling, however. Fingerprints, smudges, scratches, particles of dirt or dust, solvents, or excessive moisture all may interfere with the ability of the laser to read the data layer.

Optical discs are also vulnerable to problems with disc integrity, including separation of the layers, warping, cracking of the layers, and pinholes. These problems are made worse by exposure to high temperature, humidity and extreme fluctuations in climate.

DATA LAYERS

The type of data layer(s) used varies according to the format of the disc. Discs can be read-only (ROM), write-once (R), or rewritable many times (RW or RAM).

Read-Only (ROM) Discs

These include CD-ROM and DVD-ROM discs (both used for pre-ecorded audio, video, and computer applications). In ROM discs, the data layer is not actually separate; it is molded into the polycarbonate substrate and then coated with a metal reflective layer. In CD-ROMs and most DVD-ROMs, this reflective layer is aluminum. However, in order to put more data onto a disc, some DVD-ROMs are double-layered (on one or both sides), meaning that they have two metal reflective data layers, one of which is semi-reflective to allow the laser to pass partly through to the second fully reflective layer. In these types of discs, the semi-reflective layer is made from gold, silver alloy, or silicon.

If moisture or oxygen from the environment penetrates to the inside of the disc, the aluminum can oxidize, making it less reflective and eventually making the disc unreadable (this is known as "disc rot").

Write-Once Discs

These include CD-R, DVD-R, and DVD+R discs. In these discs, a separate data layer made up of organic dyes is sandwiched between the polycarbonate substrate and the metal reflective layer. These organic dyes are photosensitive, so marks are made in the data layer via chemical changes caused by the laser beam.

As with all organic dyes, these dyes will deteriorate slowly over time, especially if exposed to high temperatures and humidity. Extensive exposure to ultraviolet (UV) light and/or heat (*e.g.*, sunlight) will also accelerate the deterioration of these dyes. However, if they are well cared for, these discs are much more stable than rewritable discs.

Rewritable Discs

These include CD-RW, DVD-RW, DVD+RW, and DVD-RAM discs. These discs also have a separate data layer sandwiched between the polycarbonate substrate and the metal reflective layer, but this data layer consists of a phase-changing metal alloy film. While this is a complicated process, in essence the laser beam makes marks in this film by heating it and reheating it during the rewriting process.

In rewritable discs, the metal alloy film deteriorates faster than the dyes used in write-once discs, thus making RW and RAM discs less stable. The metal alloy film deteriorates in response to heat, UV light, and high humidity. In addition, the rewriting process affects the life expectancy of rewritable discs; the more times a disc is rewritten, the shorter its life expectancy.

REFLECTIVE LAYERS

The reflective layer in an optical disc reflects the laser beam to transmit the data back to the laser head. It is made from different types of metal, depending on the disc format.

Read-Only Discs

These include CD-ROM and DVD-ROM discs (both used for prerecorded audio, video, and computer applications).The data/ metal reflective layer is made from aluminum in most of these discs. Aluminum can be subject to oxidation if kept in a humid and hot environment (the polycarbonate substrate will absorb moisture in such a situation, and cracks or scratches will make this worse). In double-layer DVD-ROM discs, there are two data/reflective layers; the first is semi-reflective and made from silicon, gold, or silver alloy, which are much less subject to corrosion.

Write-Once Discs

These include CD-R, DVD-R, and DVD+R discs. Gold, silver, or silver alloy is used for the metal reflective layer in these discs as well. Silver can corrode by reacting with sulphur dioxide, a pollutant that can migrate through the substrate when it absorbs moisture. Silver alloys are somewhat less vulnerable to this corrosion. Gold is very stable, but it is expensive. All of these metals do not deteriorate as quickly as the dyes used in the data layer, however.

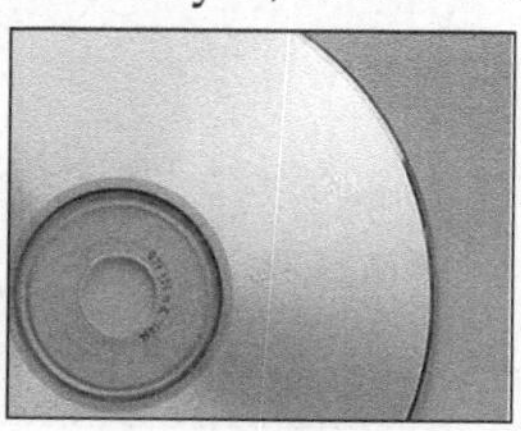

Fig. 4.14 Write-once Discs (Such as CD-R) Have a Significantly Longer Life Expectancy than Rewritable Discs.

Rewritable Discs

These include CD-RW, DVD-RW, DVD+RW, and DVD-RAM discs. Like read-only discs, these discs use aluminum for the reflective layer, which can be subject to oxidation in poor environmental conditions. However, the metal alloy film used for the data layer will likely deteriorate much more quickly.

OTHER COATINGS

Because the data layer is so close to the label side of the disc in a CD, a thin layer of lacquer is usually applied to protect the data layer from exposure to the environment. (This is not needed in a DVD, due to the presence of a polycarbonate layer on both sides of the disc.) This lacquer layer may protect the CD somewhat from damage due to writing or labeling, but care must still be taken not to damage the coating during handling. Sometimes an extra surface layer is added to a CD or DVD to provide a surface for labeling, but this also must be treated carefully. The only truly safe surface for labeling is the clear inner hub or the "mirror" band, which do not contain data.

EXTERNAL FACTORS

As with paper-based collections, external factors such as high, low, or fluctuating temperature and humidity; light exposure; the presence of pollutants; and poor storage and handling exacerbate the deterioration of film and electronic media. While these external factors affect all media collections to some extent, some of them are particularly damaging to specific types of materials, which will be the focus of this part.

Fig. 4.15 These Film Negatives are Stored in Poor Quality Enclosures and do not have Proper Support to Prevent Distortion.

ENVIRONMENT

Temperature

Higher temperatures increase the rate of the chemical reactions (oxidation and hydrolysis) that drive deterioration. This is particularly important for film-based and optical media, since many of these materials deteriorate at a rapid rate at room temperature (generally accepted as 68°F and 50% relative humidity). Cellulose nitrate film may show significant deterioration in as little as 10 years (although it may also survive significantly longer), and cellulose acetate film has a life expectancy of only about 40 years. Temperature also accelerates the fading of colour materials.

Relative Humidity

Fig. 4.16 This Audio Tape Reel has Developed Mold on the Edges of the Tape due to High Relative Humidity.

Humidity (moisture in the air) provides water to fuel the chemical reactions that cause deterioration. The more moisture there is in the air, the more quickly chemical deterioration proceeds. High humidity is a primary factor in hydrolysis, which affects binder degradation, fading of colour dyes, and deformation of film and tape supports. Fluctuating humidity levels also accelerate damage, particularly affecting distortion of CDs, DVDs, and magnetic tape backings.

Pollutants

Fig. 4.17 The Cyan and Yellow dyes in this Slide have Faded, Leaving only the Magenta Colour. The Shift of Colour dyes can be Exacerbated by Storage in a High-humidity Environment.

Film-based, magnetic, and optical media are particularly vulnerable to the effects of gaseous and particulate pollutants. Particulate pollutants cause abrasion, and many gaseous pollutants are oxidizers, contributing to the deterioration of colour dyes, silver images, the reflective surfaces of CDs and DVDs, and magnetic tape binder materials.

Light

Exposure to light greatly accelerates the fading of the colour dyes used in various types of film-based materials, as well as the dyes used in R (write once) CDs and DVDs. Exposure to strong sunlight can also cause damage due to the resulting heating of the exposed materials.

Colour slides in particular are very vulnerable to fading when projected in a slide projector (due to both heat and light exposure). It is important to note that Kodachrome slide film is very stable in the dark but fades rapidly when exposed to light, while Ektachrome slide film is more resistant to projection damage but fades more quickly than Kodachrome in dark storage. Fujichrome is generally the most stable slide film overall.

STORAGE AND HANDLING

Film and electronic media are just as vulnerable to poor storage and handling as are paper-based collections.

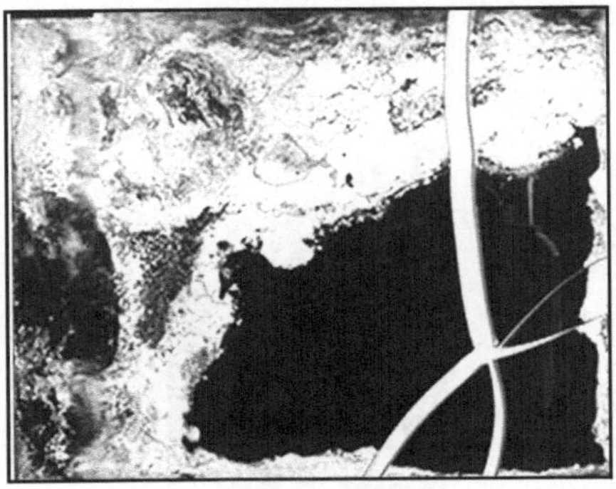

Fig. 4.18 As a Result of Water Damage, this Gelatin Glass Plate Negative Exhibits Mold Growth, Flaking and Lifting Emulsion, as Well as Breakage of the Glass Support.

Poor quality storage enclosures can damage the emulsions and image materials of film-based collections, as well as accelerate chemical damage. Poor handling can also cause problems. Glass plate negatives are vulnerable to breakage, scratching, and lifting of the emulsions when they are not handled carefully. The CDs and magnetic tapes can be damaged by being placed in strong sunlight or in close contact with heat (*e.g.*, radiators).

Magnetic media can be demagnetized if placed in contact with a strong magnetic field. Storing tapes flat for long periods of time can result in uneven distribution of the tape pack. Dirt, dust, and fingerprints can easily damage the delicate surfaces of film, magnetic, and optical media. The data layer of CDs can be damaged by adhesive labels or by labeling using solvent-based markers.

Magnetic tapes, film, and optical media have the added complication of deterioration from frequent (or sometimes infrequent) use. Every time these media are played (or rerecorded or rewritten, in the case of tapes and some CDs and DVDs) there is a danger that they will be damaged-sometimes as a result of defective playback equipment, and sometimes just from the cumulative effect of many playbacks.

EVALUATING YOUR COLLECTIONS

You have explored the mechanisms of deterioration for film-based and electronic media and briefly examined the role of external factors in collection deterioration.

In this part you will begin to relate this information to your own collections:

* *Important*: This examination of your collections is not meant to serve as a formal collection condition survey, but it will assist you in determining which materials need further attention. You may decide that one or more collection condition surveys are required for specific subsets of your film-based or electronic materials (*e.g.*, reel-to-reel tapes, photographic negatives, motion picture films). This type of inspection most often takes the form of an item-by-

item survey by a conservator with detailed knowledge of that particular type of collection.

NEGATIVES AND TRANSPARENCIES

Fig. 4.19 This Water-damaged Gelatin Glass Plate Negative Exhibits Mold Growth and Flaking Emulsion Along the Left Edge/side.

Photographic negatives and transparencies in your collection may include glass plate negatives, lantern slides, autochromes, black and white film negatives, colour film negatives, and colour slides. Older film negatives may be on nitrate film, while newer ones are likely on acetate or polyester film.

Types of physical damage you may observe include broken or cracked glass plates or covering glass, broken tape seals on lantern slides or autochromes, and cracking or flaking of glass plate emulsions. Mold growth may also be a problem.

Evidence of chemical damage due to the deterioration of nitrate film may include yellowing, stickiness, and a nitric acid odour. Nitrate films that are in an advanced state of deterioration will be soft and may adhere to adjacent films or enclosures, or they may have partially disintegrated into a brown powder. Evidence of chemical deterioration of acetate film due to vinegar syndrome may include a vinegar odour, curling, or staining. Advanced deterioration will manifest itself through bubbles on the film and separation of the emulsion from the base. Nitrate or acetate film may sometimes be identified by edge printing (it will say NITRATE or SAFETY).

Deteriorated colour negatives and slides may show evidence of fading or colour change (dye shifts).

MOTION PICTURE FILM

Motion picture film is found in several gauges (this refers to the width of the film) within collections: 35mm (commercial motion pictures), 16mm (home and educational movies), and 8mm (home movies). The 16mm and 8mm amateur films that record events of importance to an institution or person are those most commonly found in cultural collections.

Film is very vulnerable to physical damage due to projection and handling; this may include tears, damaged sprocket holes, and splices. Film can also suffer from mold growth, which begins at the outer edge and moves into the roll of film, eventually destroying the emulsion. Shrinkage of the film can occur due to low humidity, which may also make the film brittle.

Chemical damage may include evidence of nitrate or acetate deterioration and fading of the dyes used in colour films. Evidence of chemical damage due to the deterioration of nitrate film may include yellowing, stickiness, and a nitric acid odour.

Nitrate films that are in an advanced state of deterioration will be soft and may adhere to adjacent films or enclosures, or they may have partially disintegrated into a brown powder. Evidence of chemical deterioration of acetate film due to vinegar syndrome may include a vinegar odour, curling, or staining. Advanced deterioration will manifest itself through bubbles on the film and separation of the emulsion from the base. Nitrate or acetate film may sometimes be identified by edge printing (it will say NITRATE or SAFETY).

MICROFORMS

Many cultural collections include older microfilms or microfiche, which may have been produced as a preservation copy of paper-based collections or may have been surrogates for original materials that were discarded, such as newspapers. These microforms may be positives or negatives, either master or duplicate. Many of them will be silver-gelatin microfilm, but diazo microfilm (which uses dyes) and vesicular microfilm (in which an image is formed by heating the film to form bubbles) may also be present. Diazo microfilm will fade on exposure to light, and vesicular microfilm is very vulnerable to heat damage. Microfilm has been produced on nitrate, acetate, and polyester film through the years, so older microfilm must be inspected to determine its type.

Fig. 4.20 As the Acetate Base of this Microfilm Broke Down, it Shrank, the Emulsion Warped and Became Sticky, and the Film Adhered to Itself. Unwinding the Film Caused it to Tear.

Chemical damage may include evidence of nitrate or acetate deterioration. Evidence of chemical damage due to the deterioration of nitrate film may include yellowing, stickiness, and a nitric acid odour. Nitrate films that are in an advanced state of deterioration will be soft and may adhere to adjacent films or enclosures, or they may have partially disintegrated into a brown powder. Evidence of chemical deterioration of acetate film due to vinegar syndrome may include a vinegar odour, curling or staining. Advanced deterioration will manifest itself through bubbles on the film and separation of the emulsion from the base. Nitrate or acetate film may sometimes be identified by edge printing.

Silver gelatin microfilms are subject to oxidation, which can result in small blemishes (called measles). This phenomenon is made worse by high humidity and the presence of pollutants. Diazo microfilms may exhibit fading, and vesicular microfilms may exhibit image loss from heat damage.

SOUND RECORDINGS

Fig. 4.21 This Acetate Disc (Also Known as a Transcription or Lacquer disc) Exhibits Loss and a Crack in the Surface.

Sound recordings may be present in a variety of formats in cultural collections. They may include disc recordings, wax cylinders, reel-to-reel tapes, cassette tapes, and CDs. They may be commercial recordings, or they may document lectures, concerts, or other events of importance to an organization, institution, or individual.

Physical damage to sound recordings includes brittleness, cracking, and decomposition of disc recordings, damage to thin and fragile magnetic tape from playback, distortion of polyester-backed tapes, poor tape pack winding, and damage caused by defective cassette cases.

Chemical damage that may be noted includes sticky shed syndrome, in which a gummy residue is found on the surface of the tape. Sticking or jamming of the tape during playback may also indicate a loss of tape lubricant. In addition, early audiotape may be on acetate, and thus may exhibit evidence of vinegar syndrome, which includes a vinegar odour, curling, or staining. Advanced deterioration will manifest itself through bubbles on the film and separation of the emulsion from the base.

VIDEOTAPES

Videotapes are frequently found within cultural collections. The most common format is VHS, although others such as Beta and compact formats may also be found. Usually videotapes document events of importance to an organization, institution, or individual. Videotapes have a polyester base, so they are not subject to the deterioration seen in nitrate or acetate film-based materials.

As with audiotapes, chemical damage may include sticky shed syndrome, in which a gummy residue is found on the surface of the tape. Videotapes are also vulnerable to strong magnetic fields. Physical damage may include edge damage or warped tape.

MAGNETIC DISKS, CDs AND DVDs

While it is clear that magnetic disks and diskettes, CDs, and DVDs (which are all used to store various types of digital data) have limited physical lifespans, it is difficult to determine the extent of their deterioration by simple observation. If problems are noted when accessing the data or playing the CD or DVD, this should be taken as an indication that the item may be vulnerable to a more serious failure.

However, given the fact that the hardware and software to access these materials will likely become obsolete before the media themselves deteriorate, determining the condition of these materials is not the highest priority. It is very important to gather descriptive information (called metadata) about all items determined to be of long-term value. This should include physical details of the format, and the hardware, operating system, and software required to access the data. Data that is of long-term value should be copied and migrated to new formats when necessary.

5

The Building and Environment

Achieving a preservation-quality environment can be confusing and challenging. Are there specific temperature and humidity levels that must be maintained? What if your building's climate control systems cannot achieve them? How should pollutants and light be controlled? What types of fire protection and security systems are best? The quality of the environment for your collections will depend on your building's design, construction, and systems, as well as on the extent and quality of building maintenance.

If financial resources are limited, or administrative and/or facilities personnel are unwilling to make changes, you may wonder whether it is possible to make meaningful improvements. Addressing these issues may seem overwhelming, but remember that even small steps towards improving your building and environment will benefit your collections.

ENVIRONMENTAL CONTROL

All organic materials deteriorate, but research has shown that collections kept in a stable moderate climate will have a longer lifespan that those that are frequently subjected to hot and humid conditions. However, maintaining such a climate can be a challenge. Staff may be faced with older mechanical systems that are difficult to control, systems whose target set points are dictated primarily by the requirements of human comfort, and/or facilities staff who are not sympathetic to the needs of collections. In this part, you will explore "best practices" for environmental control (*e.g.*, the recommendations of preservation professionals for climate, pollutants, and light exposure in collection storage areas), and begin to consider what type of environment you are currently providing for your collections. Later in this part you will learn how these "best practices" might be achieved within your building, as well as how you might improve existing conditions even if it is not possible to attain the ideal environment.

TEMPERATURE AND RELATIVE HUMIDITY

Temperature can be defined as a measurement of how quickly molecules are moving within a material. As molecules move faster, they collide more frequently, making chemical reactions more likely. Molecules move more rapidly at higher temperatures, so heat accelerates the chemical reactions that cause deterioration. As a general rule of thumb, the rate of many chemical reactions is doubled with an increase of 18°F. Thus, a lower temperature means a slower rate of deterioration.

Relative Humidity

Relative humidity refers specifically to the amount of water vapour contained in the air (*e.g.*, 30%, 40%) at a given temperature (*e.g.*, 65°F, 80°F), relative to the total amount of water vapour the air is capable of holding at that temperature (which would be 100%). The amount of water vapour in the air is important for two reasons: moisture provides fuel for the chemical reactions that cause deterioration (*e.g.*, acid hydrolysis), and it causes physical damage such as swelling and shrinking. Organic materials such as paper naturally try to come to equilibrium with the surrounding air, so they absorb moisture as the relative humidity rises, and release moisture as it falls. Thus, higher relative humidity results in a quicker deterioration rate. Very low relative humidity can result in dessication and cracking of some materials. Frequent fluctuations in relative humidity (and temperature) are even more damaging.

Temperature and RH are Interrelated

When managing climate within collections storage spaces, it is crucial to understand that air is capable of holding more water vapour at higher temperatures. Thus, given that the absolute amount of water vapour in the air remains the same (unless moisture is added or taken away through humidification or dehumidification), the relative humidity will go down if the temperature is raised, and it will go up if the temperature is lowered.

GUIDELINES FOR TEMPERATURE AND RH

There is no national standard for climate-controlled storage of paper collections, but the National Information Standards Organization (NISO) has issued a technical report entitled *Environmental Guidelines for the Storage of Paper Records,* available from NISO. This publication gives suggested values for temperature and relative humidity for storage of paper records, which are summarized here:

Situation	Temperature	Relative Humidity
Combined stack and user areas	70 °F maximum*	30-50% RH**
Stacks where people are excluded except for access and retrieval	65 °F maximum*	30-50% RH**
Optimum preservation stacks	35-65°F***	30-50% RH**
Maximum daily fluctuation	±2°F	± 3% RH
Maximum monthly drift	3°F	3%

Note: * These values assume that 70°F is about the minimum comfort temperature for reading and 65°F the minimum for light physical activity. Each institution can make its own choice.

** A specific value of relative humidity within this range should be maintained ± 3%, depending on the climatic conditions in the local geographic area, or facility limitations.

*** A specific temperature within this range should be maintained ± 2°F. The specific temperature chosen depends on how much an organization is willing to invest in order to achieve a given life expectancy for its records.

POLLUTANTS

Like temperature and humidity, the damaging effect of pollutants on collections can be difficult to see in the short-term, but very serious over the long term. Pollutants fall into two general categories (particulates and gases) and may originate outdoors or within the building.

Particulate Pollutants

Particulates consist of organic and inorganic materials (*e.g.*, hair, skin cells, soot, fibres, pollen, metals, salts, plaster, etc.) that may come from humans, smoke, cooking, construction materials, heating systems, and other sources. Particulates are categorized by size; fine particles have a diameter of 2.5 microns or less, while coarse particles have a diameter of 2.5-10 microns. Particulates are abrasive, they attract insects, and many are acidic, reacting with moisture to worsen chemical deterioration. The effect of particulate pollutants worsens in the presence of high relative humidity and temperature.

Fig. 5.1 Deposits of Particulates Around this Ceiling Air Vent Indicate that Particulate Filtration is Inadequate.

Gaseous Pollutants

Common gaseous pollutants in the outdoor environment include sulphur dioxide (which comes from combustion of fossil fuels), nitrogen oxides (mainly from traffic exhaust), and ozone (produced by heavy electrical machinery, as well as when light reacts with nitrogen oxides). Indoor pollutants can unfortunately also be a problem. Ozone is produced by photocopiers, laser printers, and electrostatic air cleaners. Acids, ammonia, formaldehyde, and peroxides are also produced by indoor materials such as cleaning products, particleboard, adhesives, and oil paints.

The amount of outdoor pollution that actually penetrates a building and affects collections is difficult to quantify, but certainly evidence has shown that collections in urban institutions are more acidic than those in institutions located in more rural settings. Gaseous pollutants can be unpredictable; even in fairly small concentrations they may interact with each other to cause damage.

GUIDELINES FOR POLLUTANT LEVELS

There are no formal standards for pollutant levels in collection storage areas, but generally accepted levels for particulate filtration are given in NISO's *Environmental Guidelines for the Storage of Paper Records*:

Combined stack and user areas	60-80% filtration (*e.g.*remove 60-80% of particulates 1 micron diameter or larger)
Stack areas, users excluded except for retrieval	90-95% filtration
Optimum preservation areas	>95% filtration

Generally accepted levels for sulphur dioxide, nitrous oxides, and ozone (the most common gaseous pollutants in collection storage areas) have been given in numerous publications and fall in the following ranges:

Sulphur dioxide	1-10 Micrograms/cubic meter
Nitrous oxides	5-10 Micrograms/cubic meter
Ozone	2-25 Micrograms/cubic meter

It is important to be aware that the upper limits for exposure of collections to pollutants are well below the acceptable levels for human exposure set by the Environmental

Protection Agency. Thus, "safe" levels of pollutants for people are not considered "safe" for collections.

LIGHT

Light energy, in the form of waves, is absorbed by molecules within an object. This absorption of energy activates a variety of chemical reactions that have the potential to damage paper-based collections. This is termed photochemical deterioration.

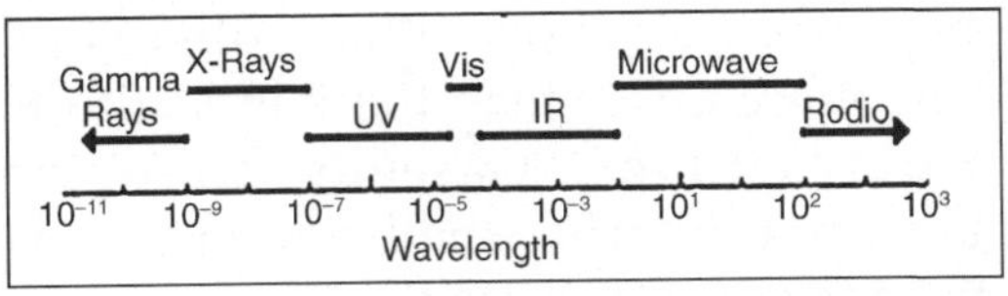

Fig. 5.2 Different Types of Light (Visible, Ultraviolet, Infrared) Fall at Different Points on the Electromagnetic Spectrum.

Visible light falls between 400 and 760 nanometers on the electromagnetic spectrum. Wavelengths below 400 nanometers have a greater frequency than visible light, and bombard an object with more energy in a shorter time, accelerating photochemical deterioration. At the other end of the spectrum, infrared light causes heating, thermal expansion, and spot desiccation. Fundamentally, although some types of light may be worse than others, all light is damaging, including visible light.

Sources of Light

Collections may be exposed to both natural and artificial light. Natural light is high in both UV and IR light, while artificial lighting varies.

There are two types of artificial light sources: incandescent bulbs and discharge bulbs. Traditional tungsten incandescent bulbs are high in IR but do not emit much UV. However, tungsten halogen incandescent bulbs may have high levels of UV. Discharge bulbs include fluorescent tubes and metal halide bulbs. Metal halide bulbs emit high levels of UV, as do many fluorescent bulbs. In fibre optic lighting, optical fibres carry the light from a single light source to various locations. Fibre optic lighting may emit some IR light, but any UV in the original light source is removed as the light passes through the fibres.

GUIDELINES FOR LIGHT LEVELS

Fig. 5.3 Sunlight Streaming in Through a Window Exposes Collections to Damaging Visible and Ultraviolet Light.

Visible light is generally measured in lux (indicating the amount of light received by a surface). UV light is measured in microwatts per lumen. Guidelines for UV light are straightforward; light sources should emit less than 75 microwatts/lumen of UV. Protecting collections from visible light is more problematic.

Certainly the most protection is provided by reducing light exposure completely (through storage in boxes or other enclosures). Light levels of 200 to 600 lux are required for comfortable vision in study and inspection areas; but storage areas can and should be as low as 10 to 50 lux. Lights should be turned off whenever possible. Ideally sunlight and daylight should be excluded completely from storage and use areas, or shades, drapes, and/or blinds should be used to reduce exposure as much as possible.

Due to the diversity of materials and their responses to light exposure, there is no standard for light levels during exhibition and use, but in general exhibition lighting for very light sensitive materials (this includes most paper-based items) should be limited to 50 lux, and exhibition time should be limited.

FIRE PROTECTION AND SECURITY

The goal of fire protection and security systems is to protect the building and its contents from damage and theft. Security and fire protection are closely related, as fire protection and security systems are often monitored by the same office or company, and security measures that discourage arson are crucial to fire prevention.

Fig. 5.4 These Files were Badly Damaged in an Office Fire.

FIRE PREVENTION

The keys to preventing fire damage are elimination of fire hazards and early detection and suppression of any fire that does occur. Fire protection systems must be monitored 24 hours a day by an outside agency (*e.g.*, an outside security company, the local fire department, or the institution's own security force) and inspected and maintained routinely to ensure that they will work properly when needed.

Most local fire departments will provide fire inspections and assist institutions in developing a fire safety programme. Hazards such as poor electrical wiring and obstructed exits must be corrected. If the fire department is familiar with the building and collections in advance, there is a greater chance that fire-fighting strategies will take collection priorities into account. Frequent fire drills and an updated evacuation plan are also very important.

DETECTION

Fire detectors commonly found in cultural institutions are manual fire alarm pulls (which provide a quick way to activate the alarm system during occupied hours), heat detectors, and smoke detectors. Often a combination of different types of detectors will be used, depending on the building construction and other needs. Detection systems often play a part in activating the fire suppression system.

Heat Detectors

Fixed-temperature heat detectors are designed to operate when the room reaches a predetermined temperature (usually a fairly high one). These do not detect smoldering fires well. Rate-of-rise heat sensors are better, since they are activated by a sudden, small increase in temperature, but in general heat sensors do not work until the temperatures in the room are quite high and the fire is likely to be well developed.

Smoke Detectors

Fig. 5.5 Smoke Detectors can Detect a Fire Before it gets out of Control.

Smoke detectors are designed to detect a fire while it is still in its incipient stages. There are several types (photoelectric and ionization) that work on different principles. Smoke detectors are usually spot units that are placed along ceilings or high on walls. A third type of detector, the air aspirating system, is very sensitive to smoke and might be considered for areas in which extremely valuable collections are stored. These units draw an air sample in, analyse it, and than return it to the space. If smoke is detected, the alarm system is activated.

System Controls

The control panel of a detection system monitors the various detectors within the system, as well as the devices that announce or respond to the alarm (bells, lights, building

HVAC controls). There are two basic types: conventional and addressable. Conventional systems usually have several zones, each of which may have a number of smoke detectors and manual pull stations. An alarm in one zone cannot indicate which specific detector was activated, so depending on the size of the zones, fire personnel may have to search for the fire. Addressable systems are more complicated and expensive, and they require more training of building maintenance personnel. However, they can indicate which specific alarm has been activated and detect any faults in the system circuits.

SUPPRESSION

A number of different types of suppression systems have been used in cultural institutions over the years. Modern wet-pipe sprinkler systems are increasingly recommended for cultural institutions due to their relative low cost, ease of maintenance, and dependability.

Sprinkler Systems

Water sprinkler systems consist of the sprinklers themselves, the piping system, and a water source. Systems are usually also equipped with water flow alarms (to indicate when a sprinkler is activated), control valves (allowing the system to be shut down), and features that allow the pipes to be drained for maintenance and tested periodically.

Fig. 5.6 In Modern Sprinkler Systems, Only the Sprinkler Heads Nearest the fire are Discharged.

Sprinkler heads are activated by high temperatures. In modern systems, sprinkler heads operate independently of each other; only the sprinklers in the immediate vicinity of the fire are discharged. On/off heads that close when the temperature is reduced are available, but they are not generally recommended due to their high cost and the fact that fire personnel normally arrive to shut down the system before the temperature is reduced enough to close the sprinkler heads.

There are three main types of sprinkler systems:

* Wet-pipe systems are the most common, the most reliable, and the easiest to maintain. Water is maintained in the pipes at all times, and when a sprinkler head opens it is discharged.
* In dry-pipe systems, the pipes are filled with air, which is released when a sprinkler head opens, allowing water to flow into the pipes and to the fire. These have a slower response time, but are useful in areas where freezing of the pipes might occur.
* Pre-action systems work with the fire detection system; when some combination of detectors indicates a fire, a valve is opened to allow water into the pipes. The water is not discharged, however, until a sprinkler head is activated. These systems are expensive to install and maintain, and they have a higher risk of malfunction.

Water Mist Systems

In recent years the water mist system has emerged as a new fire suppression option. These systems discharge water in very fine droplets at high pressure, which maximizes the water's cooling capacity and suppresses the fire with much less water than conventional sprinkler systems.

Gas Suppression Systems

Gas suppression systems extinguish a fire by flooding a space with some type of gas to reduce the oxygen concentration so that insufficient oxygen is available to fuel the fire. They can only be used in storage areas, because they pose the danger of asphyxiation to people.

In previous years, numerous institutions installed Halon gas suppression systems. New production of Halon has been phased out (due to its effect on the environment), and while several substitutes have been developed, none has emerged as a completely satisfactory replacement. Options include FM-200 and Inergen, both of which are costly and must be used at high concentrations, requiring the storage of large amounts of the gas.

Fire Extinguishers

Fire extinguishers are rated according to the types of fire they put out. Class A extinguishers are used for ordinary combustibles such as wood or paper. Class B extinguishers are used for fires involving flammable liquids (*e.g.*, oil, grease). Class C extinguishers are used for electrical fires.

Dry chemical extinguishers (also known as ABC extinguishers) are usually rated for multipurpose use. Water extinguishers (standard or mist) should only be used on Class A fires. CO_2 extinguishers are most effective on Class B and Class C fires. Staff must be trained in the use of fire extinguishers, and extinguishers must be inspected annually.

SECURITY SYSTEMS AND PROCEDURES

Unfortunately, security must be a concern in preservation of collections. A basic security policy with preventive activities and proper response procedures is critical to the protection of building, collections, staff, and patrons. Security preparations can be coordinated as part of the emergency plan or as a separate parallel security plan.

Security Systems

Automated security systems have several advantages: they can act as a deterrent to intruders, they will detect an intrusion in progress, they will notify appropriate personnel about the incident, and they can provide a means to connect other alarms (water alarms, etc.) to a monitoring station.

Security systems secure perimeter access points such as doors and windows, and they protect interior spaces via motion detectors. A system is made up of sensors, a control panel (which receives reports from the sensors and controls the alarm), and reporting devices (a traditional alarm or some type of signal to a monitoring station). A security system must be monitored 24 hours a day to be effective. This may be done by an outside monitoring company, or in the case of larger institutions, by an in-house or campus security office.

Security Procedures

While an automated security system can greatly enhance security, such a system should never be your only protection. Enhance perimeter security by increasing exterior light levels, expanding light coverage, clearing bushes and debris, and securing windows, doors, and skylights. During working hours, insist that all staff and patrons enter and exit by a single, monitored doorway. Alarm all other doors for unauthorized use. Carefully control building keys and keys to special collections areas, and keep a strict record of all keys issued and returned as employees come and go. It is also very important to register and supervise all patrons who use special collections, to track the use of these collections using call slips, and to retain all written records of use in case of loss.

PEST MANAGEMENT

The most common insects that affect paper-based collections are silverfish and firebrats, psocids (booklice), and cockroaches. Many insects are attracted to dark, small, seldom-disturbed spaces, where significant damage can be done before the problem is discovered.

Most insects are not attracted to paper itself, but rather to sizing, adhesives, and starches. However, some insects will attack cellulose (paper and cardboard), as well as protein (parchment and leather). Insect damage is caused not just by eating, but also by tunneling, nesting, and bodily secretions.

Rats, mice, squirrels, birds, and other small animals can also cause significant damage to paper collections. Rodents especially are attracted to environments that are dark, wet, dirty, cluttered, and undisturbed.

The use of pesticides to prevent pests and respond to infestations has been common in cultural institutions, but preservation professionals now recommend a strategy called integrated pest management (IPM). IPM relies on non-chemical methods to prevent and manage pest infestation.

PREVENTING PEST INFESTATION

It is always best to control pests by targeting the source of the problem, *i.e.*, the conditions that allow pests to enter and infest a facility. This strategy emphasizes ongoing maintenance and housekeeping to ensure that pests will not find a hospitable environment.

Integrated pest management focuses on sealing or otherwise blocking routes of entry to the building (*e.g.*, windows, vents, cracks), maintaining a moderate climate, avoiding water leakage or standing water (*e.g.*, pipe leaks, drains), removing or controlling food sources (*e.g.*, indoor plants, bushes and plants in close proximity to the building, staff food, trash), housekeeping (e.g, dusting and vacuuming, looking for signs of insect activity such as droppings and insect bodies), and inspection of incoming collections to ensure they are not infested.

RESPONDING TO PEST INFESTATION

Monitoring

If a few insects are observed in the building, monitor the situation with sticky traps (available in hardware and grocery stores) to determine the type of insect(s), the number of insects, and their entry points. Place traps in consistent locations, number and date them, and inspect them routinely. If results are negative, relocate the traps. Once insects have been trapped, identify them to determine what threat they pose to collections.

In cases where there is a serious insect infestation that does not respond to preventive techniques, direct treatment for insect infestation may be necessary.

Non-chemical Treatments

Controlled freezing and modified atmospheres have been used successfully to eradicate pests in cultural collections. Controlled freezing can be done in household or commercial freezers, blast freezers, or freezers with controlled temperature and humidity. Modified atmospheres (decreased oxygen, increased carbon dioxide, or use of an inert gas such as nitrogen) can be applied in a fumigation chamber or bubble, or in low-permeability plastic bags.

Heat, gamma radiation, and microwaves are used for insect control in food processing and other industries, but are not recommended for cultural collections due to their damaging effects on collections.

Chemical Treatments

Current preservation practice does not recommend extermination (chemical treatments) for pest problems except as a last resort, due to the toxic nature of pesticides.

MOLD PROTECTION

Mold spores are everywhere. Mold and mildew are types of fungi, microorganisms that depend on other organisms for sustenance. There are over 100,000 known species of fungi. The great variety of species means that patterns of mold growth and the response of mold in a particular situation can be unpredictable.

Molds excrete enzymes that allow them to digest organic materials such as paper and book bindings, altering and weakening those materials.

In addition, many molds contain colored substances that can stain paper, cloth, or leather. It is important to realise that mold can be dangerous to people and can in some cases pose a major health hazard. Mold outbreaks should never be ignored or left to "go away on their own".

PREVENTING MOLD

There are a number of factors (including high temperature, stagnant air, and darkness) that influence the growth of mold in buildings and on collections, but the single most important factor in mold growth is the moisture content of the materials on which the mold is growing. If there is sufficient moisture, mold will become active (germinating and releasing spores that spread the mold further). High moisture content is most often the result of high humidity or of dampness/wetness of collections. Paper collections are hygroscopic (*e.g.*, they absorb and release moisture) and will come to equilibrium with the surrounding atmosphere. The best way to prevent mold growth is to control humidity levels in all areas where collections are stored, and to keep the temperature moderate. General cleanliness and good air circulation also reduce the risk of infestation (although it is a good idea to limit air circulation once mold growth has occurred, to avoid spreading mold spores).

Fig. 5.7 Significant Mold Growth is Often the Result of Flooding or Other Water Problems that Cause High Humidity.

In the case of flood or other water damage, experience has shown that mold growth will occur within 48 to 72 hours if action is not taken to reduce the humidity and dry the materials, carpeting, and furnishings. You must identify and correct water hazards in your building (such as damp basement walls, leaky roofs, dripping pipes, etc.) as quickly as possible to avoid the development of mold.

RESPONDING TO MOLD

Mold must be dealt with promptly and in an appropriate manner. Under no circumstances should staff members work with moldy collections unprotected, and staff members with a known sensitivity should not work with moldy materials at all.

Health Hazards

Even small amounts of mold can be a serious health hazard to your staff and patrons. There are no federal or state regulations that govern exposure to mold, as there are for exposure to asbestos and other hazardous substances. The effects of mold will differ depending on the type of mold, the level of exposure, and the susceptibility of the person(s) exposed.

Personal Protective Equipment

A dust mask does NOT provide sufficient protection for working with mold; a respirator must be worn. If you do not have someone on staff that has been or can be fit-tested with a proper respirator, you should not clean mold in-house. Protective clothing, gloves, and eyewear are also recommended.

Many conservators and vendors choose to use a non-powered air-purifying respirator with the highest class of filter (*e.g.*, a P100 respirator, which has an efficiency of 99.97%) when dealing with mold. Be aware that the use of respirators in the workplace is governed by the Respiratory Protection Standard 29 CFR 1910.134, adopted by the Occupational Safety and Health Administration (OSHA) in 1998. This standard specifies types of respirators to be used in various situations, fit testing procedures (*e.g.*, tests to ensure that the respirator fits the wearer properly), and training procedures.

Response Procedures

You may be able to respond in-house to a very minor mold outbreak in your collection, but if you are faced with a serious mold problem that affects a significant portion of the collection and/or the building, you will almost certainly require the assistance of an outside vendor.

GENERAL BUILDING ISSUES

The design of your building has a significant effect on the preservation of the collections stored there. The indoor environment is affected by the type and extent of insulation, the presence of windows, activities taking place within the building (*e.g.*, the presence of people, pollutants generated by interior finishes and furnishings), and the capacity of the structure to resist moisture migration. In addition, the layout of collection use and storage spaces is crucial to maintaining security and environmental control. Regular inspection and maintenance of the building and systems is also very important, since it lessens the impact of weather, forestalls water damage, and ensures that building systems are working properly.

If your institution is fortunate enough to be constructing a new building or renovating an existing one, preservation concerns can (and should) be taken into account when designing new systems and spaces for collection storage and use. This is true both for your main building and for any buildings that will be used for off-site storage If your institution must work with an existing building or buildings, there are still actions you can take to ensure that those structures provide the best possible protection for your collections.

DESIGN

Following are some of the most important preservation issues to consider when designing a new building or making changes to an existing space.

Layout

To provide the best environment and the most security for collections, collection storage spaces must be separated from collection use spaces. It is best to store collections in an internal space without windows or other exposure to the outside environment. In addition, the layout of circulation, reference, and reading spaces must consider the need to supervise readers. Collections storage should be keyed separately from other spaces.

Water Control

Basement level storage areas are undesirable, due to their tendency towards flooding and moisture. If basement storage is unavoidable, excellent seals must be provided for the floor and exterior walls, and collections must be isolated from basement-level mechanical equipment. With the exception of fire suppression pipes, water-bearing pipes should not run through collections storage spaces. Cooling towers, lavatories, kitchens, janitor's spaces, and other water-carrying equipment should never be located above collections storage (including technical services, or any other areas where collections are stored for extended periods). All shelving should provide 4" floor clearance. Shelving should not be placed against exterior walls, as this can lead to condensation and other problems.

Fig. 5.8 Storing Collections in Basement is not Recommended due to the Risk of Moisture and Flooding; Overcrowding can also Pose a Fire Hazard.

Insulation and Vapour Barriers

Good insulation will reduce the effect of outdoor environmental conditions on indoor conditions. If there are windows, they should be properly insulated (*e.g.*, double-paned). Consistent use of shutters, blinds, or curtains will reduce heating from sunlight. The use of vapour barriers is also important in controlling humidity within the building. Older buildings are often sturdily constructed of hygroscopic materials (*e.g.*, wood, plaster, brick) that absorb and release moisture, while newer buildings have thinner walls and more easily allow moisture to pass through to the interior. Vapour barriers include various floor and wall coverings, such as waterproof paint or polyethylene film.

Systems

These systems are crucial to preservation and must be included in the design of a new or renovated building.

Floors and Walls

Carpeting should be avoided in collection storage spaces, as it can off-gas pollutants and absorb moisture easily. If storage areas are to be painted with collections in place, use only vinyl, acrylic, or latex paints. If areas must be painted using other types of paints, be sure to allow enough time for vapors to dissipate before returning collections to the area. Dropped ceilings are also not recommended, since they make it harder to identify leaks and can hide mold growth.

BUILDING MAINTENANCE

Periodic inspection and maintenance of the roof, walls, gutters, drains, and foundations is an investment in controlling interior conditions as well as in preserving the building itself. Every building that houses cultural collections should have a written schedule for maintenance of the exterior and interior of the building. It is also very helpful to keep an ongoing log of building problems, since this will allow staff to refer back to previous problems without having to rely on staff memories.

Working with Facilities Personnel

Particularly in large institutions, facilities personnel will likely have many responsibilities and pressures (including the need to save money and conserve energy), some of which may conflict with collection preservation needs. In addition, facilities personnel frequently hear complaints about staff comfort (*e.g,* too hot or too cold), which may make them less inclined to take seriously problems with the environment for collections. It is crucial to develop a good working relationship with your facilities personnel. Always provide accurate data to back up your arguments, and be sure that you understand the limitations of the existing building and systems, so that you do not make unrealistic requests for changes.

OFF-SITE STORAGE

Off-site storage is fairly common in libraries and archives, due to the size of collections and the fact that some collections must be retained but are not frequently accessed. Off-site storage may also be used temporarily to store collections during building renovation or in the aftermath of a disaster.

Off-site storage facilities (even temporary ones) must meet the same preservation standards as storage in the institution's main building or buildings. Time spent in poor climate conditions outweighs time spent in good conditions, so even putting up with poor climate conditions "for just a little while" can significantly shorten the life expectancy of collections. The space must also be protected against fire and theft, or catastrophic loss may occur.

A moderate stable environment (70 °F or lower, with a stable humidity between 30 and 50%) is crucial. The HVAC system should be run 24 hours a day and it must have filtration for particulate pollutants at a minimum. Fire detection and suppression, and security systems (plus water alarms if appropriate) should be provided. The building should be well-maintained, with no signs of water leaks, pest infestation, or mold. All off-site storage spaces must be checked out and approved in person by your staff before any contracts are signed. Once a space is chosen, staff from your institution should visit periodically (at least twice a week) to ensure that conditions remain acceptable.

MONITORING THE ENVIRONMENT

You have learned about "best practices" for control of temperature, relative humidity, pollutants, and light in collections storage-but how do you actually achieve these goals? Maintaining the recommended values can be difficult, even in a new building that has been designed and constructed for the purpose of storing collections with long-term value.

In this part you will learn how to monitor the environmental conditions in your building, and how to begin evaluating that data to determine which areas of your building are best for storing collections.

MONITORING TEMPERATURE AND RH

An environment with carefully controlled and stable levels of temperature and relative humidity, as well as controlled levels of pollutants and light, is generally agreed to be the single most important factor in extending the life expectancy of paper-based and related materials.

Since our subjective impressions of climate levels tend to be inaccurate, temperature and relative humidity should be systematically documented wherever collections of permanent value are stored. Monitoring involves consistent measurement of temperature and RH, either constantly or at scheduled intervals, in collection storage areas.

Recorded data will serve to establish existing environmental conditions; support the need for environmental controls (should the need exist); indicate whether climate control equipment is operating optimally, if such equipment is already in place; and/or indicate if there is a season during the year when the use of additional climate control equipment (such as portable dehumidifiers) should be considered.

It is generally recommended that independent monitoring be undertaken even if there is a monitoring system within the HVAC system. In-system monitoring may not be sophisticated or accurate enough to provide a good picture of conditions.

Climate Monitoring Devices

Monitoring devices vary greatly in cost, complexity, effectiveness, and staff time required to maintain them and to interpret the data. Some monitoring devices can be used to report immediate conditions ("snapshot" monitors), while others are designed to create an ongoing log of environmental conditions.

Examples of "snapshot" monitors include thermometers, dial hygrometers, indicator strips (useful in sealed exhibit cases), and sling or motor-driven psychrometers. "Min/max" digital thermohygrometers provide a middle ground; they can keep track of the highest and lowest temperature and humidity since the device was last reset. Thus, they can give a very general sense of fluctuations in the climate at night or on the weekend.

Recording hygrothermographs were the standard automatic recording device for many years, but in recent years dataloggers (battery operated devices that take readings at intervals specified by the user) have become the monitoring instrument of choice. This is largely due to the ease of downloading data gathered by a datalogger to a computer for graphing and analysis.

There are a number of issues that must be considered in choosing a datalogger, including memory capacity, battery life, sensor accuracy across a range of temperature and humidity, and type of display.

It is important to choose the monitoring instrument most appropriate to your institution and situation.

MONITORING POLLUTANTS

Unfortunately, there is no simple and inexpensive way to monitor pollutants in cultural institutions. Because the effect of gaseous pollutants may differ according to the level of relative humidity and/or the presence of other pollutants, most existing methods use indicators (such as silver) that are sensitive to pollutants. The corrosion of these indicators demonstrates the presence of pollutants that may damage collections. These may be useful in institutions with specialized collections that are particularly sensitive to pollutants, such as photographs.

Other options include periodic sampling of air quality over the course of a year by a specialized company, a complicated and expensive option, or the use of instruments designed to measure levels of urban pollution (*e.g.*, devices that pass air through a tube filled with a reactive substance, or electronic monitors that use corrosion detectors).

MONITORING LIGHT LEVELS

A light meter is used to measure visible light in units of lux or footcandles. A separate UV meter is required to measure UV energy in microwatts per lumen. Some UV meters can also measure visible light by changing detectors within the device. A 35mm camera with a manual light meter can also be used to measure visible light levels, as described in Protection from Light Damage.

Remember that artificial light does not change significantly, but monitoring natural light can be problematic because it differs according to the time of day, the weather, and the season.

Readings should be taken at times when the light is brightest to be sure that the highest light levels are being recorded. Another useful tool is the Blue Wool standard, cards containing samples of blue-dyed wool that fade at a known rate relative to each other (the first few samples on the card correspond to light-sensitive materials such as paper). Use of these cards can demonstrate the cumulative degree of fading caused by the intensity of light in a particular location

EVALUATING CLIMATE MONITORING DATA

The usual approach to evaluating the preservation quality of storage areas is to set specific targets for climate control, monitor the actual climate conditions, and act to correct any divergence from the targets. However, interpretation of climate monitoring data can be difficult, and correcting divergence from target values can be challenging.

Preservation professionals are increasingly arguing for a different approach. Rather than considering the climate in terms of a right or wrong set point, collections managers should determine what the climate is in each storage area (via monitoring), evaluate the effect of those conditions on the collections, and make changes or redistribute collections accordingly.

Evaluating the specific effect on collections of a particular storage area can be very difficult, however. For example, how do you determine the overall effect on collections of a storage area that cycles between 70°F and 80°F every day? How do you decide whether a storage area that is consistently 75°F and 40% RH is better or worse than one that is consistently 65°F and 50% RH?

Research conducted over the last few years by the Image Permanence Institute (IPI) has focused on answering these types of questions, and on evaluating the risks or benefits to collections of individual sets of environmental conditions.

THE PRESERVATION INDEX (PI) AND TIME-WEIGHTED PRESERVATION INDEX (TWPI)

To evaluate the risks associated with specific environmental conditions, IPI has developed two tools: the Preservation Index (PI) and the Time-Weighted Preservation Index (TWPI). The PI provides a comparative measurement of how long vulnerable organic materials (*e.g.*, those with short life spans, such as magnetic tape or newsprint) might survive under various environmental conditions. The baseline for this measurement is 68 °F and 45% RH, which results in a PI of 50 years.

As the temperature and humidity are raised and lowered, the PI changes (for example, lowering the temperature to 60 °F and the humidity to 35% results in a PI of 110, while raising the temperature to 75 °F and the humidity to 65% results in a PI of 18). It is important to remember, however, that this is a comparative measurement, not a literal measurement of years. The numbers are meant to illustrate how different storage environments can slow down or speed up deterioration.

In real storage areas, however, temperature and relative humidity do not remain the same from day to day, or even throughout a single day. Therefore IPI developed the Time-Weighted Preservation Index (TWPI), which takes into account changing conditions over time, as well as the cumulative effect of deterioration, for a particular storage area. The resulting measurement is called the TWPI.

CONTROLLING THE ENVIRONMENT

Once you are aware of recommendations for environmental control, and have monitored the environmental conditions in your building to identify problem areas, how do you achieve the desired conditions? What if you have a less-than-perfect building? If compromises in the environment are necessary, how do you provide the best conditions possible given the limitations of your building?

In this part you will learn about strategies for managing HVAC systems, controlling light, and providing cold or frozen storage for collections. You will also explore low-cost options for improving environmental conditions.

HVAC SYSTEMS

A basic HVAC system consists of:

* A heat source (steam, hot water, electric)
* A cooling source (chilled water cooled by some type of refrigeration system)
* Air handling units (for circulating the air, these include fans and dampers—as well as filters and heating/cooling coils)
* Ductwork (through which air moves to and from spaces in the building)
* Equipment for filtering the air
* Control systems (usually computerized).

Temperature and Humidity

In very general terms, an HVAC system controls temperature by passing air over a heating coil within the air handling unit. Air is humidified by introducing water vapour into the stream of air before it passes into the space. It is dehumidified by passing air over a cooling coil. The temperature of the cooling coil is lower than the dew point temperature of the air, so moisture condenses on the coil and is then drained away. The air is then reheated to the desired temperature and sent into the space.

Pollutants and Air Circulation

Particulates are removed by using various grades of filters within the air handling unit. Electrostatic precipitators can be effective, but should not be used because they generate ozone. Gaseous pollutants are removed by using adsorbers within the air handling units (beds or canisters containing granular agents such as activated carbon).

Since filtration is expensive, it is also important to reduce the amount of pollutants that enter the building. Locate air intakes away from sources of pollutants such as vehicles, industrial processes, and laboratories. The smallest possible amount of outdoor air should be used within the HVAC system; as much air should be recirculated as possible. Recirculated air should also be filtered. Air should be circulated at a constant volume throughout collection spaces, and a slight positive pressure should be maintained in storage spaces to prevent untreated air from entering them.

TYPICAL HVAC PROBLEMS

Architectural and building design features (such as windows and vapour barriers) and building operation practices (24-hour systems and the availability of heating and cooling) greatly influence the effectiveness of HVAC systems. Some typical problems with HVAC systems stem from the efforts of facilities personnel to save energy, while others may be due to ignorance or poor maintenance.

You should guard against the following:

* Raising the temperature of the chilled water will reduce the ability of the system to dehumidify the air (less water will condense out of the air when it passes over the cooling coil).
* Some systems are not able to dehumidify the air when the outside air is damp, but not warm enough for the air conditioning to go on.
* Turning systems off or setting back the temperature at night and/or on weekends will lead to damaging fluctuations in climate.
* The use of economizer cycles that bring in 100% outside air when outside conditions are moderate may result in higher pollutant levels.
* Humidifiers may be removed or disabled, perhaps due to their need for frequent maintenance. Be aware that disabling a humidifier may be a plus, if it was not working properly in the first place.
* Variable air systems may not deliver a constant volume of treated air to all collection spaces.
* Particulate and gaseous filters that are not changed frequently enough will not function properly.

* System sensors that are not calibrated may lead to undesirable levels of temperature and humidity.
* Keeping doors and windows open will keep the HVAC system from maintaining the desired conditions.

COLD/FROZEN STORAGE

Certain specialized collections will benefit from storage at lower temperatures than can be provided by a standard HVAC system. However, cold or frozen storage is only appropriate for materials that are not used frequently, since the more often the materials are brought out of cold/frozen storage and acclimated to room temperature, the less long-term benefit cold/frozen storage provides.

Types of Cold/Frozen Storage

Large collections will require specially designed insulated rooms/vaults or prefabricated chambers (which usually use a dessicant dehumidification system), but smaller collections can be stored in household-type refrigerators or freezers, provided the proper protocols are followed.

The Image Permanence Institute (IPI) has defined several levels for media storage. Room temperature storage is defined as close to 68°F. Cool storage is defined as close to 54 °F. Cold storage is defined as close to 40 °F, while frozen storage is defined as 32 °F or below. All types of storage should have a stable relative humidity between 30 and 50%.

Media that Benefit from Cold/Frozen Storage

The lifespan of vulnerable media can be lengthened by freezing or storing at extremely low temperatures. These include motion picture film, photographic film and prints. Be aware, however, that some media may benefit from cold storage, but should not be frozen. These include glass plate negatives, magnetic tape, and CDs/DVDs.

The National Fire Protection Association has guidelines for construction of cabinets and vaults to house nitrate film; these guidelines are complex and are required by some localities. For most small institutions, it is best to store nitrate films in off-site cold storage (service copies might be made onto videotape) or transfer them to an institution that is better equipped to care for them. Acetate base and colour films also greatly benefit from storage at cold temperatures, but again, this is generally not practical for small institutions with only a few films.

Packing for Cold/Frozen Storage

If cold or frozen storage is to be successful, you must be able to maintain stable low temperatures with controlled humidity. Humidity control can be managed through the careful use of packaging. Materials must be stored in a moderate relative humidity for several weeks before being packaged into moisture-proof freezer bags (this conditioning is necessary to avoid excessive moisture within the bag). Care must be taken when removing collections from storage so that condensation does not occur; the materials should be acclimatized at least overnight, or longer for a large amount of material, before being removed from the bag.

LIGHT CONTROL

Since it is not possible to keep collections completely in the dark at all times, staff must compromise to provide the minimum amount of light necessary for the tasks being performed, such as exhibition, research, or searching the stacks.

Controlling Ultraviolet (UV) Light

Controlling UV light depends on eliminating or filtering sources of light with a high UV component (*e.g.*, natural daylight, and fluorescent, tungsten-halogen, and metal halide bulbs). UV filtering film can be applied to windows. Blinds, shades, or heavy curtains will control UV light (as well as visible light and infrared light). In areas lighted by fluorescent bulbs, low-UV fluorescent bulbs or UV-filtering sleeves must be used. If filtering sleeves are used, they must be transferred to the new bulb when the bulbs are changed.

Controlling Visible Light

Natural light should be blocked completely from storage

areas. Lights should be turned off when storage areas are not in use, and light levels should be kept as low as possible. Rearrange shelving and collections so that light does not fall directly on collections. Boxing or placing materials in folders and drawers will also protect them. Any reduction of light reduces long-term damage. Each institution should develop guidelines and implement them to control light where collections are used or stored.

LOW-COST ENVIRONMENTAL CONTROL

How do you deal with a less-than-perfect heating and cooling system? Not every institution has a central environmental control system, nor does every institution have the resources to drastically improve its existing system(s)-even if the need for better climate control is clear. If installation of a central HVAC system will not be feasible in the near future, you will need to implement low or no-cost actions in the meantime.

Sealing the Building

"Letting the outside in" can contribute to the deterioration of collections. Look for air leaks around windows, doors that don't close properly, and dampness in the basement. Simple repairs and regular maintenance can make a big difference. Improvements can be made by adding weather stripping around doors and windows, insulating the attic, or installing storm windows. Simply wrapping steam and hot water pipes with insulation can minimize the effects of these localized, intense heat sources.

Reorganize Space

Move vulnerable collections out of damp basements or hot attics, and away from exterior walls. Rearrangement can improve air circulation and help maintain a uniform temperature and humidity throughout the space. Remove collections from beneath overhead water sources, away from heat registers, and out of direct light. And don't store anything on the floor. Store your most sensitive or fragile materials in the space where climate conditions are the most stable. Can you identify this space in your building?

Portable Climate Control Equipment

In winter, you should keep the heat low to ensure that humidity in the building does not fall too low. In summer (and parts of spring and fall), dehumidifiers should be used if needed to keep the relative humidity low in collections storage spaces. Dehumidifiers should be self-draining and connected into the plumbing system. Local controls like these require staff vigilance to operate the equipment and rely on a good environmental monitoring device to regulate proper conditions.

Seasonal Drift

Even in the absence of good climate control, storage in preservation quality enclosures and safe furnishings will help protect your collections from premature chemical and physical damage. Using preservation-quality enclosures and boxes effectively creates a microclimate around collection materials, buffering them from sudden changes in the temperature and humidity. A properly fitted enclosure will also help keep out dust and pollutants.

6

Collections Care

Choosing the proper storage furniture and enclosures can be confusing: there are many available choices, and the terminology can be unclear. What constitutes good-quality storage furniture? Can wood shelving be used? What type of metal shelving is recommended? What type of enclosure is best for each type of collection? What do the terms "archival" and "acid-free" really mean?

Careful handling is essential to ensuring that collections are not damaged when they are used—during retrieval, consultation by researchers, reshelving, and/or exhibition. What procedures are appropriate? More importantly, how do you make certain that staff and users are familiar with these procedures and follow them?

Storage, handling, and housekeeping are not particularly scintillating topics, but they are crucial to the long-term survival of your collections. Awareness of proper storage methods, as well as education and training of users and staff, will contribute significantly to your collections' well-being and longevity.

STORAGE FURNITURE

It is important to make sure that storage furniture is made of safe, permanent materials and that its use furthers the care and preservation of the collections it is meant to protect. Furniture has the potential to damage collections both chemically and physically.

Improper furniture materials and coatings can produce byproducts that react to form acids and other damaging chemicals in the presence of moisture and oxygen. These accelerate the chemical deterioration of collections. Furniture that is the wrong size or overcrowded can cause distortion, torn pages, worn or broken bindings, and other types of physical damage.

FURNITURE MATERIALS

Some materials commonly used to construct shelving and cabinets can actually contribute to the chemical deterioration of collections.

Wood

Wood and wood-composite materials (*e.g.*, plywood, particleboard) have traditionally been used for shelves and cabinets in cultural institutions. Although attractive, wood is the least desirable material for storage furniture because it off-gases harmful acids and other substances. Wood-composite materials may also off-gas formaldehyde from adhesives. While some woods and wood composites are less harmful than others, this is only a matter of degree. It has been argued that older wood furniture is safer, but even that can continue to off-gas damaging acids throughout its lifetime.

If wood must be used, there are treatments that can minimize damage. The wood can be sealed with a moisture-borne polyurethane, which will lessen the off-gassing but not eliminate it. Bookshelves and drawers can be lined with a barrier material, such as a metallic laminate, glass, or Plexiglas to offer collections some measure of protection.

Coatings

Various coatings used on both wood and metal furniture have the potential to damage collections. It is now thought that baked enamel (the coating traditionally used for steel furniture such as library shelving, file cabinets, maps cases, etc.) may give off formaldehyde and other volatile gases if it has not been baked long enough at high enough temperatures. Wood coatings such as oil-based polyurethanes or oil-based paints and stains can also be damaging.

Recommended Materials

The two most stable materials now recommended for storage furniture are powder-coated steel (which consists of finely divided synthetic polymers are fused onto the steel) and anodized aluminum (which is nonreactive and uncoated). While chrome-plated, open-wire steel shelving is also acceptable, particularly for storing boxes, the wires may leave marks on unprotected items.

FURNITURE CONSTRUCTION

Regardless of the materials that make up the furniture, the type of furniture used and whether or not there is an adequate amount of it are crucial to the preservation of collections.

Basic Characteristics of Good Furniture

To avoid physical damage, storage furniture must be able to support the full weight and dimensions of the materials to be stored in it, without overcrowding. Furniture should not have rough surfaces, projections, or sharp edges that might cause damage.

All shelves should be adjustable, and bottom shelves must be four to six inches above the floor. Arrange furniture within your storage area so that it allows for easy access and safe movement of collections.

Enclosed Furniture

Closed metal cabinets or bookcases provide security and protection from light, but they can pose problems stemming from the possibility of condensation within the cabinet(s) if the air inside is too humid. As the temperature in the room goes down, moisture condenses out of the air and may cause rusting and/or mold growth. Monitor closed cabinets using a small hygrometer, humidity cards, or a min/max thermohygrometer. Airing out the cabinet periodically will help, as would removing the doors. Condensation can also occur in wood cabinets, although it is less likely.

Compact Shelving

Compact shelving installations allow more collections to be stored in a smaller space by placing shelving units very close together on tracks. This type of shelving weighs significantly more than traditional shelving, so floor loading (*e.g.*, ensuring that the building is strong enough to hold the shelving) is a concern.

It is important to make sure that items do not extend beyond the edges of the shelves; that a few inches of space is provided between units to assist air circulation and discourage mold growth; and that additional smoke detectors and sprinkler heads are provided in areas with compact shelving. Take a few moments to look at the following dos and don'ts for storage. What is represented in each?

STORAGE ENCLOSURES

As with storage furniture, poor-quality enclosures, or a lack thereof, can damage collections both physically and chemically. Chemical damage such as yellowing, discoloration, or embrittlement can result from direct contact with acids produced by poor-quality storage materials, and physical damage can result when enclosures of inadequate size or shape (or no enclosures at all) are used.

When choosing storage enclosures, it is important to understand the terminology used to describe preservation storage enclosures, and to be aware of which enclosures are appropriate for which collections. What do the terms "archival quality" and "acid-free" mean? What types of enclosures are appropriate for documents, for photographs, and/or for oversize materials? These basic concepts will be covered in this part.

POOR QUALITY ENCLOSURES

While all enclosures deteriorate over time, those made from acidic paper or board can damage the collections they are meant to protect relatively quickly. Many enclosures can cause damage because they are the wrong size and do not provide proper support. In addition, fasteners, attachments, and inserts (*e.g.*, paper clips, pins, rubber bands, poor-quality bookmarks, Post-it Notes, etc.) can stain and tear paper collections.

PRESERVATION QUALITY ENCLOSURES

Storage enclosures for books and flat paper should be made of materials which are durable (strong) and chemically stable (permanent). They should fit the item(s) properly and provide good support.

When choosing storage enclosures, "archival" and "acid-free" are two terms that you will frequently encounter. There are no standards governing the use of these terms, and they are sometimes misused, so read suppliers' catalogs carefully. If there are questions about a product, ask the supplier for details. If that information is not forthcoming, find another supplier.

Terminology

The term "pH" is used to express the acidity or alkalinity of paper-based materials. It does not apply to plastics.

The pH scale runs from zero to 14, with 7 being neutral, below 7 being acidic, and above 7 being alkaline.

* Acid-free or acid-neutral enclosures have a pH of 7 to 7.5 and will absorb a limited amount of acid before they themselves become acidic and begin to decay.
* Lignin-free or low-lignin paper is produced from cotton or linen or other materials from which the lignin, a natural component of wood that darkens when exposed to light, has been chemically removed.
* Buffered or alkaline-buffered enclosures contain an alkaline substance (the buffer) to raise the pH of the paper so it can absorb and/or neutralize a certain amount of acid.

Lignin-free, buffered enclosures (pH 8.5 or above) actively reduce the sources of acid damage and are preferred for most paper-based materials.

PAT Test

The Photographic Activity Test (PAT) was developed by the Image Permanence Institute (IPI) to evaluate the suitability of enclosures for photographic materials. The PAT can be performed on paper or plastic enclosures. It indicates whether the enclosures contain harmful chemicals that will cause image fading or staining. Enclosures used for photographic materials must pass the PAT (this should be noted in the supplier catalog); those that pass would be appropriate for other types of archival materials as well.

Plastic Enclosures

Plastics used for storage enclosures vary greatly in chemical stability. Those made of polyester, polypropylene, and polyethylene are generally safe to use for storing paper and photograph collections. Plastic sleeves can allow both sides of a paper to be viewed without touching the original, and they provide additional support during handling. Evidence has shown, however, that storage in plastic can accelerate deterioration by trapping acidic byproducts of decay. The choice of paper vs. plastic enclosures may ultimately be a compromise between protection against handling and protection against chemical damage. Plastic enclosures should be free of plasticizers, surface coatings, UV inhibitors, and other materials that may interact with collections.

CUSTOM VS. STANDARD ENCLOSURES

While standard-size enclosures from conservation suppliers will normally be sufficient to provide support and protection for collections, sometimes custom-made enclosures are needed. Conservation suppliers are generally willing to work with you to produce enclosures if you have a specialized need.

Fig. 6.1 Book Boxes can be Custom made in a Variety of Materials and Styles.

The most frequently encountered custom enclosures are book boxes. These can be made by a conservator or by bookbinding companies. They are generally used for books of significant value that need a box fit exactly to size to avoid abrasion from the book shifting inside a box that is too large or damage to the book's joints and edges by a box that is too small.

COLLECTION MAINTENANCE

Collection maintenance refers to the daily care of collections: keeping the stacks/storage area neat and clean, performing general housekeeping tasks in the building, and periodically cleaning the collections themselves.

These activities may differ somewhat from institution to institution. The staff of a public or academic library may need to straighten its shelves daily, while in archives, staff must ensure that collections are in the right order and returned to the proper storage area. A library with general collections may undertake a cleaning project using student assistants, while a special collections department may contract with a conservator to clean certain materials. The common element in all these activities, however, is the need to continually observe the condition of collections and ensure that they are properly cared for.

HOUSEKEEPING

The practice of good housekeeping is probably the simplest and least expensive method of preventive conservation for any type of collection. Housekeeping will keep particulates such as dust, dirt, smoke, ash, and mold spores from gathering on or around objects in your collection. These particulates can cause abrasion of delicate objects such as photographs and will attract moisture from humid environments to form acids that cause chemical deterioration. Dust and dirt contain organic materials that serve as food for insects and mold, and therefore provide an ideal environment in which they can live and flourish.

By keeping collections clean, you reduce the risk of these types of damage. Moreover, a building that is clean and neat engenders respect for the collections within it and makes for a healthier, more pleasant environment for staff and patrons. Housekeeping is thus an excellent method to help ensure the safe, long-term preservation of your holdings.

A Housekeeping Plan

Housekeeping for the building and for collections in storage or on exhibit should be discussed and defined in a written housekeeping plan. This plan should be part of a larger building maintenance plan that includes routine inspections and maintenance of key building elements and systems (*e.g.*, roof, drainage systems, pipes and plumbing, fire protection equipment, and HVAC equipment). The housekeeping plan should carefully delineate who will do the work, how often the work will be done, and with what tools and methods it will be completed.

The plan should detail weekly, monthly, quarterly, and yearly tasks, as well as special instructions for specific materials. Keep in mind that several different people will likely be performing the different housekeeping tasks (*e.g.*, custodians, paraprofessionals, students, librarians, collections curators), and written schedules for each person and/or task may be needed.

How Often Should You Clean?

Housekeeping work should be performed on a regular schedule based on need and circumstance. For example, spaces are usually very dusty in the fall, during the first few weeks after the heating system has been turned on. Dust in the ductwork is dried out by the heated air, becomes airborne, and is then circulated throughout the building. Therefore, dusting and vacuuming will be required more frequently in the early fall than in other seasons.

CLEANING COLLECTIONS

The cleaning of general book collections is typically recommended once a year. Special collections materials may require specialized cleaning procedures because of potential damage that may occur during cleaning. In some cases they will need to be cleaned by a conservator.

Cleaning General Book Collections

It is usually not practical to clean all collections at once in a large library unless an outside cleaning service is brought in. When cleaning is done in-house, the job is often divided into specific projects, where one part of the larger collection is cleaned at a time. This prevents book cleaning from turning into a never-ending (and discouraging!) project.

In most libraries, time and staffing limitations mean that collections are cleaned too infrequently rather than too often. But remember that overdusting and overcleaning of collections increases wear and the risk for damage from handling. Active cleaning of individual special collections items should be performed only when necessary. Storing collections inside boxes or furniture or under muslin dustcovers will reduce the amount of dirt and debris that settles on the collection itself, thereby lessening the need to clean.

Cleaning Individual Paper-based Objects in Storage or on Display.

In general, cleaning of individual paper objects should not be a high priority for cultural institutions just beginning a preservation programme. Because of the potential for damage that may occur during cleaning, the cleaning of paper objects of any kind in a collection should not be undertaken lightly. A conservator should be consulted to assess all the issues relating to the care of the object(s) in question.

Objects exhibiting the following conditions should be cleaned only by a conservator:

* Pastel or charcoal media;
* Loose or friable materials of any kind;
* Loose or flaking gelatin or baryta layers;
* Active or wet mold;
* Extensive repairs; and/or
* Objects that have been rolled and will not stay flat without assistance.

In addition, if you are unable to positively identify the process by which a photographic object was made, do not attempt to clean it. Even light surface brushing can remove silver image particles from a degraded salted paper print.

STACK MAINTENANCE

The most basic function of stack maintenance in a public or academic library is to reshelve materials. The people doing this are often lower-wage employees, student workers, even volunteers, and they must be carefully trained to understand the importance of their job.

Library collections must be treated with great care and the shelves must be kept orderly, because the condition of the stacks conveys a sense of the library's commitment to the well-being of its collections.

Preservation Concerns in Stack Maintenance

When transporting collections, shelvers must use a sturdy and easily maneuverable book truck. Materials must be packed on the book truck in such a way that they cannot easily fall off.

There should be step stools and open shelves provided in the stacks so that patrons can safely access books and materials without damaging them.

Shelvers should pay attention to the following issues:

* Make sure books do not extend beyond the edge of the shelf.
* Shelve oversize books properly, usually flat in stacks of three or less.
* Straighten books that are leaning.
* Shelve books spine down; shelving spine up causes the text block to come loose from the covers.
* Use book supports (bookends) where needed.
* Do not pack books so tightly that removing them becomes difficult.
* Report overcrowded stack areas, and shift materials within the stacks when necessary to remedy this problem.

Fig. 6.2 On the left, the Crowded Shelves show Books Leaning against each other, with some shelved Spine up; this will Cause Distortion. On the right, these Books are shelved Upright and Well-supported by Bookends. Space is left on the shelves to allow for Easy Shelving and Removal.

Staff members who are reshelving books should also keep an eye out for damaged volumes that might need repair or cleaning, and they should report any storage areas that are particularly dirty and need to be cleaned by the custodial crew.

HANDLING OF COLLECTIONS

Artifacts are easily damaged by poor or improper handling. Researchers should be supplied with instructions and supervised at all times when using the collection. Staff, too, need to be made aware of proper handling techniques through regular training. This part will cover proper handling procedures for paper-based collections and for film and electronic media collections. The latter are particularly vulnerable to damage from dirt and dust, as well as to damage from playback.

HANDLING PAPER COLLECTIONS

Using Collections

As a result of both use and shelving, certain types of damage to book collections are commonly seen: headcap damage from pulling books off the shelf; spine damage from forcing books open; tearing and creasing from folding of page corners; and abrasion from being dropped. Documents may be torn, folded, or accidentally marked, while photographs may be damaged by dirt and oils from fingers. Making reference photocopies of frequently consulted documents and photographs is one way to greatly reduce this sort of damage.

Every time you handle collection materials, ask yourself the following questions:

* Do I have a valid reason for picking this up?
* What is its condition?
* What is the safest way to hold it?
* Is it too fragile to lift without a secondary support?
* Do I need a second person to assist? Do I need a cart or trolley?
* After I have lifted the object, where will I set it down again?
* Are my hands clean? Should I wear gloves?

Processing Collections

It is also important to remember that collections-processing techniques suitable for general collections should not be used on materials with value as artifacts. These procedures include painting call numbers on books; affixing pressure-sensitive labels; and attaching pockets, bookplates, and bar codes (the adhesives may damage the materials and leave a sticky residue when they fail).

Sometimes it may be difficult to know whether books with long-term research value may eventually have value as artifacts. One strategy for processing such materials is to use a polyester book jacket fastened with 3M double-sided tape no. 415 and to label the jacket. If bookplates or pockets are used in books of enduring value, they should be made of low-lignin, alkaline paper and attached with a stable, reversible adhesive, preferably wheat starch paste or methyl cellulose.

Take a few moments to look at the pictures below. What dos and don'ts for handling paper collections are represented in each?

HANDLING MEDIA COLLECTIONS

Careful handling and use of film and electronic collections is extremely important, as audiovisual media are vulnerable to even the smallest amount of dirt and dust. Cotton gloves must be used for handling, and the storage and use areas must be kept as dust-free as possible. The provision of service copies is an excellent strategy for reducing the handling of originals.

Motion Picture Film

Cotton gloves should be worn when handling motion picture film. Always hold film along its edges, being careful not to touch the sound track or the image. Do not project film to examine it, since this can further damage already-deteriorated film. Special viewing equipment is available for inspecting film, or you can commission an outside service provider to do this.

Microfilm

Always wear gloves when handling master negatives, since oils and fingerprints can damage film. Always handle film by the edges or leaders. Pulling rolled film tight on the reel can cause abrasion of the film. Do not remove more than one microfilm or fiche from its enclosure at a time, and immediately resleeve or rebox items when you are done using them.

Sound Recordings and Video

As a general rule, never touch the playing surface of any recording. Always make sure your hands are clean before you handle recordings. Be sure that all playback equipment is cleaned often and maintained properly. Cylinder recordings should be handled by putting two fingers in the center hole. Wax cylinders must be at room temperature before you touch them, as the warmth of your hand can split cold wax cylinders. Do not touch the grooves of wax cylinders.

Grooved discs (LPs, acetate discs, etc.) should be held by their edges and label areas only. Compact disc recordings should be handled by their outer edge and center hole. Reel-to-reel tapes should be handled only by the outer edge of the reel flanges and the center hub. Take care not to squeeze the flanges together, as this will damage the edges of the tape. Cassette recordings (audio and video) should be handled only by their outer plastic casing; never put fingers or other materials into the case openings. Take care not to drop tapes, and don't stack tapes on top of equipment.

CDs/DVDs

Always handle discs by the outer edges or the center hole;

never touch the surface of the disc. Take care not to bend discs when handling them, and do not scratch the label side of a disc. When cleaning discs, wipe with a clean cotton fabric in a straight line from the center of the disc to the outer edge instead of wiping in a circular motion around the disc.

STORING PAPER COLLECTIONS

What are the proper storage practices for specific types of paper collections? How do you know whether your current storage is acceptable? In this part, you will review commonly recommended storage practices for paper-based collections and use this knowledge to evaluate your own storage methods.

You will be looking for poor storage practices that are common in the collections (*e.g.*, rubber bands holding covers together, poorly supported books, overstuffed file folders, acidic inserts in books or files). Although this examination may locate individual objects that need repair or other treatment, its primary goal is to identify general needs and areas of the collection in need of remedial actions (*e.g.*, boxing, enclosing photographs, replacing manila folders with archival-quality folders and boxes, and photocopying news clippings).

If important individual objects requiring conservation treatment are identified during this process, a conservator can evaluate whether emergency care is indicated.

This review of collection storage needs is organized by type of material, since for the purposes of preservation it is usually best to store like materials together. It is sometimes necessary, however, to consider mixed collections as a whole.

BOUND MATERIALS

Shelving

The non-knifing variety of bookend, which has a lip, is preferred to the knifing variety, which allows books to be jammed onto its sharp edge. A brick covered with book cloth fastened with PVA adhesive can be a good book support. Another alternative is a piece of acid-free foam-core covered with book cloth and slipped over the upright of a knifing bookend to shield the metal edge.

Boxing

Boxes constructed of preservation-quality materials can be custom made to fit a book's measurements. They provide support for the volume and protection from dirt, dust, light, and mechanical damage. Volumes with artifactual value, where the fragile binding is to be retained in its present condition, should be boxed. Volumes that have low value or are rarely used and do not warrant treatment or repair of the binding may also be boxed.

Boxes can be made in-house or contracted out. Drop-spine boxes provide the most protection. Phase boxes are not as rigid or impervious to light or dust, but they are an acceptable cost-efficient alternative.

Ready-made rare book boxes can be purchased from conservation suppliers, but if they are to provide proper protection, they must fit the books closely and the weight of the board or card stock must be appropriate for the size of the books. Many vendors make both drop-spine and phase boxes. Deteriorated books of great value should have custom-made drop-spine boxes that fit the book exactly.

Alternatives to Boxing

Infrequently used deteriorated books can be wrapped in buffered paper or fitted with polyester book jackets. Both of these strategies will prevent dispersion of the "dust" from red rot and provide some protection from dust and abrasion. These strategies are cheaper than boxing, but they offer less protection. Among the disadvantages: a polyester book jacket does not cover the book completely; the paper and polyester film do not provide as much support as box board; and it can be difficult to replace a paper wrapping properly once it is removed for use.

If detached covers must be tied onto books as a temporary protection, ties should be undyed cotton or linen tape or undyed polyester ribbon. Any knots should be at the top or fore edge of the text block to prevent damage from pressure against other books. Never hold damaged bindings together with rubber bands; the rubber bands will deteriorate themselves and cause further damage.

PAMPHLETS

Pamphlets and small booklets can be stored in specially made enclosures, in folders and boxes, or in hanging folders in file cabinets. Pamphlets of the same cover size can be stored in drop-spine or phase boxes. Pamphlets that differ in size may be stored according to guidelines given for manuscripts and documents. Pamphlets more than about a quarter-inch thick should be stored spine down in individual folders. Pamphlets of very different size should not be stored in the same folder.

If individual pamphlets must be shelved between books, they should be individually boxed. Groups of pamphlets shelved between books can be boxed together if the guidelines above are followed. If pamphlet binders are used, they must be of preservation quality throughout, and they should never be glued directly to pamphlets. Where stitching is used to join pamphlet and binder, it should be done through the fold or, where possible, in original fastener holes.

DOCUMENTS/MANUSCRIPTS/EPHEMERA

General Recommendations

Documents should be stored in low-lignin, buffered file folders, with a maximum of about 15 sheets per folder. The folders should then be placed in archival-quality document storage boxes as close to the size of the folders as possible. All folders in each box should be the same size. Boxes should be full enough to prevent slumping of the contents; partially full boxes can be filled with spacer boards available from conservation suppliers. Do not stuff boxes. This can cause damage when sheets are removed and refiled.

An alternative to boxed storage is a standard baked enamel file cabinet equipped with hanging racks and hanging folders. Archival-quality hanging folders are available, but the conventional kind are acceptable as long as the enclosures within them are buffered.

Store objects of the same size and category together whenever possible. Archivists habitually organize collections by subject group, but objects of differing bulk and weight can cause damage from uneven pressures in a drawer or box. It is not advisable to store single sheets in the same box with books or pamphlets unless there are separate enclosures and supports for each category of material. Generally speaking, heavy objects should be stored separately from lighter objects, as should bulky objects.

Parchment and Vellum

Parchment and vellum are highly susceptible to damage from fluctuations in relative humidity and thus require stringent humidity controls. Such documents should be enclosed for additional protection. Suitable enclosures include encapsulation, folders, matting and framing, boxing, or a combination of these techniques.

Ephemera

Ephemera may have raised surfaces or three-dimensional decoration. Items should be grouped by size and type (*e.g.*, postcards, printed material, documents), enclosed to protect them from chemical migration and mechanical damage, and stored to support the structure of the artifact (encapsulated, boxed, stored flat or in hanging files). Some vendors of archival supplies offer custom-size storage boxes and sleeves for common ephemera such as postcards and stereo views, or they can produce custom-size boxes in large quantities to meet special needs.

NEWSPRINT

Because groundwood papers were commercially produced after about 1840, newsprint after that date is likely to be highly acidic. Long-term preservation of this paper is difficult at best. It is possible to treat newsprint by deacidification to retard its deterioration, but this treatment is usually economically impractical. Once paper has already turned yellow and brittle, deacidification will not make the paper white and flexible again. Microfilming is usually the preferred preservation option for bound newspaper collections or large collections of clipping scrapbooks.

Most news clippings are important because of their information, not for the value of the clippings themselves. For this reason, photocopying or microfilming are considered the most practical preservation options. All photocopying should be done on archival-quality paper; originals can then be deaccessioned at the discretion of the librarian or curator. News clippings with photographs that do not photocopy well may be physically separated from other papers in a folder by placing them inside an enclosure made of polyester. News clippings to be retained in their original form should be deacidified and stored in buffered enclosures.

OVERSIZED MATERIALS

Flat Storage

Prints, maps, broadsides, and other oversize objects are best stored flat in map drawers or in large covered boxes of preservation quality available from conservation suppliers. It is acceptable to store documents legal-size or smaller in upright archival boxes, but anything larger than 15 by 9 inches should be stored flat. Sheets smaller than 30 by 40 inches will fit into archival boxes, which come in various sizes and are cheaper than map cases. Objects should be protected in neutral or buffered folders cut to fit the size of the drawer or box, since smaller folders tend to shift position as the drawers open and close and get jammed at the back of the drawers. Several objects may be placed in a folder. Items of special value should be interleaved with buffered or neutral tissue paper.

It was traditionally recommended that some items (such as blueprints) should not be stored in alkaline-buffered folders because they are sensitive to alkaline materials and might be damaged by contact with the folders. Recent research, however, has indicated that as long as the relative humidity in the storage area is kept moderate (between 30 per cent and 55 per cent), alkaline folders should not cause damage.

Rolled Storage

If map drawers or boxes are not available, or if objects are too large to fit in map drawers, oversize objects can be rolled on tubes, as long as the paper is not too brittle to withstand unrolling. If rolling the object on a tube, use a tube longer than the rolled object and at least four inches in diameter (larger diameters are preferred). If the tube is not archival quality, the object must be wrapped in neutral or buffered paper. Carefully roll the object onto the tube, and wrap the assembly with neutral or buffered paper to protect it from abrasion. This assembly can then be stored inside a larger tube for added protection. Tubes should be stored horizontally. Alternatively, oversize objects can be rolled within a polyester folder.

FRAMED MATERIALS

Any prints, drawings, or other objects that have been matted or backed with acidic materials or wood should be removed from those mounts. They may be matted using preservation-quality materials and reframed in their original frames using museum-quality materials. These objects may also be safely stored flat (unframed, matted, or unmatted) in folders inside boxes or drawers, like oversize items.

Frames should not use eye screws or other protruding hardware for hanging, because they can cause damage to other frames or glazing. Protruding hardware should be replaced with D-rings on brackets, available from framers. Glazing should filter ultraviolet (UV) light and should never touch the artifact inside the frame.

An additional layer of preservation-quality matboard should be used behind the board on which the object is mounted. The frame should be deep enough to accommodate all the layers, and it should be sealed so that it is as airtight as possible.

Framed items should not be exhibited permanently. When not on exhibit, they should be stored vertically. Usually a padded frame rack is most practical for smaller institutions, while custom sliding storage racks (where metal grill panels are suspended from tracks) may be appropriate for institutions with larger collections of framed objects. Frame racks are available ready-made or can be constructed (be sure to use non-damaging materials). Each compartment in a frame rack should be cushioned at the bottom, and foamboard should be used between framed items within the compartments to prevent abrasion.

SCRAPBOOKS/ALBUMS

Scrapbooks pose challenging preservation problems because they frequently contain a variety of components and media. In addition, they are often unique, fragile, damaged, or of significant associational value. If they must be interfiled within archival collections, they must be well-supported and separated from direct contact with other materials.

Scrapbooks that have informational value alone (for instance, clippings scrapbooks) can be photocopied onto archival-quality paper and/or microfilmed. The originals would then be retired from use and copies made available to researchers. Scrapbooks that have enduring value in their original form should be individually wrapped in archival-quality paper and/or boxed in custom-fitted boxes. Valuable scrapbooks may have a high priority for evaluation by a conservator.

PHOTOGRAPHIC PRINTS AND NEGATIVES

Enclosures

Photographic prints and negatives are best stored in individual enclosures. This reduces damage by giving the photograph or negative physical support and protection. Enclosures can be made of paper or plastic.

Paper enclosures:

* Protect from light and buildup of moisture and gases inside the enclosure;
* Require more handling, as the object must be removed from the enclosure for examination; and,

* Are cheaper and easier to write on than plastic enclosures.

Plastic enclosures:

* Allow the user to view the image without handling it;
* Can abrade the photograph during insertion and removal from the enclosure;
* Can trap gases and moisture within the enclosure;
* Can be difficult to write on and sometimes flimsy; and,
* Usually have heat-sealed seams, which eliminate potential damage from adhesive seams.

Suitable plastics have been discussed elsewhere in this part. There are several types of individual plastic enclosures, including L-Velopes (sealed on two adjacent sides); plastic folders that can be used within paper envelopes; and plastic sleeves that are open at two opposite ends, with a self-locking fold on one of the remaining sides. There are also a number of styles of ring-binder pages for prints and negatives.

When using paper enclosures for photographic storage, conservators used to recommend that photographs be housed in low-lignin neutral paper enclosures rather than in alkaline enclosures, since it was thought that colour images, cyanotypes, and albumen prints would be damaged by the alkalinity in buffered enclosures. But recent research indicates that this is not the case. Rather than choosing enclosures according their pH level, paper enclosures should be chosen based on whether they pass the Photographic Activity Test (PAT), which determines whether the enclosures contain harmful chemicals that will cause image fading or staining.

If envelopes with adhesive seams are used, the adhesive must be stable, pH-neutral, and it must not react with silver; the seams should be on the sides or the bottom of the envelope; and the emulsion of the photograph should face away from the seams.

Boxing

Once they have been individually enclosed in paper or plastic, photographs must be placed in archival-quality boxes.

Where possible, items of similar size should be stored together; the mixing of different sizes can cause abrasion and breakage and can increase the risk of misplacing smaller items. Horizontal storage of photographs is usually preferable to vertical storage, since it provides overall support and avoids mechanical damage such as bending or slumping. The photographs should be stored flat in drop-front boxes of archival quality housed on shelves or in metal cabinets. All enclosures within a box should be the same size, fitting the size of the box. Neutral or buffered file folders may be used to organize photographs within the box.

Vertical Storage of Photographs

If necessary, vertical storage can be used. Small photographs of uniform size can be individually enclosed and placed vertically in boxes the same size as the photographs. Boxes of various sizes and types are available from conservation suppliers. For vertical storage in a filing cabinet, protected photographs should be placed in archival folders that are themselves placed in hanging file folders. Several photographs may be stored in each folder, and several folders may be placed in each hanging file. Lightly filled hanging file folders will prevent photographs from sliding down under each other in the drawer and will facilitate their handling. Alternatively, folders can be placed in archival document boxes, but the folders should not slump, and the photographs must be well supported.

Oversized Photographs

Give special care to the storage of oversized photographic prints mounted on cardboard. This cardboard is often acidic, causing the mounts to become brittle with age. Embrittlement of the support can endanger the image itself if the cardboard breaks in storage or during handling. Such prints should be placed in individual folders in archival-quality boxes of appropriate size and stored flat on shelves. They require careful handling.

Negatives

Negatives should be stored separately from prints. Larger negatives can be stored in individual enclosures and then boxed, while the smaller 35mm strips can be stored in plastic ring-binder storage pages. Nitrate and acetate negatives must be stored in paper envelopes that pass the PAT. MicroChamber or other proactive storage enclosures that contain scavengers to remove pollutants should also be considered for acetate and nitrate negatives.

Each type of film base should be stored separately, in a well-ventilated area, apart from other types of collections. This is particularly important for nitrate negatives. Both nitrate and acetate negatives should be monitored on a regular basis so that any deterioration can be identified early. If deterioration is discovered, isolate the deteriorating materials from those that are still in good condition. Nitrate and acetate negatives should be duplicated onto polyester film whenever possible, as this will provide a stable copy.

STORING MEDIA COLLECTIONS

What are the proper storage practices for film-based and electronic media usually encountered in paper-based collections? These media might include motion picture film, microforms, sound recordings, videotapes, magnetic disks, CDs, and DVDs.

Are these materials currently being stored properly? Do they need to be rehoused into preservation-quality enclosures, or can they be stored in their original enclosures? In this part you will review commonly recommended storage practices for these types of non-paper-based collections, and you will use this knowledge to begin to evaluate your own storage methods.

MOTION PICTURE FILM

Motion picture films are most likely to be on either cellulose nitrate or acetate bases. It is extremely dangerous to retain original motion picture films on cellulose nitrate base, since they are highly flammable.

For most small institutions, it is best to store nitrate films in offsite cold storage (service copies might be made onto videotape) or transfer them to an institution that is better equipped to care for them. Cellulose acetate base films are not a fire hazard, but they will deteriorate over time; this deterioration can be slowed by cold storage.

Enclosures

Like other enclosures, film containers should be chemically stable and should physically support the materials, fitting the film as closely as possible. Film containers should pass the Photographic Activity Test (PAT) to ensure that there is no damage from glues or additives contained in the enclosure.

Boxes or cans are acceptable for film storage; these may be made from acceptable plastics (polypropylene or polyethylene), preservation-quality cardboard, or non-corroding metal. Some storage containers are vented. At room temperature, this is an advantage for acetate films, allowing acetic acid vapors to disperse; at lower temperatures, venting does not make as much difference. Film containers should be stacked horizontally, with the film lying flat. In general, films should be stored with their tails out and rewound before projecting.

Be aware that the National Fire Protection Association (NFPA) has guidelines for the construction of cabinets and vaults that house nitrate motion picture film. Meeting these guidelines is complicated and expensive, and thus impractical for most small institutions, but not meeting them can be dangerous. In addition, local law may require that you meet the NFPA guidelines. Offsite cold storage or transfer to another institution is often the best options.

Handling and Inspection

Do not project old film that has been stored for many years, since projecting fragile film can cause additional damage. The film must first be inspected using special film-handling equipment. An inspection will identify edge codes that may provide clues to film base and dating, signs of mechanical damage (*e.g.*, splices, broken sprocket holes, shrinkage), signs of chemical damage (*e.g.*, vinegar odour), and/or signs of mold damage.

Duplication

Creating a new master copy of the original is the best way to ensure preservation of motion picture films. The master is used to make access copies, with the original retained in cold storage. This type of copying is a complex and very expensive process and therefore not practical for most institutions-and not justified unless the film is of significant importance. A more manageable alternative for smaller institutions is making service copies on analog or digital videotape. In the future, it may be possible to convert original films directly to digital files rather than copying them to film, but the original quality of the image and sound cannot yet be captured satisfactorily in this way.

MICROFORMS

Microfilm produced between the 1930s and the 1970s is likely to be on acetate base and thus may suffer from "vinegar syndrome", so called because of the distinctive odour given off in the deterioration process. From the mid-1970s onward, microfilm has been produced on a polyester film base. Very early microfilm on a nitrate base could be encountered, but this is highly unlikely.

General storage recommendations for microforms (roll microfilm and microfiche) are similar to those for motion picture film. All enclosures should pass the Photographic Activity Test to determine whether they contain damaging chemicals or additives. Paper or plastic enclosures are acceptable. Paper enclosures should be lignin-free and buffered or neutral; safe plastics are polyester, polyethylene, and polypropylene (not PVC or vinyl).

Microfilm reels should be boxed individually, with the film held in position by a preservation-quality paper tag fastened with a string and button tie. Do not secure the reels with rubber bands, because they contain residual sulphur and deteriorate over time. Master negatives of microfilm should be stored in a preservation-quality box in an offsite storage area with a controlled climate. Microfilm should be stored in steel filing cabinets, but, if the film must be stored on shelves, inert plastic containers can be used.

Microfiche should be sleeved individually with the emulsion side away from the interior enclosure edges; this prevents abrasion and damage from adhesives. Store microfiche enclosures in steel cabinets, and ensure that the enclosures fit into the drawers without buckling. Use pH-neutral drawer dividers to keep microfiche from curling, and compress the fiche as little as possible in the drawer. Design your filing system to minimize handling of fiche.

SOUND RECORDINGS AND VIDEOTAPES

Some collections may contain a variety of older sound recordings, from cylinder recordings to vinyl LPs, as well as various formats of videotape. Like other media, they require careful handling and a stable moderate environment.

Cylinders and Discs

Cylinder recordings should be stored standing on end; all discs should be stored vertically (on edge). Take care that shelves are solid and can bear the weight of discs: LPs can weigh as much as 45 pounds per shelf foot, and 78 and acetate discs are even heavier. Since discs tend to put most of their weight along the center line of the shelf, special shelving may be required. It should have dividers that reach from top to bottom and front to back, spaced four to six inches apart, to guard against warping of discs. Storing discs of different sizes together may also cause warping and should be avoided.

Record sleeves without text or graphics should be replaced with a high-density polyethylene sleeve. If the original sleeve must be retained, some of the polyethylene sleeves can fit inside the original sleeve.

Tape (Open-Reel and Audio/Video Cassettes)

Store all tapes vertically (on edge), in preservation-quality boxes. Do not lay any recordings flat, not even audio cassettes or videotapes. For open-reel tapes, replace reels that have slotted hubs. Only reels with unslotted hubs should be used for storage. Tapes should be played completely through, then stored without rewinding (tails out). They should be rewound just before playing them again.

When playing tapes, make sure that you are familiar with the playback equipment and that the tape is properly inserted into the machine before playing. When opening tape containers, be aware of any odour that might indicate binder hydrolysis or vinegar syndrome; such tapes should not be played. The tape should also be examined for any irregularities in the tape pack (gaps or slips, where the tape pack is not flat) that need to be corrected before playback.

Tape demagnetization is not usually a serious problem, but nevertheless, keep magnetic tapes away from any objects containing magnets of any size. Do not operate any machines (like vacuums) that might be a source of electromagnetic fields near areas where tapes are stored.

CDs AND DVDs

For the long term, discs should be stored upright (vertically) in individual storage containers. Always press down the inner hub and hold only the outer edges of the disc when removing it from the case, and be sure to return the disc to the case immediately when you are finished with it. It has been suggested that for long-term storage, label inserts/booklets should be removed and attached to the outside of the case; theoretically, the paper might attract and hold moisture in a humid climate. Never write or mark in the data area of a disc. Do not write on discs with a pen, pencil, fine-tip marker, or a marker containing solvents, as this may damage the data. Only a non-solvent-based felt-tip permanent marker should be used. Do not use adhesive labels or try to remove or reposition existing labels.

STAFF AND USER EDUCATION

Educating staff and users about preservation can be a

challenge in cultural institutions, because most damage is caused not by malicious behaviour, but by carelessness, thoughtlessness, or lack of knowledge.

The librarian, archivist, or curator has relatively little direct control over the behaviour of users. The user is normally focused on his or her own needs (which all too often are contrary to the needs of collections) and must be persuaded that the way he or she treats collections has a significant effect on how long materials will survive.

Educating staff (particularly those within the institution but outside the library, such as facilities personnel or administrative staff) can be just as challenging as educating users. In many cases, staff members have competing priorities (*e.g.*, saving energy or money) or simply too many other responsibilities to give much thought to preservation issues.

How can you implement effective preservation education programmes for your staff and users? You will explore some possible activities in this part.

EDUCATING STAFF

Preservation education for staff within an institution may take on different forms, depending on the type of institution and the responsibilities of those being targeted. Facilities personnel and administration do not need to know specifics of handling collections, while library shelvers do not need to be convinced of the need for improved climate control for the collection.

Types of Staff Education

There are a variety of ways that staff members can be educated about preservation. Workshops presented on general or specific preservation topics by outside agencies may be useful. These tend to be half- or full-day offsite workshops. Offsite training has its advantages: staff may concentrate better when removed from the regular workplace, and training from an outside "expert" may make more of an impression than in-house training. In-house training, however, has the benefit of focusing on issues specific to your institution. You might include very short presentations as part of a regular staff meeting, hour-long orientations for new staff, or hands-on training parts for student workers.

The concept of preventive preservation should always be stressed, perhaps by drawing analogies to preventive maintenance of a car or a house. Real-life examples of damaged items or other visual aids can be very effective. It is very important to keep the subject matter relevant to the audience, to keep presentations from being too technical, and to encourage discussion of concerns that staff members may have.

Pointing out that most of your institution's activities have a preservation component (*e.g.*, the decision to acquire collections, cataloging and processing, shelving and storage, circulation and use, exhibition) can make participants think about preservation in a new way. Depending on the audience, specific subjects covered might include handling books, book repair, disaster planning, preservation microfilming, and/or environmental control.

Also remember that staff members are not just being educated so that they themselves will treat materials correctly, but also so that they in turn can educate users in the proper care of collections. Suggestions for instructing users in a positive way should be presented. Sample scenarios in which staff members discuss how they would respond to different situations involving users might be helpful.

EDUCATING USERS

Education of users can be done informally or as part of a specific programme or event. Staff should model good preservation practices and correct users in a positive way whenever possible. Signs, posters, handouts, bookmarks, and bookbags can all be effective means of conveying preservation information. More formal programmes such as Web sites, temporary exhibits, and special events involve more work but can be very effective in raising awareness of preservation.

EXHIBITS

The need to exhibit books and paper artifacts complicates the goal of preservation. The display environment is often more difficult to control than the storage environment. The materials displayed have, almost by definition, special value, and preservation has historically been secondary to exhibit design. At the very least, exhibited objects are exposed to higher light levels than they would normally experience in storage. Valuable paper collections should never be exhibited permanently, since this can cause irreversible fading and accelerate acidic deterioration. Whenever possible, exhibit duplicates or facsimiles of photographs and other paper-based materials.

In this part, you will consider the three basic issues that must be addressed to ensure that exhibition damages paper collections as little as possible: environment (climate, light, and pollutants); case design; and display methods. There is a standard for exhibition of paper-based collections.

ENVIRONMENT

Fig. 6.3 Exhibited Collections should never be Exposed to Direct Sunlight; Light Levels must be Kept Low and UV Light Must be Controlled.

Light

Light levels are perhaps the most important issue for exhibition of paper-based collections. If originals must be exhibited, light levels should be no higher than 50 lux for very sensitive materials (*e.g.*, textiles, paper, dyed leather, 19th-century photographs, and colour photographs). Moderately sensitive materials (this includes only a few paper-based materials, such as carbon black inks on high-quality paper and modern black and white silver gelatin photographs on baryta paper) can be exhibited at levels no higher than 100 lux. There should be no natural light in the exhibit area, and ultraviolet (UV) light should be no higher than 75 microwatts per lumen.

Exhibit Length

Because items have different sensitivities and some may be exhibited more frequently than others, it is best to determine the length of exhibition separately for each item. Materials should never be exhibited permanently. In fact, the NISO standard for exhibition sets the maximum length for exhibition at 52 weeks, but for most items recommends a much shorter period. The standard suggests that very light-sensitive collections that are exhibited repeatedly (defined as no more than once every two years) should be on display for no longer than 12 weeks at a time.

The concept of total light exposure (TLE) can be helpful in determining light levels and length of exhibition for specific items. A yearly limit for light exposure would be set for an item, which would be calculated by multiplying the exposure time (*e.g.*, three weeks) by the light level (*e.g.*, 100 lux). Because of the principle of reciprocity, the same yearly TLE could be reached by exhibiting the item for one week at 300 lux. To use this principle effectively, good record keeping of exhibition times and light levels is of paramount importance.

Climate

The NISO standard recommends that relative humidity in the display environment (*e.g.*, inside the exhibit case) be kept at a set point between 35 per cent and 50 per cent with a variation of +/-5 per cent, while temperature should not exceed 72 degrees Fahrenheit with a variation of +/-5 degrees. In addition to monitoring the climate in the exhibition space as a whole, climate conditions inside exhibit cases should be monitored to ensure that they are not damaging. A min/max thermohygrometer will give a general indication of conditions. Exhibit cases should not contain lights, because these cause significant changes in temperature and relative humidity within the case. Fibre-optic lighting is preferable because it does not produce heat.

Pollutant levels should be limited to the greatest extent possible. Materials used to construct the exhibit cases should be as chemically stable as possible and should not off-gas damaging pollutants.

CASE DESIGN

Exhibit cases should be built of stable, pollutant-free materials and coatings. As with storage furniture, wood and wood composites are often used for exhibit cases, but they can be very damaging to collections because they emit volatile gases.

If your institution has poor-quality cases and they cannot be replaced, any wood should be properly sealed, and the interior of the cases should be lined to prevent off-gassing. Wood should be sealed with a moisture-borne polyurethane or two-part epoxy sealant. Acceptable barrier materials include polyester film, 4-ply 100% ragboard, polyethylene foam sheeting, and Marvelseal (an adhesive-free laminate that is flexible and impermeable to gases and moisture). MicroChamber boards that contain activated carbon may also be an option. Barrier materials should be attached to the sides and the floor of cases; 3M double-sided tape no. 415 is recommended.

Other items that must be chosen carefully include fabric lining for cases, adhesives, and the gaskets used to seal the cases. Fabrics should have no additives and should be washed before use. Undyed cotton, linen, polyester, or cotton-polyester blends can be used. Silk is acidic, and wood off-gases sulphur compounds.

DISPLAY METHODS

Mounts, supports, and other exhibit materials should be made from inert materials like Plexiglas and polyester, or from neutral paper or 100% ragboard.

Documents in exhibit cases should be completely supported, whether they are matted or mounted (without adhesives) to a piece of ragboard or other preservation-quality material. Edge strips or some type of corner support (photo corners will work on most small items) can be used to attach the document securely to the mounting board, but adhesive should never be applied to the object itself. Documents that are not framed should be attached. Documents can also be encapsulated for protection, but keep in mind that this can cause paper to deteriorate more quickly.

Documents to be exhibited on walls should be matted and framed using museum-quality framing and hinging techniques.

Books must be well supported to protect their bindings from strain. Wedges or cradles can be made from neutral matboard or Plexiglas. A stand or mount should support the entire cover(s) of a book as well as the spine. Reasonably good Plexiglas supports are available from conservation suppliers. Most books in general, and without exception all oversize books, should be exhibited at no more than a gentle angle.

If the book will not remain open naturally, a polyester band closed with 3M double-sided tape no. 415 can be used to hold the book open. Books can be structurally damaged by long-term exhibition in an open position, so exhibit periods must be limited. Turning the pages of a book every few days will prevent overexposure to light on one page.

7

Reformatting and Treatment

Preservation reformatting of paper collections encompasses microfilming, photocopying, duplicating, and/ or digital imaging. These options may be used alone or in combination, depending on the circumstances. Reformatting of film and electronic media (*e.g.*, motion picture film, negatives, and sound and video recordings) involves duplication onto new media, sometimes in alternate formats. Treatment options for original paper-based items include professional conservation treatment, in-house repair (also known as collections conservation), and library binding.

Reformatting and treatment can be time-consuming and expensive and may not be justified for all deteriorated collections. How do you decide which collections deserve attention? What role should reformatting and treatment play in a systematic preservation programme for paper-based collections?

PRESERVATION MICROFILMING

Despite increasing interest in new technologies, preservation microfilming remains an established and valued strategy for producing copies of deteriorated paper-based collections.

Since the late 1980s, a national Brittle Books Programme, funded through the National Endowment for the Humanities (NEH), has been in place, using preservation microfilming to produce master microfilms of deteriorated books. Overall, microfilm is an important preservation strategy for collections that have greater informational value than artifactual value and for those with such tremendous artifactual value and/or fragility that they should not be routinely handled by researchers. While microfilm is no longer the most user-friendly medium for access, it is the product of a tested technology governed by clear standards and guidelines. It provides a master copy from which relatively inexpensive duplicates can be easily made. And unlike digital media, which cannot be read without computer access, microfilm can be read by the naked eye with only a light source and magnification.

STANDARDS/GUIDELINES

Microfilming is governed by a variety of standards, but it is important to keep in mind that most of these standards were developed for commercial microfilming applications, where the microfilm being produced only needs to be retained for a limited time. Thus, certain practices may be acceptable in the production of commercial microfilm that are not appropriate in the production of preservation microfilm.

General Microfilming Standards

Preservation microfilming of paper-based collections makes up only a small fraction of the micrographics industry, so addressing preservation filming is not a high priority for standards-making organizations. The American National Standards Institute (ANSI) issues various standards pertaining to imaging materials, including microfilm, and the Association for Information and Image Management (AIIM) also issues standards for micrographics. These standards can be useful in providing general information, but it is up to the individual institution to decide what level of quality is acceptable.

Guidelines for Preservation Microfilming

For specific guidelines for preservation microfilming geared towards libraries, archives, and other institutions that hold paper collections, the Research Libraries Group (RLG) has produced three publications that have come to be considered de facto standards. The *RLG Preservation Microfilming Handbook*, the *RLG Archives Microfilming Manual*, and the *RLG Guidelines for Microfilming to Support Digitization* should be consulted by any cultural institution planning a preservation microfilming project. Another basic resource is the Association of Research Libraries' *Preservation Microfilming: A Guide for Librarians and Archivists*. All of these publications are referenced in Additional Resources.

These guidelines specify materials and procedures that must be used to ensure the permanence of the film that is produced:

* *Film Type*: All preservation microfilm must be produced on a polyester base. Types of film include silver gelatin (the most stable); diazo and vesicular (less expensive, but not as stable); continuous tone microfilm (a silver gelatin film that can be very stable and is used for filming photographs and similar materials), and colour microfilm (Ilfochrome colour film, which likely has a lifetime of several hundred years in dark storage).
* *Film Format*: The RLG guidelines are based on the 35mm roll film format, which provides a larger, better-quality image than microfiche or 16mm film.
* Film generations: Three generations of microfilm must be produced: the camera negative (*e.g.*, the film used in the camera); a duplicate negative; and one or more positive service copies for researcher use and interlibrary loan.
* *Film quality and processing*: The RLG guidelines specify requirements for reduction ratio (the number of times the original is reduced); orientation of the image on the film; the legibility of the image (background density and resolution); processing of the exposed film; and inspection of the film and correction of mistakes (*e.g.*, number of splices allowed).

THE FILMING PROCESS

For most institutions, contracting out for microfilming

services is the most efficient and cost-effective choice, since setting up an in-house lab to produce microfilm that conforms to standards and guidelines for preservation filming is extremely difficult and expensive.

The basic procedures involved in preservation microfilming are as follows:

* *Preparing Collections for Filming*: The materials are examined page-by-page to ensure that they are in the correct order and nothing is missing. Targets are created (informational sheets with bibliographic and condition information that are photographed with the item to assist the user), and reel breaks are determined. During the review process, special instruction for the filmers are noted. The materials are shipped to the vendor.
* *Filming*: A planetary camera (where both the camera and the materials are stationary during filming) is most commonly used. Bound materials may be filmed using a book cradle. Manual exposure is usually necessary for collections with variations in paper colour, texture, and/or ink.
* *Film Processing*: Silver gelatin film processors may be tabletop or deep tank models. They develop, fix, wash, and dry the film. Filmers should use control strips daily to check the performance of the processor.
* *Polysulfide Treatment*: This treatment was developed to combat the formation of redox spots or rings on silver microfilm, which are a result of poor environmental conditions and exposure to pollutants. Polysulfide treatment (which converts the silver to a form that better resists oxidation) can be used during initial processing, it can be provided for the master and duplicate negatives after all quality control inspections have been done, or it can be applied to older film, as long as it is not yet deteriorated.
* *Quality Control*: Before duplication, the master

negative is inspected for proper resolution and density; a methylene blue test (for residual thiosulfate from processing) and a polysulfide test are conducted; and the master negative is inspected frame-by-frame to ensure that each document has been filmed in the correct order and each frame is legible. If necessary, mistakes are corrected using ultrasonic splicing.

* *Duplication*: The choice of film for duplicates will depend on cost and use patterns. Silver film is preferred for duplicate negatives, and should receive a polysulfide treatment. Diazo and vesicular films, which are cheaper and less prone to scratching than silver films, are often used for service copies. Duplicate films are inspected for resolution, density, and completeness as required in ANSI/AIIM and RLG standards and guidelines.
* *Return of Film and Originals to the Institution*: Original materials are generally returned at the same time to facilitate in-house inspection of the film, but master negatives should never be shipped in the same box, or on the same day, with their service copies or duplicate negatives. If possible, master negatives should be shipped by the vendor directly to off-site storage.
* *Post-filming Activities*: You must conduct in-house quality control inspections once the film is returned. These should include a general inspection of the film, packaging, and labeling, as well as a more comprehensive technical inspection that might include testing for density and resolution, as well as scratches, problematic splices, and other problems.
* *Storage*: Once materials have been filmed, house all preservation microfilm in archival enclosures, maintain microfilm readers regularly, and insist that researchers use the microfilm instead of the original materials. Master negatives must be stored off-site, preferably under the proper temperature and humidity conditions.

PAPER REPRODUCTIONS

PRESERVATION PHOTOCOPYING

Photocopying in-house onto permanent durable paper can provide a paper copy of fragile or brittle documents that are not easily usable in microfilm format (*e.g.*, news clipping collections, indexes, finding aids).

In archival collections, preservation photocopies can be used to provide initial access so that researchers can identify which materials they need to see; to reproduce unstable documents (*e.g.*, faxes); to provide copies of valuable documents that should be stored more securely; or to provide surrogate copies for materials that are too fragile to handle.

Traditional preservation photocopying, however, does not provide a master negative from which additional copies can be made, as microfilm does. If the photocopy becomes unusable, the original must be copied again, which can be problematic for fragile or brittle items.

PRESERVATION FACSIMILES

The production of preservation facsimiles is an option for brittle books that are heavily used (*e.g.*, for which a paper copy would meet the users' needs better than a microfilm copy). This type of reproduction is normally contracted out to a vendor. Production of a facsimile is appropriate when reprints are expensive or unavailable, duplicate copies are not available, and other editions cannot provide an adequate substitute. Ideally, the item should be filmed as well, either by your institution or another.

Preservation facsimiles were traditionally done using a photocopier, but now they are produced using digital scanning. Items are normally disbound, then scanned and printed on alkaline paper on a digital laser printer. This produces a digital file that can then be used to print additional paper copies in the future without rescanning the originals. Keep in mind, however, that if the digital file should become inaccessible for any reason and the paper copy wears out, the original must be reproduced again, or the information may be lost.

STANDARDS/GUIDELINES

A high-quality preservation photocopy or preservation facsimile requires the use of permanent paper, as well as equipment and procedures that will ensure a long-lasting copy. Although there are no specific standards for preservation photocopying or for the production of preservation facsimiles, there are related standards and guidelines that cover elements of the process.

Paper used for preservation photocopies or facsimiles must comply with ANSI/NISO Z39.48 1992 Permanence of Paper for Publications and Documents in Libraries and Archives. The standard sets out requirements for pH, tear resistance, alkaline reserve, and amount of lignin permitted. A partial list of papers that meet the ANSI/NISO standard is available online in an excerpt from North American Permanent Papers, 3rd ed. Procedures for ensuring the quality of scanned images in preservation facsimiles should follow guidelines and best practices for digital imaging that are generally accepted within the preservation community.

Copiers used for preservation photocopying must be kept in the best condition possible and should not be used for other types of copying. Carbon black toner must be used, and the adhesion of the image to the paper must be tested periodically.

PRODUCING PHOTOCOPIES AND FACSIMILES

It is best to contract out the production of preservation facsimiles, since complex machinery and procedures are involved. Small-scale preservation photocopying can be done in-house, but staff must be well trained in the proper procedures and the equipment must be properly maintained.

The basic procedures involved in producing preservation photocopies and facsimiles are as follows:

* *Preparation*: The materials to be copied are examined page-by-page to ensure that they are in the correct order and nothing is missing. If there are foldouts or other oversize materials in a bound volume, these are measured.

* *Photocopying*: Books are normally disbound for copying. During the photocopying process, a daily peel test (sometimes called a tape pull test) is recommended, to ensure that the image is adhering properly to the paper. When photocopying two-sided pages, care must be taken to ensure that the placement of the text or image on the verso and recto sides of the pages are maintained in relation to each other. Oversize and colour materials may be copied separately as needed.
* *Scanning*:When scanning, items are also normally disbound (unless their value warrants reproducing them without disbinding). The institution must specify how illustrations will be scanned (gray scale, colour), at what size foldouts will be scanned, etc.
* *Inspection*: Once copying or scanning has been done, the finished product is inspected to ensure that there are no pages missing, the copies are legible, the contrast is good, and the general quality is acceptable compared to the original.
* *Binding*:Paper copies are bound according to the NISO standard for library binding. A statement is placed in the copy identifying it as a preservation photocopy; this should be noted in any catalog records as well.
* *Storage*: The copy or copies should be stored according to guidelines for paper-based collections. The original items may be retained after photocopying in case additional copies or another type of reformatting is needed in future. For books that have been disbound, the loose leaves can be foldered and boxed.

DIGITIZATION

Many collections managers, particularly those in small institutions, have been confronted with a member of the board of trustees who asks: "Why don't we just buy a scanner? Then we wouldn't have to worry about preservation."

The short answer to this question is that while digitization (the conversion of analog data into machine-readable binary code) is an excellent tool for researcher access, it cannot yet stand on its own as a viable preservation reformatting strategy, particularly for small institutions with limited resources. For the future, the preservation community envisions a gradual partnership between preservation microfilm and the evolving technology of digital imaging.

Digital scanners and cameras are ubiquitous, however, and numerous digital initiatives, on varying scales and with varying goals, are occurring in cultural institutions.

Key challenges of digital preservation include:

* Creating digital objects worthy of the effort and expense required to preserve them;
* Creating effective systems for accessing the digitized images; and
* Dealing with the problem of rapid obsolescence of the hardware and software that support those access systems.

STANDARDS/GUIDELINES

Unlike preservation microfilming and photocopying, there are no formal standards that govern the capture, processing, and storage of digital images.

There are, however, a number of projects and publications that have set forth best practices for creating high-quality digital images, access systems, and storage systems. If you choose to undertake a digitization project, you will need to create your own technical guidelines that reflect your institution's needs and your project's goals. Explore Cornell University's Moving Theory into Practice: Digital Imaging Tutorial.

DIGITIZATION PROCEDURES

Despite the possible variations in technical requirements, there are several standard steps in digital imaging. As with other reformatting methods, most institutions will find digitization too complex and expensive to undertake in-house; contracting with a vendor experienced in working with historical paper-based collections is recommended.

The Digitization Process

The basic steps in digital imaging are as follows:

* *Image capture*: The document(s) or other materials are captured in digital form using a scanner or digital camera. Decisions made about the desired image quality during benchmarking (*e.g.*, the type of scan, the resolution of the scan, the bit depth) are implemented.
* *Image processing*: This includes image editing if necessary (*e.g.*, compression of files, sharpening of images) and the creation of metadata (sometimes defined as "data about data"). Metadata indexes and describes the scanned materials. A table explaining the types of metadata can be found within Moving Theory into Practice: Digital Imaging Tutorial.
* *Image delivery*:This is the process of getting the scanned images to the user through computer networks, monitors, and printers. Delivery methods, file formats, file compression, and acceptable image quality will differ depending on various user characteristics. It is crucial to consider image delivery needs during project planning, not after the images have already been created.
* *Quality control*: This involves both initial and ongoing evaluation of whether the technical requirements for image capture, processing, and delivery are being met. At the beginning of the project, it is a good idea to digitize a representative sample of documents to be sure that all quality requirements are being met.

Storage and Maintenance

After digital objects are created and appropriately indexed and described, they must be stored on-line, near-line, and/or off-line. Over time, however, obsolescence of hardware and software (the technology chain used to access digital objects) becomes a far greater concern. If a CD-ROM survives intact for 50 or even 100 years, but no device survives that can retrieve the data, then the data have effectively been lost.

At present, there are significant obstacles to maintaining the integrity and functionality of the technology chain. Upgrading to new hardware and software platforms may prove prohibitively expensive over time. To further complicate matters, a practical and universally reliable way of migrating existing digital data to newer hardware and software platforms has yet to be developed. Even if migration procedures were more standardized, they would necessarily involve a significant commitment of time and resources, making them challenging to implement.

HYBRID OPTIONS

Given the challenges of digital preservation, it makes sense for most institutions to use digital imaging as an access tool while simultaneously relying on more traditional approaches such as microfilming for preservation. Over the past 15 years, several grant-funded projects have explored the possibility of combining microfilming and digital imaging technologies.

Yale University's Project Open Book studied the feasibility of converting existing preservation microfilm of 19th- and 20th-century brittle books to digital images (known as the "film-first" method). Cornell University's Digital to Microfilm Conversion Project studied the feasibility of scanning the same type of collections and producing computer output microfilm (known as the "scan-first" method).

These projects proved that both methods could be used successfully. Detailed technical guidelines for filming first and scanning first were devised, and information was gathered about costs and workflow. The project administrators concluded that the choice of where to begin a hybrid project would depend on the condition of the original materials, whether or not preservation microfilm already exists, and whether or not disbinding of bound volumes is permissible, among other issues.

REFORMATTING MEDIA COLLECTIONS

This is partly because, unlike paper-based collections,

many audiovisual materials must be played in machines to retrieve their information.

Even minimal playback leads to wear and tear, and playback machinery can become obsolete in a relatively short time. Magnetic and optical media may also be subject to catastrophic failure without any warning. In addition, new still and moving images and sound recordings are now frequently being produced in digital form. These are then subject to the difficulties of preserving digital information.

Duplication or reformatting onto appropriate media is an important preservation activity for audiovisual collections. Reformatting can provide service copies for deteriorating materials, preservation-quality copies on a more stable medium, and/or preservation masters to replace deteriorating or obsolete formats.

PHOTOGRAPHS AND NEGATIVES

If photographic prints do not have negatives, it is important to produce a negative so that the image will be preserved even if the original is lost or damaged. Conversely, prints should be made from negatives when an original print does not exist. Duplicate prints of deteriorating historical photographs may be needed if the original is in very poor condition and/or if it is subjected to frequent use. Deteriorating negatives (such as broken glass plate negatives or nitrate- or acetate-based negatives) may also need to be duplicated.

Duplicating Photographs

There are several options for producing use copies of photographs. Duplicate prints can be produced, a microfilm index of photographs can be created, or a database of digital images can be prepared. A very inexpensive (albeit lower-quality) option is to produce photocopies in-house that can be used to identify which photographs are needed by the researcher. You may be able to find a local photographer or camera lab that provides copying services for historical photographs. It is a good idea to use a service provider that has experience dealing with older materials. If the duplicate photograph is intended to be used as a preservation copy, it should be printed on traditional photographic paper, not on a digital printer, since prints from a digital printer or a colour photocopier will not last as long as traditional processed prints.

Duplicating Negatives

Duplication inherently involves a loss of image quality and detail, so it is crucial that duplicate negatives are printed on stable materials and that the reproduced image is the highest quality possible. As with all reformatting, choose a vendor who is experienced with historical collections.

Methods for duplicating negatives include:

* Producing a print and photographing the print using a large-format camera to produce a copy negative;
* Making a direct duplicate negative using duplicating film;
* Contact-printing the original negative onto film to produce a positive image, called an interpositive. The interpositive is then contact-printed onto film to produce a duplicate negative. This has the advantage of producing a master (the interpositive) and use copies

MOTION PICTURE FILMS

The optimum scenario for motion picture film preservation is to undertake film-to-film duplication, producing a preservation master, a new viewing print, and additional access copies. Film-to-film duplication is very expensive, however, and will be justified only for the most valuable and significant historical films.

Videotape Service Copies

For most small institutions with limited resources, the best option will be to have service copies of films made on videotape and to store the originals in cold storage offsite. Since the two media are very different, the copy will not be a completely accurate reproduction and thus cannot be considered a preservation copy, but it will allow access to films that would be unavailable otherwise.

While videotape copies can be created on VHS videotape (which is well known to users and can be played on equipment already found in many institutions), you should also consider creating the first copy on better-quality tape, which can then be used as a master to make additional copies as needed. BetaCam SP (a half-inch analog tape) has often been used for this purpose, although in recent years some institutions have begun to use DigiBeta (a half-inch digital tape) because of its increasing presence in the broadcasting industry.

Analog and digital reproductions each have advantages and disadvantages. Analog systems are much simpler than digital systems and reproduce the content more accurately—digital copies by definition sample the original information rather than reproducing it exactly—but digital formats can be easily transmitted over the Internet, copied to other media such as DVD, and recopied many times without data loss.

Digital Preservation

As many other materials are converted to digital format, the question arises of whether to simply convert film to digital for preservation purposes, rather than film to film. For now, the answer is that current digital technology cannot yet capture all of the images and sounds of an original film adequately. In addition, the problems of digital preservation would also apply to digitized films.

AUDIOTAPES AND VIDEOTAPES

For audiotape and videotape that is deteriorating rapidly and/or becoming obsolete, create a preservation master, which will then be used to produce use copies for viewing and listening. The preservation master should be stored in a stable and moderate environment and restricted from use.

Copy Formats

As with motion picture film, preservation masters and service copies can be made either in digital or analog format, each of which has advantages and disadvantages.

It is generally recommended that sound recordings be reformatted via analog recording onto quarter-inch polyester standard-play tape with a ferric oxide coating. The preservation master should reproduce the original as accurately as possible, while the service copy can be altered to improve the sound quality if desired

Videotape can be copied onto VHS videotape, or you can create the first copy on better-quality tape, which can then be used as a master to make additional copies as needed. BetaCam SP (a half-inch analog tape) has often been used for this purpose, although DigiBeta (a half-inch digital tape) can also be used.

LIBRARY BINDING

Although it is primarily a strategy for general collections, library binding can be used for deteriorated historical volumes that have informational rather than artifactual value. Damaged books that have artifactual value, however, should not be library bound, but should instead be treated by a professional conservator.

The long-term preservation and usability of re-bound volumes has increasingly become a primary concern in library binding. While older library binding techniques were strong and economical, they sometimes resulted in books that did not open well and could be damaged by handling and photocopying. Also, the bindings were too strong for the text blocks they were meant to protect. Today's library binders have addressed these issues and provide bindings that are more durable and longer lasting.

STANDARDS/GUIDELINES

The binding industry has adopted formal standards for library binding. The binding industry has adopted formal standards for library binding. At present, ANSI/NISO/LBI Z39.78-2000 Library Binding is the library-binding standard of record..

The goals of modern library binding are:

* To produce a durable and economical binding;

* To alter the text block as little as possible;
* To ensure that the binding itself is as nondamaging as possible; and
* To produce a re-bound volume that will open easily To 180 degrees and stay open as the researcher is working.

Because the *Library Binding* standard is geared primarily towards professional library binders, it became clear that staff of collections-holding institutions would benefit from additional explanation and discussion of the standard so they could make informed binding decisions. In response, the Library Binding Institute (LBI) sponsored a *Guide to the Library Binding Institute Standard for Library Binding*, originally published in 1990. This publication is in the process of being updated, and a draft version can be reviewed at the LBI Web site.

BINDING OPTIONS

The many options available for library binding of historical items can be confusing to those with little experience in the field. Always remember that if a volume has artifactual value, it should never be library bound; it must be treated by a conservator instead. Any volumes to be library bound must have paper that is not too brittle and is strong enough to withstand the binding process. When making binding decisions, keep the following general guidelines in mind.

Preserve the original signatures and sewing by choosing from the following options:

* *Recasing*: If the original sewing is intact, the volume should receive a new case (*e.g.*, new boards and covering that are attached to the text block by gluing them to the endsheets).
* *Resewing and recasing*: If the sewing is deteriorated, the book should be resewn through the original sewing holes (by hand or machine) if possible, even though this can be an expensive option. The volume should then be recased.
* *Double-fan adhesive binding*:Volumes that cannot be recased should usually be double-fan adhesive

bound. In this type of binding, the spine is milled, and a machine applies adhesive to the leaves as they are fanned back and forth.

* *Oversewing*:This technique (machine sewing of single leaves at an angle through prepunched holes) could be needed for very heavy and thick text blocks, but oversewn volumes often do not open well, and the sewing can easily tear the pages if they become brittle in the future. This option should be avoided if at all possible.

When rebinding materials from historical collections, there are some additional issues to consider:

* *No-trim policy*: Specify that the binder should not trim the edges of the text block unless the page edges are damaged or the pages are uncut. Otherwise, any images or text that extend to the edges of the pages will be lost.
* *Paper repairs*: If paper repairs are needed, a paper-based pressure-sensitive tape with acrylic adhesive should be used (document repair tape, available from conservation suppliers). It is important, however, to remember that these repair tapes are only reversible with the use of organic solvents. A conservator would be needed if a volume is later reclassified into special collections. If the book has value as an artifact and would merit page repairs done with Japanese paper, it should not be library bound.

CONSERVATION TREATMENT

It is important to differentiate between conservation of general collections and conservation of special collections. The former refers to the repair and protective housing of general library collections that are shelved in open stacks, while the latter refers to treatment by a professional conservator of library materials that have been separated from the general collection because of their value as artifacts, as well as archival materials, scrapbooks, photographs, etc.

Collections conservation (also sometimes known as in-house repair when on a smaller scale) can be an important element of a systematic preservation programme for academic and public libraries.

For those institutions that are concerned primarily with special collections materials, however, in-house repair is usually not appropriate. In all cases, it is important to follow proper procedures for repair, since unintended damage can result from improper repairs.

Professional conservation treatment, while not appropriate for every deteriorated item, should be considered by any type of institution for deteriorated materials that possess significant artifactual, historic, associational, legal, aesthetic, or financial value as artifacts. A conservator's goal is to chemically stabilize and physically strengthen the item(s) being treated. Conservation treatment by a professional conservator is time-consuming and costly, so it must be limited to those materials that are the most valuable and the most deteriorated.

PRINCIPLES OF TREATMENT

Special Collections Conservation

The primary goal of conservation treatment for special collections is twofold: to stabilize the item in the collection so that it survives over the long term and is available for use, while at the same time changing its physical characteristics as little as possible. All repairs should be obvious to the trained eye (although they should not clash aesthetically with the item). It is important not to mislead the researcher into thinking the item was never damaged.

Conservation treatment must maintain the integrity of the object to the extent possible; thus, conservators follow the principle of minimal intervention.

Specifically:

* *Do no harm*: Use stable materials, and, in the event that the treatment turns out to be damaging over time or improved treatment options become available in the future, use reversible treatments wherever possible.

This caution arises in part because some conservation treatments used in the past (*e.g.*, the use of silking, soluble nylon, and lamination to reinforce brittle paper) have caused unforeseen damage to collections.

* *Less is better*: Consider the effect that treatment will have on the aesthetic and physical characteristics of the object. Sometimes limited treatment, or even no treatment, may be the best choice.

Ultimately, it is important to remember that compromise is unavoidable; a conservator must weigh all factors before making a treatment decision and then work with the institution to make the best decision.

General Collections Conservation

While collections conservation shares the goal of stabilizing an item so that it can be accessible in its original format, there is less emphasis on maintaining the integrity of the object and more emphasis on lengthening the useful life of the item (*e.g.*, producing a durable item that will withstand heavy use). The need for relatively quick and low-cost treatments is a factor, as is the need for an organized workflow and the ability to treat materials in batches. Thus, compromises in treatment techniques are sometimes made that would not be acceptable in special collections conservation.

COLLECTIONS CONSERVATION/IN-HOUSE REPAIR

Collections conservation is normally carried out by either a collections conservator (a professional conservator specializing in general library collections) or a conservation technician (someone with more limited training who is knowledgeable about specific techniques). In small institutions, in-house repair is often carried out by a regular staff member who has been sent to one or more workshops; this can be problematic, though, because the training is usually brief and ongoing supervision unavailable.

Collections Conservation

There are a number of procedures that are carried out as

part of collections conservation, including preparing new materials for library use (binding pamphlets, attaching book pockets, etc.); preparing books for library binding; constructing protective enclosures; and carrying out basic book repair.

Look at the following sites to explore what is involved in implementing a book repair programme. How do the sites differ?

What activities do you think might be appropriate for your institution?

* University of Illinois at Urbana-Champaign
* Dartmouth College
* University of California, Berkeley
* Cornell University

IN-HOUSE REPAIR OF HISTORICAL COLLECTIONS

In the context of historical collections, "safe" in-house techniques are limited to rehousing objects in appropriate enclosures and simple cleaning of books and some paper using preservation-quality procedures and materials.

Instructions for simple page repairs and surface cleaning can be found on the Northeast Document Conservation Center's (NEDCC) Web site, but these activities should be undertaken only when absolutely necessary and after training and extensive practice on unimportant items. In reality, most institutions will have higher-priority preservation needs than the repair of individual items.

PROFESSIONAL CONSERVATION TREATMENT

There are a number of treatments typically carried out by professional paper, book, and photographs conservators. These might include surface cleaning of paper, removal of damaging backings or mounts, removal of adhesive tape, washing in water, alkalization, mending or backing weakened items, bleaching to reduce stains, retouching areas of loss, re-sewing book pages, re-backing books with damaged covers or spines, and full rebinding of damaged volumes.

MANAGING REFORMATTING

Managing preservation reformatting involves identifying

collections in need of reformatting; setting priorities among those collections; choosing the appropriate reformatting method(s); finding funding for the project; and carrying out the project. Because institutions are usually working with a limited budget, and numerous collections may be good candidates for reformatting, selecting the materials to be reformatted and setting priorities are often extremely challenging. In this part, you will identify strategies for effective selection and project management.

SELECTING PAPER COLLECTIONS

Identifying Collections in Need of Reformatting

Reformatting can provide preservation copies of collections that have only informational value, service copies to lessen handling of valuable originals, and/or security copies to guard against loss of information.

To identify collections that are good candidates for reformatting, consider the following:

* Is the collection extremely deteriorated?
* Does the collection have informational or artifactual value?
* How important is the collection to the institutional mission?
* Is the collection frequently used?
* Is the collection important in the context of other local, regional, or national collections? Is it a good candidate for a cooperative reformatting project?
* Have the materials been reformatted elsewhere?
* Is the collection a particularly good candidate for grant funding (perhaps because of its format or subject matter)?
* Does the collection have copyright or donor restrictions?
* Are there a variety of formats within the collection, and how easily can the materials be filmed, scanned, or copied?

Choosing a Reformatting Method

Once you have prioritized a particular collection or collections for reformatting, the next step is to decide which of the various options for preservation reformatting is the most appropriate. Keep in mind your overall goals of ensuring continued access to the information, protecting the original from additional damage, copying originals in poor condition only once, and creating a copy or copies that will last as long as possible.

In general, it is best to start by thinking about the end results of the project. Is microfilm needed for security or preservation purposes? Is a hard copy also needed? Is an exact reproduction needed (*e.g.*, do images need to be colour, or is black and white sufficient)? Is an enhanced version of the material, such as online searchable text, needed? In many cases, a combination of more than one reformatting method will be appropriate, such as preservation photocopying and microfilming, digital imaging and microfilming, or digital imaging and creation of a bound copy on permanent paper.

SELECTING MEDIA COLLECTIONS

Reformatting audiovisual materials is very expensive, and there is rarely enough funding available to reformat large numbers of items at once. While general concerns about level of use and importance to the institution apply to all types of collections, selection issues to be considered for specific types of audiovisual collections include:

Photographs and Negatives

Cellulose nitrate or cellulose acetate negatives that already exhibit signs of deterioration should be a priority, as should colour photographs, slides, and negatives. Deterioration of acetate negatives can be very quick, so frequent monitoring of their condition is essential. Priority for duplication may also be given to valuable negatives and to negatives that are frequently used, whatever their type. If you cannot store nitrate negatives according to the guidelines given by your insurance company and local authorities, their duplication and disposal should be a priority.

Motion Picture Films

For films, cultural significance must be determined, as well as whether or not the institution's copy is the best surviving copy. Completeness of the copy, the number of generations your copy is from the original, and the physical condition of the film must be considered. Films on nitrate or acetate base that already exhibit signs of deterioration should be a high priority. In general, if materials can be placed in cold storage, individual films can be copied as time permits, with the most significant and deteriorated films duplicated first. As is the case with nitrate negatives, if you cannot store nitrate films according to the guidelines given by your insurance company and local authorities, their duplication and disposal should be a priority.

Audiotapes and Videotapes

In addition to determining cultural significance, you must identify damaged tapes, recordings made on obsolete or unusual formats, recordings made early in the life of a format (these may be of inferior quality), older tapes, and unique copies (*e.g.*, the only master). All of these should have priority for copying.

WORKING WITH A VENDOR

For most small institutions, contracting out to an experienced vendor for preservation reformatting will be easier and more cost effective than trying to reformat in-house.

Evaluate the Vendor's Experience and Services

High-volume commercial microfilmers do not have the equipment or expertise to film fragile materials without damaging them. For valuable collections and/or materials that are being filmed because they are too fragile to withstand extensive handling, it is best to use a special service filmer who is experienced in dealing with hard-to-film collections (*e.g.*, tightly bound books, faded documents). For digital imaging, the vendor should have experience working with historical materials, as well as current equipment and the expertise to use it.

For audio and video recordings, an audiovisual or multimedia lab experienced with library and archives collections (as opposed to commercial customers) must be chosen. Professional-quality equipment and properly trained staff are essential to the production of preservation masters and service copies for audio and video recordings. Video recordings are especially vulnerable to data loss during the copying process because of the large amount of data in video signals.

Similarly, a specialized commercial film laboratory is needed for film duplication. Some duplication laboratories have developed particular specialties, such as specific formats or types of film (*e.g.*, 8mm film, colour film, nitrate film, soundtracks).

Contact several different vendors to compare costs and services. You will need to estimate the size of the project, which will allow the vendor to provide a cost estimate. Visit the vendor to make sure that housekeeping, environmental control, and security are acceptable for temporary storage of the collections. This is especially important to prevent damage to original materials that will be retained rather than discarded after reformatting.

Draw Up a Contract

Once you have identified the vendor you wish to use, negotiate a contract. Be sure to find out whether your institution has specific procedures that must be followed for bidding and contracts.

You will need to specify standards and guidelines to which the vendor must adhere (*e.g.*, for image quality, quality control measures, etc.) in the contract. Insurance and shipping requirements must be covered in the contract, as well as any special services (such as the creation of microfilming targets) that the vendor will provide.

MANAGING REFORMATTING PROJECTS

For institutions that contract with an outside vendor for

reformatting services, the basic elements of project management are:

* Selecting the collections to be reformatted;
* determining which reformatting method is most appropriate;
* Creating a project plan (often as part of preparing an application for grant funding);
* Preparing the collections for reformatting;
* Keeping in touch with the vendor during the reformatting process to ensure that all is proceeding as planned; and
* Examining the final result to ensure that all technical specifications provided by the institution were met.

Planning a Reformatting Project

Begin with the following questions: Will you be instituting a systematic ongoing reformatting programme or undertaking one or two special projects? Do you have the expertise in-house to determine the condition of collections and decide which merit reformatting? Will you need a collection survey by a specialist prior to making reformatting decisions?

Who will plan and manage the reformatting project(s)? A professional staff member is usually recommended, but in some cases a paraprofessional may perform this function. Choose someone who can successfully interact with other institutional staff as well as with the outside vendor.

What will be the responsibilities of various staff members within the institution during the project? How will you fund the project(s)? You will need to estimate the size of each specific project and determine how much in-house staffing and time will be needed. If the project is to be grant funded, this will be done as part of your grant application. Most importantly, what are your goals for the project? This is particularly important for projects that include digitization, where you must begin by deciding what products and results you want from the project, and then determine the technical requirements for producing those results.

MANAGING CONSERVATION TREATMENT

Managing conservation treatment of paper-based collections involves:

* Identifying collections in need of treatment;
* Setting priorities for treatment among those collections;
* Choosing a conservator;
* analysing use and preservation needs, and choosing the appropriate preservation strategy;
* Finding funding for the project(s);
* Interacting with the conservator or technician during the treatment process; and
* Integrating the treated item back into the collection after the project.

For most small institutions, in-house repair and library binding should be used only minimally for historical collections, and professional conservation treatment should be reserved for those materials of greatest value to the institution. For medium to large institutions, a collections conservation programme, a library binding programme, and/or individual special collections treatment projects may be appropriate.

SELECTING COLLECTIONS FOR TREATMENT

General Collections Conservation

Because library collections conservation programmes handle a larger volume of material, and because these programmes focus on general circulating collections, all staff must have a role in identifying collections in need of treatment. Circulation staff, shelvers, and interlibrary loan staff should all be trained to identify damaged volumes (*e.g.*, loose hinges, torn or detached pages, broken spines, damaged corners).

Depending on whether the book is worth keeping (a bibliographer's opinion may be needed), whether the book is needed by patrons, whether there are other copies available, and whether the needed repair is simple or complex, repair may not be the best option. Alternatives include ordering a replacement copy, sending the book for commercial binding, reformatting the book, and/or rehousing the volume.

As books are flagged for repair, damaged items should be sorted into groups by type of repair (*e.g.*, pamphlet binding, hinge tightening, page mending, etc.) for efficiency.

Special Collections Treatment

Deciding which special collections merit treatment by a conservator can be challenging. There may be a variety of reasons for undertaking conservation treatment: if an item is fragile and must be frequently handled; if a reproduction cannot substitute for the original deteriorated item (*e.g.*, when physical characteristics of the item such as the binding or ink may have meaning for researchers); if the item has special characteristics such as colour illustrations or foldouts that preclude reformatting; and/or if it is necessary to repair the effects of past damaging treatments.

Treatment methods for individual items must be decided in consultation with a conservator experienced with paper collections (or books or photographs, as appropriate). The choice of a particular treatment will depend on the value of the object in its original form, the importance of the information it contains, the condition of the object, the potential for treatment to cause additional damage, and—realistically—the funds available for conservation.

For any item, there are usually several possible levels of treatment. When a conservator examines an object, he or she will provide a treatment proposal that sets out these options and their varying costs.

CHOOSING A CONSERVATOR

Since professional conservators usually specialize in a particular type of collection (*e.g.*, photographs, books, art on paper, paintings, furniture), and because qualified conservators may have been trained in various ways, it can sometimes be difficult to find the right conservator for your treatment project. When choosing a conservator, you will want to get information about the conservator's training, experience, and professional involvement.

Education and Experience

Conservators receive their training through graduate-level degree programmes (two to three years of coursework, plus an additional year of hands-on experience) or through lengthy apprenticeships. Apprenticeship is particularly common in book conservation, since formal educational programmes in that field are limited. Whatever the type of training, gaining hands-on experience in treating materials in their chosen specialty is an important part of a conservator's education. When choosing a conservator, be sure to ask about the conservator's practical experience, and obtain client and peer references.

Professional Membership

There are a number of respected professional organizations for conservators, including the American Institute for Conservation (AIC), the International Institute for Conservation (IIC), and various regional organizations. Membership in such organizations can indicate a conservator's interest in keeping up with current developments in the field.

Locating a Conservator

There are several ways to locate a qualified conservator. Getting recommendations from other institutions with similar collections is always a good idea. You should also consult the American Institute for Conservation's online guide to conservation services. This resource does not endorse specific conservators, but will provide you with a list of professional conservators in your area, along with their specialties. There are also a number of regional conservation centers that employ conservators in different specialties to provide conservation services.

If you are located in an isolated area, you may need to get referrals from a broad geographic area. Regional centers and many conservators have experience in packing, shipping, and transporting fragile collections and can provide advice.

MANAGING TREATMENT PROJECTS

Planning a Collections Conservation Programme

Because of the complexities of planning such a programme, management issues can only be touched on here. Issues to address include the following: where in the institutional structure the collections conservation programme will be located; what staff will perform collections conservation activities; how staff will be trained; what space and equipment will be provided; what repair procedures will be performed (simple or complex?); and how damaged collections will be identified. The answers to these questions will depend in large part on the size and financial resources of your institution.

Planning Special Collections Treatment

As with other reformatting and treatment options, organization and funding are crucial. Who will plan and manage treatment projects? A cooperative relationship between the project manager and the conservator will be very important. How will you fund the project(s)? Will you apply for grants? Do you need a collections survey to determine treatment needs?

If you are applying for a grant, items will have to be taken or sent to a conservator for a detailed examination; in some instances, a conservator may be willing to come to your institution. The conservator will produce treatment proposals, perhaps with options, which you will incorporate into your grant application.

Once you have funding, you will sign and return the treatment proposal. As treatment proceeds, unexpected changes in the treatment plan are sometimes needed (for example, if the object does not respond as expected to the proposed treatment). The conservator will consult the project manager if changes are required. When the material is returned, the conservator will provide a treatment report describing what was done to the item(s), which must be retained permanently.

Planning for Library Binding

Binders should be members of the Library Binding Institute (LBI), which is the primary membership organization for library binders. To become a certified member of LBI, binders must undergo a certification process in which their work is inspected to ensure that it meets the *Library Binding* standard. The binder must pledge to adhere to the standard when undertaking work to which the standard applies.

Your institution should have a contract, or at least an informal agreement, with its library binder that specifies the institution's preferences for leaf attachment and the other binding issues noted in the Exploring part of this part. Books returned by the binder must be individually inspected for quality of work and adherence to these specifications.

8

Disaster Planning

RISK ASSESSMENT

Every institution has its own unique set of hazards (*e.g.*, threats to the building and/or collections). Risk assessment studies the probability that specific hazards will result in disaster. The most likely disasters and their potential effects should be identified during the risk assessment process.

When assessing risks, focus on the following questions:

* Which of the identified hazards are the most significant to the site or the collection
* What risk of disaster is posed by each of these hazards?
* Which sources of risk can be eliminated or moderated?
* Which risks must be addressed in the emergency plan?

EXTERNAL HAZARDS

External hazards can be natural or manmade. They may be common (*e.g.*, flooding) or uncommon (*e.g.*, oil leak). They may happen suddenly (*e.g.*, tornado), or there may be prior warning (*e.g.*, hurricane). They may be a result of geography, physical location, or even the political environment. As you consider the external hazards to which your institution might be vulnerable, remember that there may be unexpected risks.

REAL LIFE EXAMPLE

The worst water damage to the Boston Public Library in 120 years occurred when a water main dating from 1895 burst and sent tens of thousands of gallons gushing through the basement of the recently renovated McKim Building shortly after midnight on August 16, 1998. Three feet of water saturated the first three shelves of almost every basement book stack. Loss and damage included about 350,000 paper lost GPO documents, 3 million pieces of damaged or destroyed microfiche, and 250 drawers of damaged maps.

Following are some risks to which your institution might be subjected:

* *Hurricane*: Hurricanes are slow moving, severe storms with high winds that are a serious threat to the East Coast and the Gulf Coast of the United States from approximately June to November of each year. Those affected usually have 24 hours or more to prepare, with hurricane watches and hurricane warnings issued well in advance.
* *Severe winter storm*: Winter storms often involve heavy snow, sleet, or freezing rain. Very heavy snow accompanied by high winds and extreme cold is termed a blizzard. When rain falls on surfaces with a temperature below freezing, an ice storm can occur. A nor'easter is a specific type of storm characteristic to the East Coast of the U.S., which can bring heavy snow (or rain), hurricane force winds, and coastal flooding.
* *Flooding*: Flooding often develops over a number of days, as a result of prolonged heavy rain or melting snows that create high river, stream, or reservoir levels. Flooding, particularly flash flooding (which occurs very quickly with little warning), can be extremely dangerous and damaging; even shallow floodwaters can sweep away cars or people. Flash flooding occurs most often from storms that produce large amounts of rain in a short time, but can also be caused by some sort of catastrophic event, such as a dam failure.
* *Earthquake*: Earthquakes measuring 6 or more on the Richter scale are considered major; earthquakes with a magnitude of 8 or more on the Richter scale can result in catastrophic damage. Buildings that are constructed on unconsolidated landfills, old

waterways, or other unstable soil are most at risk. Trailers and manufactured homes not tied to a reinforced foundation anchored to the ground are also at risk. Certain areas of the United States are prone to earthquakes, but history has also shown that damaging earthquakes do not always occur on well-known fault lines.

* *Wildfire/Forest Fire*: Institutions located in a rural wild land or forest area face a significant risk from wildfires, of which the major causes are human negligence (*e.g.*, smoking or improperly extinguishing a campfire) and lightning. Adjacent properties may pose a danger to your building and collections if the property owners do not take steps to prevent the spread of the fire. In addition, a rural location may be far from fire stations and water supplies. Finally, wildfire firefighters may be unaware of actions needed to protect cultural buildings and collections.
* *Water Main Break*:Since many underground water mains are very old and deteriorated, they often break unexpectedly. It is also possible for a water main to be broken accidentally by digging or construction in the area. The primary threat to institutions and collections is flooding, which can be significant, particularly if some time passes before workers can cap the water main.
* *Sewer System Backup*: Sewer system backups often occur because of heavy rains that increase the water pressure in the sewer system, causing sewage to flow into buildings through the basement drains. If there is a widespread power outage in the area, the sewer system may fail due to lack of power to parts of the system. Sewer backups can also result from inappropriate materials being disposed of down the drains or from shrub or tree roots cracking or breaking the sewer lines.
* *Proximity to Hazardous Materials or Activity*: Hazardous materials are used in a wide range of

activities, including manufacturing, agriculture, medicine, and research. Many products that are routinely used in homes or workplaces contain hazardous chemicals (*e.g.*, cleaning products, paint removers and thinners). Most serious accidents involving hazardous materials are the result of transportation accidents (involving air transport, highways, trains, and/or waterways) or accidents in manufacturing plants.

* *Terrorist Attack (or Riot/Civil Disturbance)*: Most terrorist attacks that have occurred in the United States have been bombing attacks, but chemical or biological attacks are possible. If an institution is located near railways, highways, waterways, power plants, government buildings, or other prominent public facilities, there is some risk of terrorist attack. If an institution is located in a public facility or in proximity to a controversial organization, there may also be risk of a riot or civil disturbance.

INTERNAL/BUILDING HAZARDS

Hazards internal to your institution fall into several categories. They might relate to the building and/or mechanical systems (*e.g.*, leaky roof, inadequate electrical system); detection and alarm systems (*e.g.*, fire, security); personnel and procedures (*e.g.*, inadequate backup of records, poor staff training); or maintenance issues (*e.g.*, insufficient inspections and repairs). When evaluating the relative importance of internal risks, consider the frequency and occurrence of past problems. Again, remember that there may be risks that have not previously occurred to you. Take a moment to look at the pictures below—what hazard is represented in each?

PREVENTING/MITIGATING DISASTER

Once you have identified institutional, take action to protect your collections. While you may need to guard collections against specific types of disasters (*e.g.*, bracing shelves for earthquake protection, building window coverings in case of hurricane), it is generally most effective to begin with general prevention efforts, with a focus on those risks you identified as most serious in your risk assessment.

Facilities improvements, increased vigilance, and changes in procedure can all prevent or lessen damage to collections in a disaster. Be aware that you may need to devise both short- and long-term solutions to the problems you have identified. For example, you may need to relocate collections or cover materials with plastic sheeting until money is available for roof repair. To help you consider what might be done to protect your own collections, sample scenarios and prevention checklists for some of the most common types of damage are provided here.

WATER DAMAGE

Water damage can be the result of many different disaster scenarios, ranging from hurricane or flooding to roof leaks or clogged pipes. Paper-based collections are highly susceptible to damage from water, which causes swelling and distortion of bound volumes and cockling of paper. It also dissolves water-soluble inks and pigments and causes coated papers to adhere to each other. Photographs may separate from their mounts, emulsions may dissolve or stick together, and items may be stained. Mold growth can be an additional danger, developing within 24 to 48 hours if the relative humidity is high and the materials remain wet or damp. Mold can be highly dangerous to people and causes staining and other damage to collections.

FIRE DAMAGE

Fire damage can also be caused by a variety of scenarios, including fire in an adjacent building, sparks from renovation work, faulty electrical wiring, or even arson. Collections may not survive fire damage at all, and if they do, they may be charred, covered with soot, brittle from exposure to high heat, and smell of smoke. Often they are also wet from water used by firefighters or even moldy.

THEFT AND VANDALISM

While no staff member likes to think it could happen in their institution, theft and vandalism unfortunately occur more frequently than might be imagined. Trusted patrons, students, and even valued staff have stolen or vandalized collections. Valuable collections might be stolen to be sold or added to a private collection, while magazines or books might have pages torn out because someone wanted the information.

DATA PROTECTION

It is likely that much crucial data is stored electronically in your institution. This may include collection descriptions, financial information, scanned collections, or "born-digital" collections. The provision of backups to replace or reconstruct data is crucial to preventing a serious loss of data. Issues to consider include storage of backups (onsite and/or offsite), frequency of backups, the number of backups to be created for each type of data, and maintenance of backups (*e.g.*, periodically checking backups for deterioration).

PREPARING FOR DISASTER

You have learned that good building maintenance and careful procedures may prevent disasters from occurring or at least lessen the effect of any disaster that does occur. But is there more you can do? Consider how you would react during an actual disaster. Would you know what to do? Would you have the information you need close at hand? A calm, quick, and reasoned response to an emergency can make the difference between a minor event and serious ruin. This part will help you prepare for an effective response

EMERGENCY PROCEDURES

If the fire alarm goes off in your building, do you know what to do? If you discover a water leak while working late one night, do you know who to call and how to respond? Advance preparation of emergency procedures, wide distribution of these procedures, and staff training in implementing them are crucial to disaster preparedness.

Basic Procedures

At a minimum, you will need to prepare the following procedures:

* Building evacuation procedures—specify who is responsible for clearing each floor/area of the building and indicate where staff and visitors from each floor/area should gather outside.
* Emergency call list—provide staff names and after hours phone numbers, with those who can respond most quickly listed first.
* Basic water damage and fire response procedures.

Additional Procedures

Emergency procedures can be prepared for many possible scenarios, including mold outbreak, terrorist attack, power outage, gas or oil leak, various natural disasters, etc. For disasters with advance warning (such as hurricanes, some types of flooding, and wildfires), you can also prepare a list of actions to take once a warning is received. In general, you should prepare procedures for those hazards you identified as the most serious during your risk assessment.

SUPPLIES AND SERVICES

Who would you call if you had wet documents that needed to be dried? What is the after-hours number for the library's plumber? Who would you call if you needed computer data restored, or if you discovered a gas leak? You should gather phone numbers for essential services, as well as sources for necessary supplies and equipment, before disaster strikes. During the disaster planning process, assign someone to gather information about services and supplies, including their cost.

Basic Services

At a minimum, include telephone numbers and after-hours contact information for:

* Fire department
* Police department

* Ambulance
* Security company (or in-house security)
* Insurance company
* Electrician
* Plumber
* Heating and cooling service company
* Utility companies
* Conservation/preservation assistance
* Local freezer facility (where wet collections can be frozen quickly until they can be transferred to a vacuum freeze drying service)
* Vacuum freeze drying service
* Any other crucial services

Additional Services

In the event that your building is inaccessible for some time, you may want to arrange for alternate locations to which phone service, telecommunications, and/or computer operations could be moved, so that your institution can continue to operate while collections and the building are salvaged.

Depending on the scope of your collections, other services that might be needed include microfilm salvage, videotape salvage, and/or computer media recovery.

Supplies

It is a good idea to keep a limited number of supplies on hand for immediate response to minor water emergencies. A separate list should be kept of names and numbers for sources of additional supplies.

INSURANCE

Is your institution insured against damage to your building and collections? Do you know how to file a claim? Do you know what procedures you must follow in the event of a disaster (*e.g.*, are you allowed to begin salvaging damaged collections before the insurance adjuster arrives)? Insurance is a complex subject and can be very confusing. It is *very important that you consult with your insurance agent* to determine precisely what coverage is right for your institution.

Types of Insurance

An institution can be self-insured, purchase commercial insurance, or have a combination of the two. Self-insurance refers to the practice of putting funds aside within the institution to be used in case of loss. Some larger institutions or those that are part of a larger entity (*e.g.* a university or a government agency) choose self-insurance or a combination of commercial and self-insurance. Commercial insurance is more common for smaller institutions that do not have the resources to allow for self-insurance.

Materials Covered

Different collection materials may need different types of insurance coverage. In libraries, special collections are often covered by a Valuable Papers and Records policy that is separate from the policy for general collections. Do not neglect insurance for your building, machinery, and equipment (*e.g.*, furnishings, photocopiers, microfilm readers). Sometimes a separate computer rider is needed to cover replacement of computer hardware and software. You should also consider business interruption and extra expense insurance; these cover loss of income and extra expenses that may be incurred while providing services during the period of repair and restoration after a disaster.

Regardless of the materials covered or the method of insurance coverage, your institution must:

* Establish the value of the item(s) to be insured,
* Decide on the appropriate type of coverage, and
* Establish the procedures and documentation that will be required in the event of damage or loss.

PRIORITIZING MATERIALS FOR SALVAGE

Imagine that you are confronted with damp and soaked collections due to damage to your building from high winds and heavy rains. Which collections will be your highest priority? Setting salvage priorities is one of the most difficult tasks connected with disaster planning and recovery. To prevent delay and disagreements among staff during a crisis, it is best to identify high priority holdings in advance of an emergency.

Prioritizing by Type of Collection

High priority materials will vary from institution to institution. However, all organizations must give priority to vital records (*e.g.*, accounts payable, payroll and personnel records, legal documents).

Without these materials, it may be difficult to restart operations in a timely manner. Don't forget to include computer data in your salvage priorities. Data salvage priority should go to data that is not backed up at all and does not have offsite backups.

Following are types of collections that may be high priority:

* Materials that support your institution's primary mission
* Unique collections
* Heavily used collections
* Collections with legal retention requirements
* Collections that are difficult or expensive to replace
* Collections with scholarly research value
* Collections with monetary or artifactual value
* Formats that are particularly vulnerable to damage (*e.g.*, leather bindings)
* Materials that are particularly fragile
* Materials on loan

Methods for Setting Priorities

As a first step, set priorities by department or by parts of the collections. Since it is most likely that an emergency will affect only a portion of the collections, these priorities can serve as a basis for setting overall collection salvage priorities for the institution. This should be done by a committee made up of representatives from each department and/or area of the collections.

If your institution has an up to date collection development policy or retention/disposition schedules (in the case of archivists and records managers), use them to help determine which collections are most important. As a general rule, do not to try to set salvage priorities on an item-by-item basis. While there may be the occasional object of value that deserves to be considered on its own, it is much more practical to designate groups of items for salvage. A colour-coded map can be used to identify the location of high priority items (although this information must be protected to avoid creating a "shopping list" for thieves). Collection priorities should be shared with the fire department prior to an emergency.

Rethinking Priorities During a Disaster

During a disaster you may find that some collections are beyond salvage, particularly if they have spent significant time in adverse conditions. Exposure to fire can damage some formats (such as negatives and microfilm) so that salvage is impossible. Materials that have been wet for a long time may also be too badly damaged. If books with coated paper have been wet and begun to dry, their pages may block together, making them unsalvageable. In cases like this, you will have to move on to the next priority collection and concentrate on those materials that can be successfully salvaged.

RESPONDING TO DISASTER

We have seen some of the steps that should be taken prior to a disaster.

Explore these additional links that discuss the damage suffered by cultural institutions during Hurricanes Katrina and Rita last year and the ongoing recovery efforts:

* The Society of American Archivists' Report of Hurricane Katrina Damage Assessment—an assessment of damage to record-keeping facilities on the Mississippi Gulf Coast
* The Library of Congress' Learning from Katrina — first-person accounts of response and recovery from conservators with suggestions for best practices.

INITIAL RESPONSE AND ASSESSMENT

During a disaster, what steps need to be taken to deal with the affected materials? The primary directives are to stabilize the condition of collections so no further damage occurs and to salvage the maximum number of valuable materials. Time is a crucial factor. If conditions are wet and warm, mold can develop in less than 48 hours. A mold outbreak will compromise your ability to recover collections materials successfully and can also pose serious health risks.

It is helpful to assign responsibility for response and recovery efforts in advance of an emergency. A designated emergency recovery director (and an alternate) should be in charge of implementing the plan and coordinating recovery efforts. This person could be the institution's director, or it might be someone else who reacts calmly in an emergency.

Initial response lasts from the time an emergency is first noted to the time that packing and removal begins. Depending on the scope of the disaster, some of these actions may be carried out concurrently, while some may not be needed at all.

* *Notify the appropriate personnel*: Use the emergency call list to contact those appointed as initial responders. If it is outside of working hours, keep calling until you find someone who can respond.
* *If necessary, get clearance to enter the site*: If serious damage has occurred, it may be necessary to wait until the appropriate officials declare the building safe to enter. Re-entry to the site may also be delayed if hazardous materials are present, or if the building is a crime scene (as in the case of arson). If re-entry to the building is delayed, work must proceed from an off-site command center that has been designated ahead of time.
* *Begin to determine the extent of the damage*: What actually happened? How serious is the damage? How many and what type of materials are affected (*e.g.*, general collections, local history materials, audio/

visual materials, computers and data, plain paper, coated paper)? What kind of damage is it (*e.g.*, water, fire, smoke)?

* *Make a detailed damage assessment*: Remember to take photographs or video and document the damage in writing.
* *Call the insurance company or in-house contact (for self-insurance)*: Contact information should be provided in the disaster plan.
* *Get advice from a preservation professional*: Unless the disaster is very small, it is likely that you will want to contact a preservation professional to ensure that you are responding properly. In the event of a major disaster, you may need to arrange for a professional to provide on-site assistance.
* *Determine what additional personnel will be needed*: Staff members, volunteers, and/or temporary workers may be needed. Develop a system to keep track of personnel and ensure that everyone is properly trained.
* *Establish a command center for the recovery effort*: Potential sites should have been identified ahead of time.
* *Establish security procedures for the recovery site*: Only authorized persons should be allowed to enter the site; some type of identification (*e.g.*, badges, vests) should be arranged.
* *Decide what will be salvaged and what will be discarded*: Remember that the salvage priorities that were determined ahead of time may need to be adjusted according to the extent and/or type of damage.
* *Decide how the materials to be salvaged will be treated*: Treatment options will be discussed in this part. For wet collections, sort the materials, separating those to be frozen from those to be air-dried. As you begin sorting and moving materials, it is essential to keep track of collections at all times.
* *Determine if it will be necessary to relocate collections*: A large space may be needed for air-drying, or

collections may need to be stored elsewhere temporarily to protect them from danger while the building and damaged collections are salvaged.

* *Gather supplies and arrange for services*: Again, information should have been collected prior to the disaster, and an emergency supply kit should be available.
* *Stabilize the building and environment*: Do not turn up the heat; this will not dry out the space and may encourage mold growth. If the outdoor humidity is low, open the windows. If the climate control system is working, use it to provide as much cooling and dehumidification as possible. Your goal should be to keep the temperature below 70°F and the humidity as much below 50% as possible. Wet carpeting should be removed and wet furniture and standing water should be removed. If the climate control system is not sufficient to reduce the temperature and humidity to the desired levels, building dry-out services will be needed. Monitor the temperature and humidity in the recovery area several times a day to ensure that the desired conditions are reached and maintained for the duration of the recovery effort.
* *Communicate with the media and the public*: It is important to inform patrons and other interested parties of the extent of the damage and the progress of recovery efforts. It is also crucial that one person be responsible for all interaction with the media and the public.

SALVAGING COLLECTIONS

Once you have determined what needs to be salvaged, what are your options for stabilizing damaged materials? In most cases, you will be dealing with water-damaged collections that need to be dried. It is very important to realise that collections will not be restored by the drying process. If response was slow and collections became significantly distorted, they will remain distorted when dry. If collections are dried quickly, however, visible damage may be minimal.

General Drying Options

Several methods are available for drying wet books and records:

* *Air Drying*: most appropriate for small numbers of damp or slightly wet collections
* *Dehumidification Drying*: most effective for buildings that have suffered extensive water damage and for collections that have suffered only slight to moderate water damage
* *Freezer Drying*: suitable for a modest number of books that are damp or moderately wet
* *Thermaline or Cryogenic Drying*: a new drying technique designed for rare book and manuscript collections, particularly leather and vellum
* *Vacuum Freeze Drying*: the best option for large numbers of wet books and records and for those with water-soluble inks and/or coated paper.

Recovering Specific Types of Collections

Different types of collections have specific recovery needs. Drying methods that work well for some books and documents may not be appropriate for other types of collections. It is essential to familiarize yourself with salvage recommendations for all types of materials held by your institution.

Salvage of Specific Collections

Explore the Minnesota Historical Society's Emergency Salvage Procedures for Wet Items web page. This page provides salvage instructions for the various types of collections found in libraries, archives, historical societies, and other cultural institutions.

RECOVERING FROM DISASTER

Once collections are salvaged and dried and/or cleaned, how do you return to normal? Once wet collections have been dried, they cannot just be put back on the shelf. Depending on the nature and extent of the disaster, returning to normal may be relatively quick and easy, or it may take a great deal of time and effort. It will be necessary to examine all the items that have been salvaged to determine their additional needs.

AFTER REHABILITATION OF COLLECTIONS

Catalog records and finding aids will need to be updated to reflect any withdrawals, replacements, or other changes. Furnishings and shelving will need to be cleaned, repaired, and/or replaced. Finally, the collections themselves will need to be reshelved or refiled.

PLANNING FOR REHABILITATION

It is difficult to plan ahead for specific rehabilitation activities, since it is impossible to know the extent or nature of the disaster in advance.

If you are confronted with a disaster, you will need to ask the following questions:

* What specific steps are needed for each rehabilitation activity?
* Who will carry them out, and who will supervise the work?
* Where will the work be done?
* Will temporary storage space be needed?
* Who will have authority to discard badly damaged items?
* What funds will be available? Will they come from the operating budget or insurance?
* How should rehabilitation priorities be set to allow quick resumption of essential services?
* How much of the work can be done by staff and how much needs to be contracted out?

PREPARING A DISASTER PLAN

In this part you will pull together the concepts you have explored and consider how you might create a disaster plan for your own institution.

Once you have completed this part, you will have an understanding of the disaster planning process, a sense of your institution's priorities for disaster planning, and even have some individual elements that can be used in your actual disaster plan.

THE DISASTER PLANNING TEAM

The first step in creating a disaster plan is to gain institutional commitment to the planning process. The administration must approve the expenditure of the time and money required to draft and implement the plan, as well as provide for staff training.

Members of the Team

The disaster planning team should be comprised of staff with responsibility for collections care. The team may be large or small, depending on the size of the institution. Small institutions might consider cooperating with other small organizations within the community, so that they can pool emergency resources and help each other to stay on schedule when preparing a plan. In a large institution, the disaster team might include library professionals, a conservator, a facility manager, and a technology support representative. Input from fire safety professionals, police, and other interested parties will provide added energy and visibility to the planning process and broaden perspectives on various issues.

Assigning Tasks

The disaster planning team should be led by a disaster planning manager, appointed by the institution's director. This person is responsible for setting objectives, coordinating the project, establishing a budget, and approving expenditures. The team must prepare a realistic timetable for the completion of each task or goal, including testing and future updates of the plan.

Each member of the team should be assigned responsibility for a specific category or part of the plan: assessing risks, devising prevention activities, gathering information on supplies and services, preparing response procedures, etc. Tasks should be assigned according to the ability of various staff members to best handle them. It is usually a good idea to assign one person the responsibility of pulling together all the information gathered by the team into a written plan.

WRITING A DISASTER PLAN

A disaster plan must include both prevention activities and response instructions. A written document containing this information must be prepared by members of the disaster planning team and approved in writing by senior management. The plan should list all staff members (and any others, such as fire department contacts) who will be given a copy, and it should indicate where the plans will be stored. Copies should be placed in all departments and at all points of contact (*e.g.*, reference desk, circulation desk), and copies should also be stored off site. Writing a disaster plan can be extremely complex and time-consuming. While you cannot complete your plan as part of this part, you have already begun the process.

You can use the information you have collected as the basis for your disaster plan by:

* Expanding on it to create your own plan, or
* Using dPlan, the Northeast Document Conservation Center's online disaster planning template. Input the information you have collected, along with additional information, and dPlan will generate a plan for you.

MAINTAINING THE DISASTER PLAN

Once you have prepared a disaster plan, remember that it will not be effective without reviewing and updating, whcih should occur yearly (at a minimum). It is often a good idea to assign each member of the disaster planning team responsibility for updating a specific part. Once updating is complete, make sure that you replace all existing copies of the plan (in all locations) with the new version.

The importance of training all staff in emergency procedures and implementation of the disaster plan cannot be overstated. Staff members are often the first line of defence against disasters, because they observe problems as they occur. At a minimum, hold periodic staff meetings to review basic preventive measures and proper implementation of the disaster plan (*e.g.*, how to recognize a potential threat, how to respond, how to report a problem, who to call, how and when to activate the plan). Also review specific evacuation routes and general emergency procedures.

Periodic emergency drills and testing of the plan can give your staff confidence, as well as point out "weak spots" in your plan. Even if a full-scale disaster drill cannot be held, consider a "table-top" exercise, in which staff members meet to go through a scenario and discuss how they would respond.

Real Life Example

The Seattle Art Museum, which has an extensive disaster plan, found several weak spots during emergency drills: its public address system was not sufficiently audible in all rooms; its "buddy system", in which staff members check on each other to ensure that all areas in the building are clear, was not working properly because staff members forgot about it in the rush to leave the building; and arrangements had not been made for access to emergency cash or credit outside business hours.

9

Building a Preservation Programme

You have learned about the factors that cause or accelerate the deterioration of collections, as well as strategies that can be used to prevent or mitigate damage. In this part, you will learn how to pull together these building blocks to create a systematic and well thought out preservation plan for your institution. The preservation planning process has several explicit goals: to determine preservation problems and needs; to identify activities that will solve those problems and meet those needs; to allocate resources to implement preservation activities; and to prepare a detailed plan for carrying out the necessary activities.

The planning process also has the implicit goal of educating staff members and administration about preservation issues. Preservation cuts across existing organizational divisions and affects virtually every aspect of an institution's operations. Thus, creating an environment in which all staff members apply preservation knowledge and skills in their everyday work is very important. This can significantly improve the condition of collections even without large expenditures of funds.

To achieve your preservation planning goals, it is best to undertake the planning process by consensus, involving a range of institutional staff, including the institution's senior management (*e.g.*, director, board of trustees). This helps to increase staff understanding of preservation issues and builds support for the inevitable changes the plan will bring.

PRESERVATION PLANNING

Even in the smallest institutions, a preservation programme needs administrative coordination in order to be effective. If individual preservation activities are undertaken in the absence of an overall plan, one or two preservation activities (such as preservation microfilming or rehousing collections) may be well developed, while others (such as monitoring improvement of environmental conditions) are neglected.

The process of development and ongoing review of a preservation plan helps ensure that preservation is considered an integral part of institutional activities, rather than in competition with other activities (such as collection development) for time and resources.

THE PLANNING PROCESS

* *"Planning Provides a Rational Process to Analyse Needs Systematically to Minimize the Problems and Maximize the Opportunities."* —Jutta Reed-Scott, "Planning for Preservation in Libraries," in *Preservation: Issues and Planning*

In her article, Jutta Reed-Scott sets forth the basic components of the preservation planning process:

* Identify and assess preservation needs (through some type of survey)
* Set priorities among preservation needs according to the institution's mission
* Evaluate existing preservation activities
* decide what preservation functions are needed within the institution and how they will be organized
* Allocate resources for preservation
* Write a plan and determine how the plan will be implemented

Identifying and assessing needs is an information-gathering process: what collections does the institution hold and what is their condition? How are collections housed? What are the environmental conditions within the building(s)? Is there a disaster plan? Are collections protected from fire and theft? Are repair, binding, and/or conservation treatment undertaken regularly? How much funding is allocated for preservation? How much staff time?

Once you have discerned your preservation needs, you must consider potential solutions to the problems you have identified. What answers are most appropriate for your particular institution and situation? What existing activities already have a preservation component, and how should existing preservation activities change to meet the needs you have identified?

As part of this process, you will need to assess your institutional mission and goals and the personnel and monetary resources currently available, as well as potential future resources.

Once all the relevant issues have been considered, you should set preservation priorities and pull together a preservation strategy that includes an action plan and timetable. A systematic preservation plan will allow you to respond effectively to preservation needs and take advantage of preservation opportunities that might otherwise have been missed.

PRESERVATION STRATEGIES

Developing a Preservation Strategy

While the basic elements of a preservation programme are fairly straightforward, the emphasis placed on each of these elements will vary according to the institution and situation. The relative importance of each component for your institution will depend on the type, value, and condition of your collections; the importance of specific collections to your institution's mission; the type of access you need to provide (open stacks, closed stacks, offsite storage); and the amount of use the collections receive.

You will need to develop an appropriate preservation strategy for your institution. In general, preservation programme elements that benefit all collections (such as environmental control, security, disaster planning, and proper storage and handling) should be thought of as the basic "umbrella" components of a programme. Other strategies, such as microfilming, library binding, or treatment would be used for individual (or groups of) items as needed.

Strategies for Different Types of Institutions

Preservation needs and responses are specific to a particular institution and each collection within that institution. Some repositories may see their primary responsibility as preserving unique and/or comprehensive collections over the long term, while others may place more emphasis on serving academic teaching and research needs or services to the general public.

In general, institutions with archival or historical collections assume an obligation to preserve those collections over the long term. These institutions will place a strong emphasis on strategies to stabilize the collections as a whole (*e.g.*, holdings maintenance/collections care, environmental control, security, emergency preparedness), with a secondary focus on preservation reformatting (usually microfilming) and/or conservation treatment for the specific collections that require it.

The primary mission of small- to mid-sized public or academic libraries, on the other hand, is to provide access to collections for as long as the materials are needed. These libraries generally have a high level of use and collect basically rather than comprehensively. In these libraries, reference collections and materials related to current courses receive the most use. These institutions will also need to focus on umbrella issues such as storage and handling, environment, security, and disaster planning-but in addition they will undertake library binding, basic book repair, withdrawal of brittle titles that are no longer needed, and replacement of brittle titles with reprints, photocopies or purchased microfilm. Preservation microfilming and conservation treatment will generally not be a priority, unless the institution also holds historical or other unique collections.

Like smaller academic and public libraries, large research libraries strive to provide users access to collections for as long as the materials are needed.

In addition, they assume responsibility for building and maintaining research collections that are meant to survive over the long term. For these institutions, an even wider range of preservation options will be needed, including umbrella strategies such as environmental control, storage/handling, and disaster planning, as well as preservation reformatting, replacement, library binding, book repair, and conservation treatment.

PROGRAMME MANAGEMENT

Managing a preservation programme involves developing policies, assigning preservation responsibilities to staff members, and documenting preservation activities. Budgeting and identifying funding for preservation activities is also important, but this will be considered separately.

Remember that if preventive preservation is to be effective, it must become part of all activities within the organization. Part of your job will be to make your colleagues aware of their roles in the preservation programme. In other words, preservation should not be an "add-on" activity-it must be an integral component of the day-to-day operations and responsibilities in every department, office, and division.

POLICY

The development of written preservation policies and documentation is crucial to the planning process. Written policies provide guidance for carrying out specific activities, help to codify procedures, and ensure that staff members accept them and carry them out.

Overall Preservation Policy

One of the first steps in the planning process must be to develop an overall institutional preservation policy. This document will provide a framework for setting preservation priorities and preparing a detailed preservation plan.

It should reflect the institution's mission and goals and should include:

* A general description of the preservation problems facing the institution
* Definitions/explanations of key preservation concepts and terms
* The general principles and practices that will guide the preservation programme
* A general outline of the preservation programme that includes responsibilities for preservation activities and describes how preservation relates to other functions within the institution (*e.g.*, provision of access, processing of new collections)

Once an overall preservation policy has been developed, more detailed polices will be needed to provide staff with written guidelines for carrying out specific preservation activities as part of everyday collections care efforts. This is particularly important in smaller institutions where there is no separate preservation department. The policy-development process may also facilitate change within the institution, educating staff and administration about the damaging effects of current practices and procedures. Essentially, the preservation policy articulates the overall goals of the preservation programme. This policy should be revisited periodically, as the institution and circumstances change and as preservation goals are achieved.

Policies for Specific Activities

Preservation should be a part of all activities including, but not limited to:

* Acquisition (use of nondamaging spine labels, etc.)
* Binding (use of archival materials and nondamaging binding techniques that allow the book to open completely, etc.)
* Shelving (storing oversized books flat or spine down, using proper bookends)
* Photocopying (using an "edge" photocopier with an edge platen and being careful not to damage the spines of books)

* Exhibition (supporting collections properly and using nondamaging exhibit techniques, etc.)

Once an overall preservation policy has been developed, strategies will be needed for specific preservation activities, which will provide staff with written guidelines for carrying out these activities as part of everyday collections care efforts. Written policies are best developed over time as preservation activities are systematized.

Following is a list of potential policies and procedures that have a preservation component (all of these may not be needed for every institution):

* Disaster planning and recovery
* Collection acquisitions and processing
* Donor forms and agreements
* Exhibit guidelines
* Rights and reproductions policies
* Book repair policy
* Selection for conservation treatment
* Documenting conservation treatment
* Binding quality check
* Microfilming selection and quality
* Selection for digitization
* Handling materials for digitization
* Food and drinks policy
* Security policy
* Patron access/use policy
* Loan policy
* Environmental monitoring
* Collection storage and rehousing.

In general, clear and well-considered policies that are universally enforced will make preventive preservation measures routine and lengthen the useful life of collections.

ORGANIZATION AND STAFFING

Larger Institutions

There are a number of models for staffing a successful preservation programme at a large institution. The Association of Research Libraries (ARL) 1991 publication *Preservation Programme Models: A Study Project and Report* set out organizational and staffing models for four libraries of varying size, and it is still referenced in the library literature. ARL preservation statistics published annually show that many large research libraries have preservation departments of various sizes, ranging from part-time to full-time preservation administrators, along with library assistants, conservation technicians, and/or conservators.

Smaller Institutions

Identifying an effective staffing model for a preservation programme in a small or medium-sized institution can be more challenging. In archives, historical societies, public libraries, and small college libraries, it is usually not realistic to have a separate preservation manager. In fact, many small institutions (this is particularly the case in archives) may have only one professional staff member who is responsible for all activities, including preservation. In these situations, preservation management will be a part-time responsibility for one or more staff members.

If the institution does not have a full-time preservation manager, it is best for one person on staff to be responsible for acquiring preservation information and making preservation decisions. Even though a number of staff members may carry out preservation activities as part of their regular duties, it is important to have one person responsible for coordinating these activities.

In some institutions and situations, however, a committee may be more effective in managing preservation activities. In this case, each member of the committee would oversee a specific area of preservation (*e.g.*, disaster planning, environmental control, housekeeping).

If you are responsible for managing preservation in a smaller institution, it is likely that preservation will be only one of many "hats" that you wear. Try not to be discouraged by the scope of the preservation problem. Instead, break tasks down into manageable projects that can be completed in a reasonable amount of time. Your preservation plan will help you to do this and will give you a sense of accomplishment.

Assigning Responsibility

Remember that it is pointless to assign preservation responsibilities if staff members do not have the time to carry them out. Your institution will need to make a commitment to providing staff time for preservation activities, as well as appropriate training. Job descriptions should include preservation activities, and the preservation manager should be at a high enough level within the organization that he or she can effectively work for change.

DOCUMENTATION AND STATISTICS

Ongoing documentation of preservation activities ensures that data is available to support any changes that may be needed. Documentation may involve describing existing preservation procedures, keeping statistics on preservation activities, maintaining records of conservation treatment and other activities, and providing photo documentation.

Documentation of preservation activities is important because it:

* Provides crucial information for new staff in case of reorganization or staff turnover
* Documents current practices so that they can be compared to future practices
* Supports necessary product, equipment, or technology changes
* Provides information that can be used to determine future budgeting and staffing levels

Preservation statistics can be very helpful for planning and budgeting, but you must carefully consider how many to keep, in what categories, and how you will use them.

PROGRAMME FUNDING

Effective preservation requires a dependable budget with active administrative coordination, even if the budget is not large at the beginning. While it is possible to improve conditions to a certain extent through changes in existing procedures, funding will be needed for supplies, training, and equipment if anything more than very basic preservation projects are to be undertaken.

In this part you will learn about budgeting for preservation, identifying outside sources of funding, and writing grants for preservation projects. Keep in mind, however, that although grant funding is an excellent resource for individual preservation projects, it should be used to supplement institutional funding, not to replace it. Institutional commitment to the preservation programme through the allocation of funds for preservation activities is very important.

THE ROLE OF FUNDING IN SETTING PRESERVATION PRIORITIES

Setting preservation priorities involves many cost-related questions. Will you tackle lower-cost preservation options first? How will you plan for higher-cost activities? If your institution needs a preservation survey, will you pay for a professional one or will in-house staff conduct it? If you need to establish an ongoing library binding or book repair programme, how much will it cost, and is your institution willing to bear the charges? Would outsourcing of some preservation activities be cheaper than doing the work in house? How will you fund special projects such as preservation microfilming or conservation treatment? Is outside funding available?

Remember, however, that cost is only one of the factors in setting preservation priorities; you must also consider each activity in the context of the entire preservation programme. Is the activity a critical need? Will it provide a significant benefit for a large number of materials? If it provides a limited benefit, but is also low cost, should it be done anyway? The cost of a preservation activity must also be balanced against the risk of not undertaking the activity; neglecting an activity because of high cost (such as roof repair or installation of fire protection equipment) may have serious negative consequences for all or part of your collection over the long term.

BUDGETING

Budgeting is one of the most challenging aspects of preservation management. You must decide what preservation activities are needed within your institution, how much they will cost, and how you will pay for them. You will also need to decide what work will be carried out in house and what might be outsourced.

Preservation Spending: How Much Is Enough

In an era of declining budgets and staffing, there are never enough resources to address all preservation needs. To determine whether your institution is on the right track in terms of preservation spending, it can be helpful to compare your efforts to those of other institutions.

The Association of Research Libraries (ARL) issues an annual report on preservation statistics in ARL member libraries, which primarily represent libraries that hold two million volumes or more. These reports collect statistics on the organizational structure of library preservation programmes, staffing levels, preservation expenditures, conservation treatment, and preservation reformatting.

ARL statistics gathered over a number of years have shown that research libraries with active preservation programmes spend approximately 5 to 10 per cent of their total budget on preservation (*e.g.*, prevention of deterioration, preparing materials for use, and repairing/copying materials). This statistic does not include costs related to the building and systems that enable the library to maintain a preservation-quality environment. The larger the library, the higher the percentage of total library expenditures that tends to be directed to preservation. While these figures obviously do not apply directly to other types and sizes of institution, they are useful as a general model.

Reallocating Existing Funds

Remember that initiating new preservation activity does not always have to involve allocation of new funds. When planning a preservation programme, review your institution's budget to identify any activities that could be redirected to assist in meeting preservation goals. For example, most archives already purchase folders and storage boxes, and many libraries purchase pamphlet binders or other enclosures. A change in the type of material bought and/or training of staff to use the enclosures properly may greatly improve the overall protection of collections with little or no additional cost.

Since reallocation of existing funds may cross departmental lines, it must be undertaken as part of a cooperative preservation planning process that is coordinated with the institution's overall strategic plan.

Cost Analysis

Cost analysis is crucial to effective budgeting for preservation. In order to decide how best to accomplish a particular preservation goal, a preservation manager must be able to analyse a preservation activity and its associated costs.

A cost analysis might be needed in any of the following situations:

* Submitting a budget proposal for a preservation activity within the institution
* Preparing a response to an institutional request for cost reductions
* Developing a cost estimate for a grant proposal
* Comparing the costs of carrying out an activity in house versus using a vendor

The process of carrying out a cost analysis is explained in detail in *The Preservation Manager's Guide to Cost Analysis*. After identifying the product, service, or other activity to be analysed (for example, to determine the costs of producing book boxes in-house), the preservation manager must gather detailed information on the procedures for carrying out the service or activity.

Costs may include supplies and equipment; services; labour; or indirect costs (*e.g.*, overhead). In each of these categories, the cost of each resource needed to complete the activity should be calculated on a per-item basis. Remember to include "hidden" costs (*e.g.*, supply costs may include not just the cost of the items, but shipping costs or custom order fees).

All assumptions made must be documented (for example, if the cost of staff time is not included in a comparative cost analysis because it is the same in both scenarios), and the effectiveness of the cost analysis must be measured by comparison with actual costs or with similar activities at another institution.

FUNDING SOURCES

There are various potential sources of funding for preservation activities; these include internal sources (your parent institution, or possibly fees for services and/or other income-generating projects) and external sources (federal and state grant programmes, as well as local corporations and foundations). For external funding sources, your primary goal should be to develop a network of funders that matches your goals and ideas, and that can provide regular small grants supplemented by periodic larger grants.

Federal Funders

The three major federal sources for preservation funding of paper-based collections are:

* The National Endowment for the Humanities (NEH) Division of Preservation and Access. NEH has a number of grant categories, including Preservation Assistance Grants, Stabilization of Humanities Collections Grants, and Grants to Preserve and Create Access to Humanities Collections. Note that the Preservation Assistance Grants are designed specifically for smaller institutions—they provide funding for preservation surveys; purchase of preservation supplies, equipment, and storage furniture; and other activities.
* The Institute of Museum and Library Services (IMLS). IMLS funds the Conservation Assessment programme and the Conservation Project Support

programme (both for historical societies, museums, and state/local governments), as well as the Save America's Treasures programme and National Leadership Grants. IMLS also administers the Library Services and Technology Act (LSTA), through which funds are provided to state libraries, which then make re-grants to individual institutions for various purposes, including preservation.

* The National Historical Publications and Records Commission (NHPRC). NHPRC makes Archival and Records Project Grants to archival institutions to preserve records and make them accessible.

Other potential federal funders include the National Endowment for the Arts (NEA) and the National Science Foundation (NSF).

State Funders

There are numerous state preservation grant programmes around the country; these generally provide funding for preservation planning surveys, and subsequently for implementing survey recommendations. The type and extent of these programmes varies greatly, so it is best to consult your state library or archives to determine whether or not a preservation grant programme exists in your state.

Foundations

Remember that private organizations may also be a source of funding. There are several types of foundations: large general-purpose organizations such as the Ford Foundation or the Mellon Foundation; special-purpose foundations; company-sponsored foundations; community foundations (which usually fund within a specific geographic area); and family foundations (which are often informal and unstaffed).

Many small/local foundations or corporations have specific interests and you may be able to find one that matches your needs. For example, if you are trying to preserve a local history collection, you might consider approaching local businesses or others with an interest in the community. As with federal or state funding, you may have to provide funds to match the grant. Also remember that foundations may help in ways other than providing money directly for preservation activities, including providing funding for printing costs, furniture, or equipment.

GRANTWRITING

The key to writing a successful grant proposal is to understand what needs to be included in each part of the proposal, as well as what the proposal reviewers will be looking for when reading the document.

A grant proposal is a written presentation asking for support of a programme, project, activity, or function that an institution wants to undertake in response to a need. The proposal must articulate this need and provide a plan for carrying out the desired activity. The activity to be funded must have a clear relationship to your institution's mission and purpose. Your written proposal should be clear and realistic and should focus on what you can accomplish.

The general components of a preservation project proposal are as follows:

* *Objectives*: This part includes both your goals (a broad-based statement of the ultimate result of the activity) and objectives (a narrowly defined, measurable, time-specific outcome that your institution expects to accomplish as a result of the grant). Be sure to identify the community being served and to state the results of the project, not the activity itself.
* *Plan of Work*: This is a detailed description of the activities and services to be undertaken to achieve your goals and objectives. It should explain why you chose these methods, and it should enumerate what facilities, personnel, and equipment will be used. It should include a timeline for the process and define tasks and subtasks.
* *Budget*: This provides estimated costs for the activities listed in the plan of work. The forms and guidelines

of the funder should be followed; government funders usually require more detail than foundations.

* *Evaluation*:This part describes your plans for evaluating the project to determine whether or not it was successful. You may need to measure whether staff members changed or improved their skills, knowledge, etc., or you may need to measure facts such as items rehoused or treated, materials developed, supplies consumed, etc.
* *Sustainability*: This part indicates how you will maintain the project or programme at the end of the grant period. Will the activities continue? If so, how will they be maintained, and what funding/resources will you provide?

Helpful Hints for Grant Writing

* There should be one writer, even if there are many contributors.
* Follow the funder's guidelines.
* Do your research and get the facts right-be knowledgeable about the most current preservation practices.
* Be aware of related preservation projects.
* All ideas should flow from one central need.
* Avoid jargon.
* Be compelling, but not overdramatic.
* Get an outside person to edit the proposal and review the budget.
* Be thorough, clear, and concise.

Remember that a good proposal doesn't necessarily result in getting a grant; other factors, such as the number of proposals received or the current priorities of the granting agency, may come into play. Ask the granting agency for feedback, and resubmit if necessary.

EDUCATION AND TRAINING

Preservation education and training of staff and others is necessary to successful preservation efforts. Facilitating preservation awareness for the institution's administrator(s) and/or trustees can be very helpful in encouraging institutional commitment.

Certainly all staff members with preservation responsibilities (*e.g.*, book repair, administering preservation microfilming projects) must be trained in proper preservation techniques. Staff members with management responsibility for preservation activities should also participate in professional activities, which will allow them to keep up with current preservation information and network with peers.

EDUCATING STAFF AND ADMINISTRATORS

One of the most important steps an institution can take is to support the ongoing education and training of staff members with preservation responsibilities. Some preservation projects such as weeding and shelf maintenance do not require a large investment in equipment or supplies, but they do require that staff members have knowledge of preservation principles and proper procedures for care of collections. An investment in training for those who carry out preservation activities will serve to extend the useful life of the collections. The staff member or committee in charge of preservation should coordinate this training.

Staff training and education can be undertaken in-house or through outside workshops, and avenues for raising preservation awareness among administrators may be similar. Administrators and board members or trustees may be interested in attending half- or full-day workshops on general preservation topics. A presentation by the preservation manager at a board of trustees meeting, or a preservation exhibit within the institution, may also be effective at setting the stage for training or raising awareness.

RAISING AWARENESS AND MANAGING CHANGE

While holding training parts and attending workshops is a relatively straightforward activity, you may find that it is much more of a challenge to get staff members and administrators to fully implement and support the preservation programme when it involves changes to the status quo. Staff members may be resistant to changing the way they have always done things, and they may see the change as a threat to their position(s).

How can you make the case for change and handle the transition to new policies and procedures? First, you must be sure that you understand your institutional culture (*i.e.*, how your institution operates). Is the institution's mission formal or implied? Is the organizational structure hierarchical or lateral? Rigid or more flexible? What is the institutional style of communication? Oral or written? Interpersonal or by committee? E-mail or memos? The answers to these questions will help you figure out how to effectively persuade staff and administrators and build consensus.

When introducing new activities or changes to existing preservation activities, try to be aware of how specific staff members may be feeling about the change. Who is having the hardest time with it? Try to acknowledge the difficulty, provide lots of information, and give everyone a part to play in the new arrangement. It is usually a good idea to make the actual change quickly, rather than dragging it out. In managing the change, it may be helpful if you can find out how transitions (*e.g.*, automation, building renovation) have been handled in the past within your institution.

PROFESSIONAL RESOURCES

Ongoing preservation education and professional activities will help you carry out your preservation management duties more effectively. In particular, interaction with other preservation managers can provide encouragement and reinforcement, especially if you are the only person responsible for preservation in your institution.

You can update your skills and knowledge (and network with other preservation managers) through workshops, other continuing education programmes, and participation in professional organizations and listserv discussions.

Many workshops are given by regional or state preservation organizations. There are a number of regional organizations throughout the United States that have joined together to form the Regional Alliance for Preservation (RAP). There are a number of regional organizations throughout the United States that have joined together to form the Regional Alliance for Preservation (RAP). Statewide preservation programmes began during the 1980s and 1990s in a number of states throughout the country, based on a number of different models. Many of these have provided grants and workshops, often through the state library or archives. Examples include the New York State Library Programme for the Conservation and Preservation of Library Research Materials and the Massachusetts Board of Library Commissioners preservation advisory services, workshops, and grants. Consult your state library or archives to determine whether or not similar programmes exist in your state.

Both the American Library Association (ALA) and the Society of American Archivists provide resources for preservation professionals:

* ALA's Association for Library Collections and Technical Services division (ALCTS) includes the Preservation and Reformatting Section (PARS). PARS has a number of preservation committees and sponsors workshop and conference programmes. PARS also sponsors two e-mail discussion groups: the Preservation Administrators Discussion List and the Preservation Educators Discussion List.
* The Society of American Archivists (SAA) also has an active preservation part that provides opportunities to get involved with the professional community. SAA also maintains the Archives and Archivists Listserv.

Bibliography

Acemoglu, D.: *Definitions of Conservation*, New Delhi: Oxford University Press, 2002.

Ahluwalia, J.: *Libraries and Scholarly Communication in the India: The Historical Dimension*, New York: UNDP, 2008.

Bardhan, P.: *Selecting and Appraising Archives and Manuscripts, Amritsar*: Guru Nanak Dev University, 2006.

Batra, G.: *Preservation of Library and Archival Materials: A Manual*, London: BBC Books, 2005.

Bhalla, G.S.: *Collections Policies and Preservation*, Cambridge: Cambridge University Press, 2006.

Canagarajah, S.: *Library Resources and Technical Services*, New Delhi: Council for Social Development, 2006.

Chadha, G. K.: *Preservation: Issues and Planning*, New Delhi: Oxford University Press, 2004.

Dahlman, C.: A *Glossary of Archival and Records Terminology*, London and New York: Longman, 2000.

Dasgupta, A.K.: *The Future of the Past: Preservation in American Research Libraries*, London: Yale University Press, 2008.

Dearden, L.: *Photographs: Archival Care and Management*, London: University College London, 2004.

Gupta, R.: *The Artist's Handbook of Materials and Techniques*, London: Sage Publications, 2002.

Gupta, S.P.: *Permanence of Paper for Publications and Documents in Libraries and Archives*, Chicago: University of Chicago Press, 2006.

Krueger, O.: *The History of Bookbinding as a Mirror of Society*, Cambridge: MIT Press, 2000.

Nayar, Baldev Raj.: *The Film Preservation Guide: the Basics for Archives, Libraries, and Museums*, New York: Greenwood Press, 2000.

Pursell, G.: *Preservation Microfilming: A Guide for Librarians and Archivists*, London: Sage Publications, 2002.

Rao, M.: *Magnetic Tape Storage and Handling: A Guide for Libraries and Archives*, Cambridge: Cambridge University Press, 2006.

Reynolds, Paul D.: *Video Preservation Handbook*, Kansas City: Kauffman Center, 2005.

Rodrik, D.: *Care and Handling of CDs and DVDs: A Guide for Librarians*, London: Yale University Press, 2007.

Sanjaya, Lall: *Guide to Environmental Protection of Collections*, Princeton: Princeton University Press, 2003.

Shankar, A.: *Collections Security: Planning and Prevention for Libraries*, London: Picador, 2002.

Tan, H.: *Step-By-Step Workbook: Achieving a Preservation Environment for Collections*, London and New York: Longman, 2005.

Index

A

B

C

D

E

F

G

H